Sasaki Associates:

Integrated Environments

Text by Melanie Simo

Dialogues by David Dillon

S P A C E M A K E R   P R E S S

Washington DC

Cambridge MA

Front cover: Cleveland Gateway
Photo by Alan Ward

Publisher: James G. Trulove
Designer: Sarah Vance
Assistant Designer: Elizabeth Reifeiss
Editor: D. Sperry Finlayson
Print Coordinator: Susan McNally

Printer: Palace Press, Hong Kong

ISBN 1 888931 08 6

Acknowledgments

The editors wish to thank everyone
who assisted in the production of this
book. Special thanks are due to the
following individuals for their efforts
in documenting the projects presented
and without whom this book would
not be possible: Kenneth E. Bassett,
Darrell Bird, M. Perry Chapman,
Stuart O. Dawson, Neil J. Dean,
David Dillon, Roberta Doocey,
Joanna Fong, Cynthia A. Fordham,
Maurice Freedman, Alan Fujimori,
Richard F. Galehouse, Terri Gray-
Pearce, Stephen E. Hamwey,
Nancy K. Harrod, Gregory Havens,
David M. Hirzel, Jessica Horwitz,
Daniel R. Kenney, Mark Maniaci,
Alistair McIntosh, Julia Monteith,
Don Olson, Dennis Pieprz,
Vicki Rugo, Robert Sabbatini,
Melanie Simo, N. Scott Smith,
James A. Sukeforth, Sarah Vance,
Roy V. Viklund, Peter Walker,
Alan L. Ward, and Larry R. Young.

Contents

4 Preface

5 Dedication

7 **Sasaki Associates:
Integrated Environments**

11 **Portfolio:
Planning and Urban Design**

36 **Campus Planning**

38 The University of Colorado
40 The University of Illinois at
Urbana/Champaign
44 The University of South Florida
at Tampa
46 California State University,
Monterey Bay Campus
48 The Ohio State University

52 **Urban Design**

54 The Dallas Arts District
Urban Design Plan
58 Taipei Terminal
60 Babelsberg Media City
62 Oerlikon
64 Megaproyecto Puebla Plus
66 Cleveland Gateway

70 **New Communities**

72 Sea Pines Plantation and
Harbourtown
74 The Landings
78 Costa Smeralda
82 Brambleton
84 Sugarloaf/USA
86 The Virginia Coast Reserve
88 Lowry Development Plan
90 The San Nicolas Master Plan

93 **Dialogues**

97 **Portfolio: Design**

134 Deere & Company
Administrative Center
136 TRW Corporate Headquarters
138 Frito-Lay Corporate Headquarters
140 GTE Telops Headquarters
142 Western Wyoming College
146 Boston College: Sports Facilities,
Theater, Dormitories, and Entry
148 College of the Holy Cross:
Edith Stein Hall
150 The University of New Hampshire:
Student Housing, Arena and
Recreation Center
152 University of California,
Santa Barbara: Recreation and
Aquatics Center
154 Interlochen Center for the Arts
156 Greenacre Park
158 Christian Science Center
160 Pennsylvania Avenue
162 Reston Town Center
164 Lima Downtown Civic Center
165 Scudder Stevens & Clark
166 The DART Transitway Mall
167 San Francisco Waterfront
168 Boston Waterfront
172 Newburyport Downtown and
Waterfront
174 Kuwait Waterfront
176 Central Indianapolis Riverfront
178 Charleston Waterfront

181 Employees 1953-1996
190 Notes
191 Photography Credits
193 Translations

Preface

This monograph on the work of Sasaki Associates sets forth the scope of a collaborative practice that has spanned over four decades and touched the lives of hundreds of professionals. The materials selected for this book include projects that have established the prototypes for solutions to large-scale and complex planning problems as well as projects that demonstrate a design sensitivity to the setting and the needs of users. The research and dialogues that have contributed to the writing of this book offer insights into a practice that looks to the future while mindful of the founding principles that have guided the growth of the firm over 45 years.

In considering how to organize the book, we asked ourselves what is distinct about Sasaki and the projects we chose to highlight. The answer can be found in the very philosophy on which Sasaki Associates was founded: the belief that small, focused teams, comprised of talented professionals from various disciplines, working collaboratively, are capable of creating exemplary environments.

The projects in this book range from early projects such as the University of Colorado, the Costa Smeralda resort, and the corporate headquarters for John Deere to more contemporary work such as the Cleveland Gateway, the Charleston Waterfront projects, and the recreation center at the University of California Santa Barbara. Selection of the projects to be included in the monograph was a complicated process. Ultimately, we chose projects that represent our goal of making comprehensively planned and highly integrated environments. These projects are emblematic of a practice that has evolved to include the disciplines of planning, landscape architecture, architecture, civil engineering, and interior design.

The text written by Melanie Simo and David Dillon provides a perspective far more objective than we could have written ourselves. Melanie's introductory essays, based on previously published materials, her own careful research and numerous interviews with Sasaki's principals, reveal the human side of our collaborative practice. David's interviews with Mayor Joe Riley of Charleston, South Carolina, and Hunter Morrison, long-time planning director for the City of Cleveland, Ohio, both illustrate the clients' perspective and offer a glimpse of the dynamics of a project from the planning stage to completion. These essays are retrospective. They are intended to give the reader an understanding of how Sasaki Associates and our philosophy have evolved.

This volume celebrates the work of Sasaki Associates' past and present. The work of the future will be built on a foundation we believe to be broad-ranging and strong. It is our corporate philosophy—our belief that the whole is greater than the individual parts—that will make the next 45 years as successful and enriching as the first.

Kenneth E. Bassett
President
January 1997

This book is dedicated to

Hideo Sasaki who, as teacher,

nurtured our talents; as visionary,

encouraged our imaginations; and

as leader, brought us together and

demonstrated how talented

individuals, working as a team,

can create extraordinary places.

Sasaki Associates: Integrated Environments

By Melanie Simo

In 1988, on the occasion of Sasaki Associates' thirty-fifth anniversary, Pietro Belluschi sent his congratulations along with a few memories of the firm. "I was in Cambridge at the time of its birth," he wrote to architect/planner Richard Galehouse, "and [I] have followed very closely its growth and successes—all due to unusual combinations of talent and common sense in solving the many problems facing our environment."[1]

From the vision of one man, Hideo Sasaki, the firm had grown through a succession of partnerships and corporate entities—Sasaki & Novak, Sasaki and Associates, Sasaki, Walker and Associates, Sasaki, Dawson, DeMay Associates—to Sasaki Associates, dating from 1975. Today a multidisciplinary planning and design firm with offices in metropolitan Boston (Watertown), Dallas, and San Francisco, Sasaki Associates is known for its work in campus planning, urban design, the development of new communities, environmental assessments, and the design of individual buildings, gardens, plazas, and corporate and commercial landscapes, as well as interior planning and design.

The firm is also known for some of the specific projects that, over time, have become "classics" of their type or era: small discrete projects, such as the roof garden of Place Bonaventure, in Montreal, Quebec (1967) and Greenacre Park, in New York City (1971); significant portions of urban and institutional contexts, such as Constitution Plaza, in Hartford, Connecticut (1959) and Quincy House, at Harvard University, in Cambridge, Massachusetts (1959-60); and large-scale works on previously undeveloped land, such as Foothill College, in Los Altos, California (1957-60); the Deere & Company Administrative Center, in Moline, Illinois (from 1963); and the waterfronts of Boston and Charleston, South Carolina (from 1973 and 1979). As these and other exemplary projects have matured, they have contributed to the cumulative, evolving identity of the multidisciplinary firm, Sasaki Associates.

Less evident, perhaps, is the firm's historic role in developing the fields of campus planning and urban design. With its multidisciplinary organization and its early ties to the development of postwar theory at Harvard and MIT, Sasaki Associates has been one of the most important centers of experiment for planning and design in the United States and abroad. In addition, a continuum of teaching and practice, outlined below, has broadened the vision of two generations of landscape architects—colleagues and students of Sasaki—who have gone on to work with architects, engineers, and planners in the major postwar development of institutions, government, and industry.

In *Campus Planning* (1963) and *Environmental Design* (1969), Richard Dober documented this work (by Sasaki's firm and others) with plans, photographs, and descriptions. Dober, formerly a student of Kevin Lynch at MIT and a colleague in Sasaki's firm, also revealed something of the idealism—as well as the pragmatism—that underlay these postwar efforts in campus planning and urban design. The opening of the Joint Center for Urban and Regional Studies at MIT and Harvard, in 1957, was only one of many hopeful signs. At that time, Belluschi was Dean of the School of Architecture and Planning at MIT. Josep Lluis Sert was Dean of Harvard's Graduate School of Design. Sasaki (soon to be chairman of Landscape Architecture at Harvard) worked amicably with both men in those confident years, when it seemed that there was no problem that could not be solved by rational means and a truly collaborative spirit.

Left to right:
Upjohn Corporation 1957
Kalamazoo, Michigan
Foothill College 1957
Los Altos, California
Constitution Plaza 1959
Hartford, Connecticut
Place Bonaventure 1967
Montreal, Canada

Those were also the years of the "heroic," or highly individualistic phase of modernism, characterized by the work of Eero Saarinen, Paul Rudolph, I.M. Pei, Minoru Yamasaki, Gordon Bunshaft, and others—the great form-givers. Sasaki worked with these men and enjoyed their respect without aspiring to quite the same form-giving role. This was most evident in campus planning, where Sasaki frequently worked with Belluschi to design the broad framework of new development—such as the planned expansion of The University of Colorado at Boulder (from 1960). More thoroughly than most designers of that time, both Belluschi and Sasaki looked beyond the individual building or clearly defined space to the broader context of a project. They would seek to establish connections and linkages within and beyond the property lines of a campus. And in their siting of new structures—heterogeneous, often monumental and isolated buildings—they would strive for a degree of harmony and wholeness in the larger environment.

Such was the legacy of the association between Belluschi and Sasaki and his colleagues, over many years. Its traces can be seen in the more recent work of Sasaki Associates, including the expansion of Western Wyoming College, in Rock Springs; the Interlochen Center for the Arts, in Michigan; and other projects featured in this monograph. In all of these collaborative projects, the design of the architecture and the site has evolved from a layered appreciation of the larger environment—natural and cultural.

Focusing on the built environment, Belluschi surveyed the projects of Sasaki Associates over time: "They all have convincing, timeless qualities which, in my opinion, is the test of architecture as a great Art of our time, beyond fashions and trends." [2] Sympathetic to this view, Sasaki passed it on to his partners and associates, along with other values he shared with Belluschi: respect for the larger context; appreciation for simplicity, restraint, proportion, permanence; and a belief in the collaborative process. In many respects, Belluschi became his role model; Sasaki, too, served as "chief design critic" within his own firm, subtly giving structure and form to the built environment. But Sasaki was also acutely aware of the land itself. His training, though varied, was centered on landscape architecture.

"Ah, yes," people in his firm are quick to respond, "but he never considered himself a landscape architect." On some level that may be true. But the historical evidence, lodged in old memoranda, long-forgotten essays, and transcribed interviews over many years, suggests otherwise. The planning and design of land—not as commodity, but as natural resource, as setting for human action, and as repository of personal and cultural memory—was fundamental to the founder's view of his profession and his firm. In practice, of course, the pragmatic side was more often emphasized. As Sasaki reminded planner Richard Dober in 1959 (when Dober was not yet executive director of the firm), "All buildings, cities, institutions, houses, etc., must go upon the land. If we could provide competent and needed services, there need be no limit to our growth." [3] A month earlier, Dober had noted, "our chief function as design consultants is and should be related to landscaping and site planning. A second area in which we should be involved is that of urban design—i.e., a continuing process of evolving a richer physical environment, linking the personal and private to the communal and public." [4]

As it happened, Dober and Sasaki would not always agree. However, Sasaki welcomed a diversity of views, expressed with civility and openness to other views.

It seems fitting, then, to introduce the diversity of views, ambition and project types of the current firm, Sasaki Associates, by first considering the vision of its founder—an extraordinarily ambitious young man who was also modest, rather shy. He was determined to transform a profession that often seemed too limiting, at times lethargic. But he also knew his limitations; he could not do so alone.

In 1953, when Sasaki opened the practice that would become known as Sasaki Associates, he had traveled a long way from the Central Valley of California, his birthplace. In adolescence, during the last years of the Great Depression, his intellectual curiosity had led him from general studies in junior college to college courses in business and fine arts. He had also been intrigued about the new field of "planning," which drew him from southern California to the University of California at Berkeley. There he was introduced to architecture and landscape architecture as well as planning; and a personal inclination toward working with ideas and the natural elements drew him closer to the field of landscape architecture.

These studies were abruptly interrupted in December, 1941, when the United States entered World War II. Sasaki spent a period of time in the internment camp for Japanese-Americans at Poston, Arizona. Then a series of jobs in and around Denver and Chicago led him to complete his studies in landscape architecture at the University of Illinois, in Champaign-Urbana, just after the war, in 1946. Factories were then rapidly making the transition from wartime to peacetime, and the resources and the will to plan and build were evident. Having received his bachelor of fine arts degree, summa cum laude, Sasaki accepted a scholarship for graduate work at Harvard. Up to this point, he appeared to be moving through the proper channels to assume a responsible position in a fine profession. He had some reservations, however.

At the University of Illinois, Sasaki studied with several mature, highly competent professors, including landscape architect and planner Karl B. Lohmann, and Harland Bartholomew (who took one month a year from his planning practice to teach). Professor of landscape architecture Stanley White had worked for the Olmsted Brothers, in Brookline, and later worked briefly on planning projects and the federally-sponsored new town of Greendale, Wisconsin, with such planners as Jacob Crane, Elbert Peets, and Bartholomew. Through his studies and his part-time jobs for Lohmann, Sasaki saw how the planning and design continuum could operate on a relatively large scale, among professionals who had built their own substantial careers on a base of landscape architectural studies. And on his own, Sasaki pored over the writings of Frederick Law Olmsted, finding precedents for planning and design of city-wide park systems—in Boston, Buffalo, Chicago, and elsewhere—along with insights into the social, cultural, and psychological value of the designed landscape, at whatever scale, public or private. [5]

But if Olmsted and the Illinois professors had been reassuring, the old *Transactions* of the American Society of Landscape Architects were not. There, Sasaki detected a distinct sense of inferiority among landscape architects, vis-à-vis architects and engineers. This led him to write an essay, "The Inferiority Complex of Landscape Architects." It was never published, but the determination to rectify this state of affairs remained with him at Harvard. In fact, that determination became intensified.

At Illinois, Sasaki had met educators and practitioners who had made the transition from Beaux-Arts methods of planning and design to fresh attempts to deal with emerging problems of the contemporary environment, without worrying about modernist theory or formal expression. White, a broadly educated man, conversant in the arts and the sciences, emphasized design at the large scale and design that fit the site, unbeholden to preconceptions and theories. At Harvard, however, modernism was an issue. At the Graduate School of Design, Walter Gropius and his former students represented a revolutionary force, driven by aesthetic and social ideals previously defined at the Bauhaus. This energized the postwar students while also posing a threat to the older generation of educators in landscape architecture. At that time, landscape architecture was still taught in a "classical sort of way," Sasaki recalled. City planning was a separate department (it had grown from a few planning courses taught initially in the department of landscape architecture). Meanwhile, in architecture, at least since the late 1930s, students had been struggling with problems of urban renewal, housing, new communities, and so on. In such an environment, Sasaki gravitated toward students and faculty in architecture and planning. He listened intently to the lectures of Gropius, and he learned a great deal from fellow students in architecture, who would later bring him commissions for site planning and design. [6]

After receiving his M.L.A. degree from Harvard in 1948, Sasaki spent another five years gaining experience in practice and teaching before setting up his own office in the environs of Harvard, in 1953. He had worked at both the New York and the Chicago offices of Skidmore Owings & Merrill (SOM), and taught at the University of Illinois and at Harvard. On the side, he had worked with planner Reginald Isaacs on urban renewal projects and research efforts in and around Chicago. It was Isaacs who, as the new chairman of City Planning and Landscape Architecture at Harvard, brought Sasaki back to teach there in 1953. And it was to Isaacs that Sasaki made his first proposals to transform the profession of landscape architecture—by beginning with professional education at Harvard, where many of the next generation of educators and practitioners would earn their advanced degrees. Among other things, Sasaki recommended a new balance among personalities and skills at the school—the kind of balance that he would also seek within his firm. Ideally there should be at least four instructors (full- and part-time): "a man of creative genius, an energetic and productive person, a highly technical man, and a moderate." The man of creative genius would be someone of the caliber of Roberto Burle-Marx. The moderate would be Sasaki. [7]

The details of Sasaki's efforts to transform professional education and practice in landscape architecture are given elsewhere. In summary, a close colleague, Charles W. Harris, wrote, "Under the leadership of Hideo Sasaki, the decade of evolutionary change (1958-1968) had an almost revolutionary impact upon the nation's major educational programs and professional offices." [8] These transformations depended on a uniquely symbiotic relationship. While chairman of the department of landscape architecture from 1958 to 1968, Sasaki supported the department with part-time instructors and financial resources from his firm. He enriched both the teaching and the learning process by inducing busy practitioners and specialists in new fields, such as aerial photo interpretation and computer applications, to teach for brief periods. The most promising students would be offered part-time work at his office and jobs after graduation—at which time they would be asked to teach part-time (for little or no pay), and thus give back something to the institution that had nurtured them.

In this process, the traditional barriers between practice and teaching became permeable, even as the traditional distinctions among landscape architects, architects, planners, engineers, and others became less sharp, at times irrelevant. As Sasaki recently observed on a visit to Sasaki Associates, "At that time, there was a spirit of inquiry and excitement, whether it was with architects or landscape architects. It didn't matter whom you worked with. Some were generous in their credit for something. We would work together to achieve a solution that we thought was the most appropriate or creative for a particular situation." [9]

With characteristic modesty, Sasaki has described the evolution of his multidisciplinary firm as something quite natural, occurring without a precise plan, but rather with a sense of the possibilities opening for teams of differently trained, highly skilled professionals, united in their belief that a better environment could (and must) be created. Gropius had long upheld the collaborative ideal of the Bauhaus and, since late 1945, had been engaged with his former students in the new firm, The Architects Collaborative (TAC). Before long, TAC had brought in people from different disciplines, as had SOM before them. One major departure from this precedent, however, was that Sasaki's firm had been founded on a base of landscape architecture. This base, Sasaki believed, allowed the multidisciplinary firm to move beyond the tradition that grew directly from the industrial revolution and mechanization. For many modernists, inspired by such books as Siegfried Giedion's *Mechanization Takes Command* (1948), "Nature was something to be licked," Sasaki recalled. "But our notion was that nature is to work together with our economy." [10]

Before long Sasaki hired planners, graphic designers, architects and engineers, initially to work on land planning and site design, but eventually, as requests came in from long-standing clients, to design buildings as well. In time, the engineers would undertake complex technical problems, such as the bulkheads of urban waterfronts and the lengthy environmental impact statements, from the 1970s onward. In that decade, another departure from common practice in multidisciplinary firms was evident: the principals agreed to promote at least one professional in each of the firm's disciplines to the level of principal—a share-holding and decision-making position.

By the 1970s Sasaki was no longer writing for publication. In his few published articles, virtually all from the 1950s, Sasaki did, however, outline the range of opportunities specifically for landscape architects, from environmental planning to urban design. "There needs to be an ecological survey based upon the natural forces operative upon the site or area to be planned," he wrote in 1953. "Such a survey may determine how the cultural forms may be most favorably adjusted to the natural forces so that the various ecological tensions operating may be gotten from such a study to stimulate the creation of more appropriate design-forms than most which we evidence in our scene today." In 1955, he underscored the cultural dimension: "The landscape architect can contribute his skills and, together with others, may create a good environment, not only in terms of economic functioning, but as a visually satisfying expression, which in some respects is the measure of cultural achievement of a civilization." [11]

In the 1950s, while he and his firm worked on projects in Boston, Philadelphia, and Chicago, Sasaki reflected on some of the underlying urban problems. As a function and as a cultural expression, the city was endangered, he wrote in 1955. In 1956, he specifically addressed the new field of urban design. "The landscape architect, because of his specialized knowledge, may contribute greatly to the field of urban design. . . . He may, together with the planner, determine the relational aspects of the use of the land, and may further determine the design structure and form of the overall project." [12]

In April, 1956, an urban design conference at Harvard's Graduate School of Design brought together Richard Neutra, Garrett Eckbo, Jane Jacobs, Lewis Mumford, Charles Abrams, Edmund Bacon, Charles Eliot, and others to seek a common basis for the joint work of architects, landscape architects, and planners. The host, Dean Sert, was at that time collaborating with Sasaki's firm on a number of projects at Harvard, involving both urban design and campus planning and design—Holyoke Center, the married students' housing, the Center for the Study of World Religions, and other projects. At this conference, Sert emphasized the need for large teams of specialists to solve urban design problems. "After many years of individual, isolated work, we are logically coming to an era of synthesis," he noted. Urban design, the "most creative" if the least explored of the phases of city planning, should bring about a process of recentralizing the city, to which Sert was committed. In his view, the city was a contributor to America's greatness—not only as a place of business, but also as a center of culture and learning. [13]

Sasaki took this occasion to emphasize a few disturbing developments of modern times. He regretted the meaningless conformity of architectural style (conforming to present as well as past eras), which he called "eclecticism without meaning." Also disturbing was "monumentality without meaning," or lack of scale. Sasaki saw that buildings of a technological scale might express a dimension never witnessed before; but it was human beings who would have to live in and understand these buildings. A third disturbing development was lack of relation with surroundings. Once aware of these surroundings, one might choose to act humbly or rather, with boldness and daring. However, to seek the spectacular for novelty's sake was, to him, an abhorrent design notion. [14] These points (much distilled for the pages of Progressive Architecture) offer some insight into the reasoning, analytical mind and the humane sensibilities of Sasaki Associates' founder.

Indeed, the humane aspects of his planning and design practice were of overriding importance to Sasaki. The harmony and wholeness that he sought to elicit from the larger environment were also qualities he tried to maintain in his firm. This was a difficult, delicate matter (as he freely admits), for the talented individuals he gathered around him were often men of strong personality and volatile temperament. Again, mindful of his own limitations and commitments, Sasaki chose as his second-in-command landscape architect Paul Gardescu, a calm, fair-minded person of recognized integrity. For over twenty years, as executive director, then as president, Gardescu attended to human relations, contracts, and other uncelebrated aspects of the business of design with an equanimity and a degree of otherworldliness that are still fondly remembered by his colleagues at Sasaki Associates.

Sasaki retired in 1980 but remains a consultant to the firm. Gardescu retired in 1984, whereupon James A. Sukeforth, C.P.A. and M.B.A., was elected president and served for nine years. By his own admission, Sukeforth could not lead the firm on his own; rather he would balance his own financial leadership with the professional leadership of four heads of disciplines: Richard Galehouse, planning; Kenneth Bassett, landscape architecture; John Orcutt, architecture; and Maurice Freedman, engineering. "The five of us essentially ran the organization," Sukeforth explained. [15] After he stepped down as president, at the end of 1992, another form of balance was achieved; Kenneth Bassett became president, but continued to confer frequently with his predecessor. Bassett and Sukeforth now occupy adjoining offices.

Bassett, currently president of Sasaki Associates, has moved easily from one project type to another within the firm. He takes pride in his ability to listen, to understand the broad framework of a given situation, and to carry forward Sasaki's legacy on his own terms. "Our culture is born out of the balancing act between the disciplines," he observed. "It's a culture where probably there has to be a 'loose hand on the tiller.' The best will come out of a place like this when you give some breathing room to people who may be very driven by the discipline they're in, yet at the same time you have to gently pull them back in and say, 'But there's also the whole here. You do have to temper your behavior and your attitude and your way of working to recognize that, if we're all in this together, then we're part of a team, and you have to behave in certain ways.' But you don't drive this place in a rigid way. You do it by paying attention to a number of different concerns. I like that." [16]

In the following pages, more will be heard from the current principals at Sasaki Associates, interpreting the work and vision of the firm in their own words. Here, three views of Sasaki's legacy—a mixture of philosophy, ambition, and human relations—may serve as summary. "I remember talking with architects who loved to work with Hideo in the early days," architect/planner David Hirzel recalls. "They said it was so refreshing to work with someone who believed in collaboration, participation, and support, as opposed to competition. The great egos of architects were very happy to have that. And those traits of Hideo really reflected who stayed and who left. Those who wanted to do their own thing and have their own name on the door passed through this place." [17]

Peter Walker, a landscape architect who left, looks back with pride. "Just as Thomas Church's San Francisco atelier ushered modernism into the field of landscape architecture in the 1930s and '40s, Hideo's neo-Olmstedian vision has defined the purpose, the form, and the nature of landscape practice for all of us since 1955, embracing the challenge of the great postwar expansion. The Bauhausian ideal of a collaboration among design equals, rarely achieved on a base of architecture alone, has been sought by four decades of dedicated landscape architects, architects, planners and engineers, and endures to this day at Sasaki Associates. It is a sustaining dream of a finely built world, seen as a whole." [18]

And Don Olson, a landscape architect who stayed, looked back in 1981: "Not many offices have followed our tracks—nor we theirs. Offices in existence prior to ours presumably were in a better position to respond to the same growth opportunities. Thus, it seems that the special qualities of the man were essential for it to all come together."

Portfolio

Planning and Urban Design

The University of Colorado

The University of Illinois at Urbana/Champaign

The University of South Florida at Tampa

Cleveland Gateway and North Coast Harbor

Cleveland Gateway

Sea Pines Plantation

The Landings

Costa Smeralda

Costa Smeralda

Sugarloaf/USA

Sugarloaf/USA

Campus Planning

"The justification for a university is that it preserves the connection between knowledge and the zest for life, by uniting the young and the old in the imaginative consideration of learning. The university imparts information, but it imparts it imaginatively.... A fact is no longer a bare fact; it is invested with all its possibilities. It is no longer a burden on the memory; it is energizing as the poet of our dreams, and as the architect of our purposes."

– Alfred North Whitehead

This passage was used as the epigraph to a draft master plan for Cleveland State University, dated June 28, 1968. Sasaki, Dawson, DeMay Associates (SDDA) was then working with architects Don M. Hisaka & Associates on that urban campus. From the master plan, Sasaki's firm would move on to provide landscape architectural services on a new physical education building and design a plaza for a new university center. This was a major commission at the time. Today it could be yet another footnote to Sasaki Associates' impressive history of campus planning and design, were it not for the transcendent idea of a university's function, articulated by Whitehead, and then rediscovered as an expression of the values in Sasaki's office.

At that time, M. Perry Chapman was a young architect/planner who had been hired by Sasaki's firm in 1964, initially to work on the master plan for the University of Rochester. Soon he became immersed in the complexities of campus planning and design, by far the most rapidly growing area of practice for the firm in the 1960s. Thirty years later, when Chapman decided to write an essay on postwar American campus planning, he interviewed Sasaki and wrote a draft that began with the prolific decade of the 1960s. An editor then prodded him to begin further back in time. "When I started to delve into the '50s," Chapman recalled, "I realized that some very interesting and significant things happened in campus design in that period."[1]

Chapman's essay, "Social Change and American Campus Design" (1994) may eventually lead him to a book-length study.[2] Here, the early contributions of Sasaki's firm should be noted. Shortly after Hideo Sasaki began teaching at Harvard in 1953-54, he invited the new dean at MIT, Pietro Belluschi, to see what he and his students were doing in the studios at Harvard. Belluschi accepted that invitation, found in Sasaki a kindred spirit, and began to seek Sasaki's assistance on projects that came to him, mainly from campus administrators. American colleges and universities were then experiencing phenomenal growth due, in part, to the presence of veterans then studying under the G.I. Bill of Rights. Belluschi, recently resettled in Cambridge after building up a significant practice in Portland, Oregon, had no local office of his own. In the late 1950s and early 1960s he would work with associate architectural offices, such as Robinson, Green & Beretta, on the new dormitories at the Rhode Island School of Design (RISD), or Carl Koch's office, on a the new Bennington College library. In each case, Belluschi engaged his friend Hideo Sasaki as landscape architect.

Soon the presidents of these and other institutions requested advice on the larger issues of campus growth and planning. Belluschi turned to Sasaki and his then small office to staff and formalize these investigations and organize the multidisciplinary teams needed to address such issues as infrastructure, parking, pedestrian movement, open space, and the siting of buildings.

Several studios at Harvard, conducted jointly between the schools of design and education, had begun to explore the relationship between educational programming and three-dimensional physical planning. The results of these explorations soon informed the work of Sasaki's firm; for Sasaki and some of his colleagues there—Richard Dober, Jack Robinson, Kenneth DeMay, and Don Olson—were also students or part-time instructors at the School of Design. Sasaki brought organizational and practical building skills to these studies. He also viewed his own office as a kind of school, where an exploratory frame of mind and a pragmatic interest in research were critical for dealing with the emerging issues of campus planning:

rapid growth, historical continuity, infrastructure and building implementation, and the control of visual quality in architecture and the landscape. These studies were done with various models of staffing by consultants and university officers. A process of determining the building program was developed. Campus advisory committees were formed to oversee different stages of the work. The focus was no longer on buildings alone, but on ensembles, sequences, circulation, and outdoor spaces. A new framework for development emerged.

The results of these investigations accumulated rapidly, forming a body of theory and clinical data that Dober used to write *Campus Planning* (1963). Chapman, reading this book soon after it appeared, was intrigued. The book's impact was like that of Jane Jacobs' *The Life and Death of Great American Cities* (1961) and Gordon Cullen's *Townscape* (1961). These were works that expanded one's horizons while bringing one back to small, important details of daily life. They offered the big picture and the vignette, the sustaining ideals and the facts. And so they quickly penetrated the design professions.

The magnitude and the freshness of the new work in campus planning and design rapidly gained Sasaki a nationwide reputation for comprehensive and yet humane physical planning and design, services much in demand. The office grew, attracting graduates from Harvard, MIT, and other schools. After a few years in the Watertown office, some of these young planners and designers moved on to jobs in their native regions. Some left to teach. Some accepted jobs within institutions and then turned back to Sasaki Associates to help them carry out their new planning responsibilities. [3]

The young planners and designers who stayed at Sasaki's office were able to work on some exceptional projects for new and existing campuses in several regions of the United States, as well as in Canada. Foothill College, in Los Altos, California, for example, became a prototype for something more than a collection of academic buildings. Beginning in 1957, Sasaki and his colleagues worked closely with the architects, Ernest J. Kump & Associates, and Masten and Hurd, to integrate Foothill's buildings and outdoor spaces on the regraded summits of two hilltops. The theatre, the library, the gymnasium (where the San Francisco Symphony would occasionally perform), and the plazas and courtyards, large and ceremonial or small and intimate, all became gathering places for students and other members of the surrounding communities. Before long Foothill was recognized as a true Acropolis; it was, in Allan Temko's view, a "high place" consecrated to the highest values of its young community." And so Foothill set the standard for the development of a new type of institution—the two-year junior college that would serve as a "multipurpose cultural resource" for the community and the region. [4]

After Foothill College came a long series of large, complex, and multi-stage projects of campus planning and design that would engage Sasaki's firm for many decades. And, among Sasaki's associates in the early 1960s were some young professionals whose talents and natural inclinations were well suited for such work, notably Richard Galehouse and Jack Robinson, who had been trained in both architecture and planning. These men, along with Chapman and Kenneth DeMay, played leading roles in the development of the firm's practice in campus planning and design. The University of Colorado, at Boulder, began as a project of master planning for the postwar expansion of the campus. It then led to a series of architectural projects in collaboration with a number of prominent architects, including

Pietro Belluschi, Harry Weese & Associates, and DeMars and Reay, and the emerging Colorado firms of William C. Muchow Associates, Hobart D. Wagener & Associates, and others. In retrospect, perhaps no campus work of the early years gained more recognition and garnered more awards than Foothill and the University of Colorado. But many other significant projects came into the office in the 1960s and '70s. Including the expansions of the University of Massachusetts, at Amherst; new buildings at the University of Rhode Island, in Kingston, and the University of Virginia, in Charlottesville; and master planning as well as building design at the Amherst campus of the State University of New York, at Buffalo.

Galehouse, who served as planner for several of these projects, including the University of Massachusetts, at Amherst, has fond recollections and many stories that shed light on the ways in which problems were solved in the process of collaborating with strong-willed, eminent professionals with unlike backgrounds. Galehouse has said much less about his own role in those early days, however, than about his senior colleagues, Sasaki and Belluschi, two men who shared a deep commitment to collaboration and appeared to thrive in that kind of working environment. "Belluschi was such a gentleman, an old world gentleman," Galehouse sighed. His style and skill were amazing. I think he really enjoyed his relationship with Hideo. There were *two* such gentlemen." [5]

In several articles, Chapman has noted the firm's major achievements in campus planning, decade by decade. In the 1950s and early '60s, master plans that gave new structure to open spaces and circulation often led to further commissions for landscape and site design and sometimes architectural design as well. By the late 1960s, commissions for some academic buildings came into the firm, independent of master planning jobs; and the architectural discipline, aided by greater strength in civil engineering, would soon emerge as a force in its own right. In the 1970s, with the accumulation of campus unrest over the war in Southeast Asia, economic recession, inflation, energy crises and dwindling endowment portfolios, campus planning subsided for a while. By the end of the '70s, some universities asked Sasaki Associates for assistance in developing their outlying land to accommodate mixed-use development (commercial, corporate, research and development, etc.), so as to generate employment in their communities and new sources of revenue.

The 1980s and '90s have brought a return to campus planning, often on more stringent budgets and with new concerns: for adaptive re-use rather than new construction; for facilities that would help campuses compete for students at a time of declining enrollment; for "selective expansion" rather than grand schemes built on greenfield (virgin) sites; for the use of more traditional materials and forms that would fit into an existing context; for low-maintenance planting; and for greater security. Moreover, there was a need for strategies to integrate computers and other technological apparatus in existing spaces, while also encouraging more personal, face-to-face exchanges—which have traditionally been at the heart of academic life.

Many principals at Sasaki Associates consider the creation of places for meeting and congregating—for simple, enjoyable human contact, at whatever scale, on campus or beyond—to be at the heart of their multidisciplinary practice. Chapman likes to quote a town planner who recently asked, "Why are we not concentrating on the need for public space with the same energy that we're concentrating on the need for cyberspace?" "It's only anecdotal," Chapman admits, "But I think there's something there."

The University of Colorado

Location: *Boulder, Colorado*
Client: *The University of Colorado*
Project Dates: *1960-1970*
Sasaki Staff: *Hideo Sasaki, Stuart O. Dawson,*
      Jack Robinson, Kenneth DeMay,
      Harry Porter, Carlisle Becker,
      Dick Dober

In Association
With: *Pietro Belluschi*
Architects: *Moore & Bush; William Muchor*
      (architectural associates in
      Colorado); Meyer & Ayres;
      Harry Weese & Associates;
      Hobie Wagner Associates;
      Murphy & Mackey; DeMars and Reay
Awards: *Award Citation, Progressive*
      Architecture, Education category,
      1963

Boulder, Colorado

The "Colorado style" blends with the Rocky Mountain backdrop

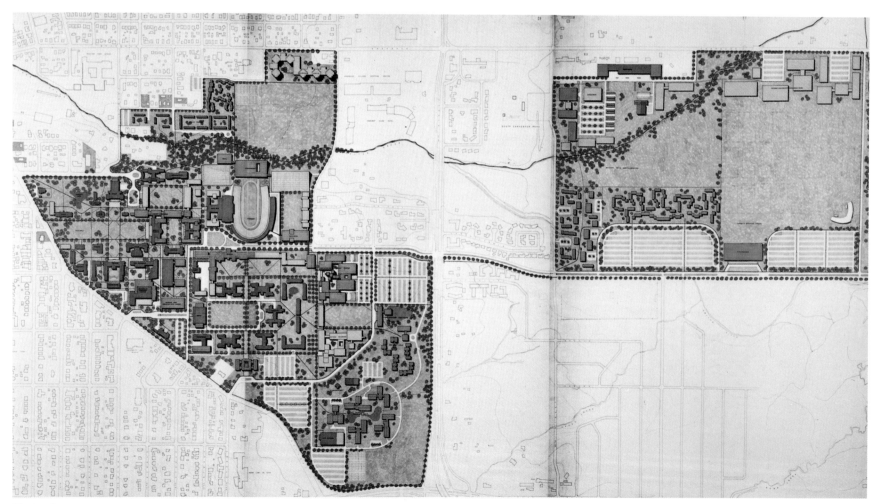

Master plan

0   1000 feet ▲

The Boulder campus of the University of Colorado sits on a spectacular plain at the base of the Rocky Mountain Front Range. Like many early U.S. land grant institutions, the campus consisted of a loose and undistinguished assortment of buildings constructed between its founding in 1876 and the early 1900s. The great transformation that made Colorado one of America's most beautiful campuses was a consequence of the campus plan prepared by Charles Klauder of Philadelphia in 1919. The Klauder plan organized buildings around a network of *Beaux Arts* open spaces and established an architectural vocabulary of sandstone facades and red tile roofs adapted from the "Tuscan vernacular" style. This ingenious translation of a Mediterranean building form fit exquisitely into the semi-arid foothill setting. Klauder went on to design 15 buildings at Colorado, and set architectural guidelines that have endured to this day as the "Colorado style."

In 1960, Sasaki Associates was retained as consultant for planning and design to define how the university could accommodate an expected doubling of enrollment to 20,000 students in the following ten years. Pietro Belluschi collaborated as consultant for architecture. The team's design affirmed the principles established by Klauder, extending the spatial framework with new buildings and maintaining the warm palette of architectural materials. The Sasaki plan sustained the pedestrian scale of the expanding campus by linking the major spaces with a unified system of landscape materials and by introducing site features such as plazas and pools to provide focus and variety at important junctures in the network of campus spaces. New buildings were placed to frame quadrangles and courtyards, with major structures positioned to visually anchor primary pedestrian axes.

The principal challenge in the early 1960s was to maintain the integrity of the Colorado style in the design and placement of the larger, more complex facilities necessary to accommodate a new generation of academic, research, residential, and public functions. The solution was to break down the scale of facilities into component volumes in scale with the traditional forms of the campus, while adhering to the rich textures introduced by Klauder. The first and most notable example is the Engineering Sciences Center, a 440,000 square-foot complex designed as an assemblage of shed-roofed volumes organized around a series of small courtyards. The soaring "mine tipple" form is dramatically rooted in the foothill environment, while expressing a modern collegial function. The design recaptures the Tuscan vernacular style in its articulated massing and in the detailing of the stone facade.

The Sasaki plan for Colorado included updating design review procedures and guidelines to fit the contemporary needs of the growing institution. The university's diligence in maintaining the review process has resulted in the preservation of a remarkable legacy throughout an era of extraordinary growth and change.

Connections to older campus

Memorial Courtyard is one of many nodes of student activity

Campus context

Kitteridge Dormitory pond

Old Quad

Memorial Courtyard fountain

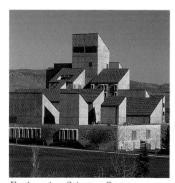
Engineering Sciences Center

Kitteridge Dormitory Commons

The University of Illinois at Urbana/Champaign

Location: Champaign, Illinois
Client: The University of Illinois
Project Dates: 1985-1990
Sasaki Staff: M. Perry Chapman, Stuart O. Dawson,
                 Joseph A. Hibbard, Martha Lampkin,
                 Dennis Swinford, Anne Casey

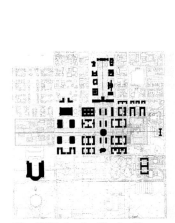

The 1927 plan by Charles Platt
extended the axial order of the
Quad

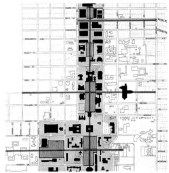

The main axis of the Quad draws
the various areas of the campus
together

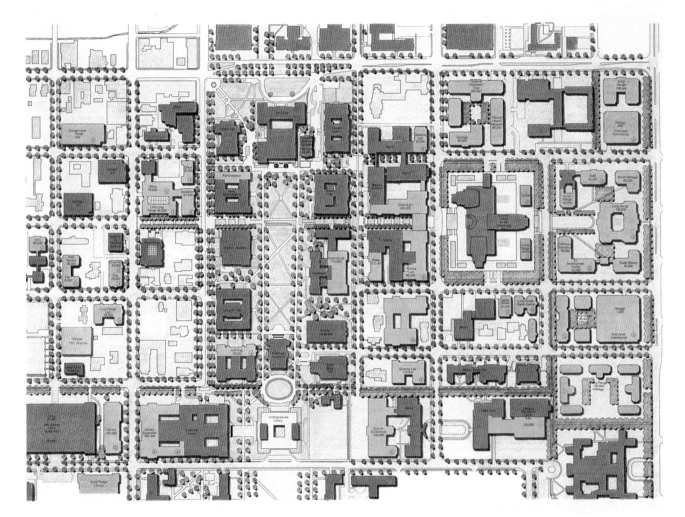

The plan for the Central Campus is integrated
with the surrounding street grid

The University of Illinois at Urbana/Champaign is an example of the classic midwestern American public university. Established in 1867, the university has grown from an agricultural land grant college to a comprehensive research institution serving 35,000 students. The campus environment is both urban and rural, consisting of an 800-acre academic and residential "core" interwoven with the street grid of Urbana and Champaign and over 2,700 acres of agricultural land to the south. The university came to a watershed in its physical development in the early years of the twentieth century when plans prepared by James White, and later, Charles Platt, organized the layout along a north-south central axis intersected by a cross-axis extending the campus to the east and west. The axial framework prevailed as the foundation for the university's development through the expansive post-World War II decades.

In 1985, Sasaki Associates was asked to initiate the first of a series of district plans for long-range development of various sectors of the campus with the axial framework as the armature joining the districts together. The first plan, for the north campus, provides for significant growth in the university's engineering instruction and research programs. The priority was to site several proposed research facilities, notably the Beckman Institute for Advanced Science and Technology, then representing the largest capital donation ever made to a public university. The plan extends the central axis north from the core of the campus with the Beckman Institute as its northern anchor. The congested and fragmented area that had been the northern periphery of the campus was organized into a system of open spaces that form a unified matrix of building sites. Space was identified for future research enterprises that would be drawn to the university.

The plan for the central campus focused on the undergraduate heart of the university around the main quadrangle. The plan preserves the traditional spatial order of the university, extending the core beyond the quad into the urban street and block structure of Urbana and Champaign on designated sites. Future facilities for the sciences, the arts, continuing education, the bookstore and other uses are accommodated by the extension beyond the quad area.

The Quad in the early 20th century

The University of Illinois at Urbana/Champaign

Pedestrian walks frame the major campus spaces

The Quad is the central organizing space of the university

The midwestern landscape is a unifying theme

Main axis of the Quad

The Quad

Ornamental planting unifies varied building edges

Side courts connect the Quad with peripheral areas of the campus

Building entries

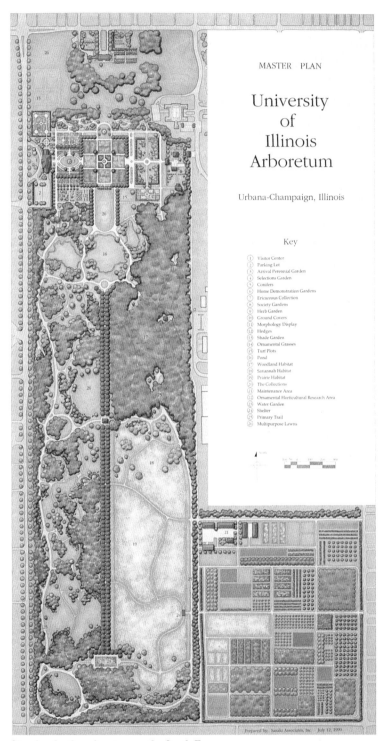

MASTER PLAN

University
of
Illinois
Arboretum

Urbana-Champaign, Illinois

Key

1 Visitor Center
2 Parking Lot
3 Arrival Perennial Garden
4 Selections Garden
5 Conifers
6 Home Demonstration Gardens
7 Ericaceous Collection
8 Society Gardens
9 Herb Garden
10 Ground Covers
11 Morphology Display
12 Hedges
13 Shade Garden
14 Ornamental Grasses
15 Turf Plots
16 Pond
17 Woodland Habitat
18 Savannah Habitat
19 Prairie Habitat
20 The Collections
21 Maintenance Area
22 Ornamental Horticultural Research Area
23 Water Garden
24 Shelter
25 Primary Trail
26 Multipurpose Lawns

Prepared by: Sasaki Associates, Inc.   July 12, 1990

Site plan for the arboretum on the South Farms

The south campus plan accommodates the broad range of academic, residential and recreational functions that span the east-west cross axis. The plan links the urban groupings of academic and residential facilities clustered in the vicinity of the main quad with the dispersed sports facilities and fields at the western and southern periphery. The connecting theme is the reinforcement of the campus street and open space grid with a consistent landscape fabric and the development of strategic sites for academic buildings.

The South Farms area contains the university's agricultural lands, the arboretum, state survey facilities, athletic and recreation fields, and a proposed research park. Agricultural lands are now organized in relation to such factors as soils, drainage, and ecological considerations. An ordered framework for built facilities is defined. The vast holdings of the South Farms area called for a regional scale landscape system to tie the area together. Major arterial highways traversing the site are lined with a unifying tree-scape that echoes the windrow vocabulary of the rural midwest. New destination open spaces such as the arboretum and the sports complex provide regional amenities.

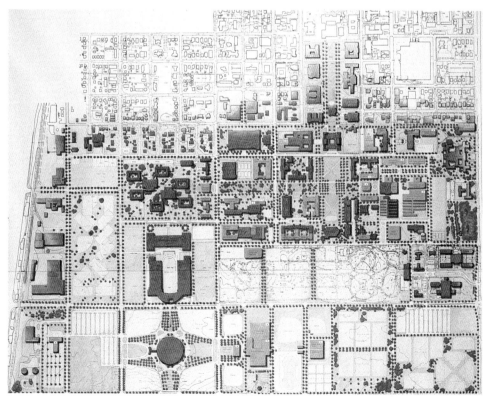

Illustrative plan of the South Campus

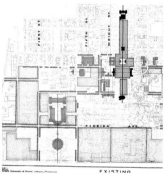

Open space structure of the South Campus

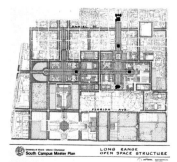

Circulation structure of the South Campus

The University of South Florida at Tampa

Location: Tampa, Florida
Client: The University of South Florida
Project Dates: 1993-1996
Sasaki Staff: M. Perry Chapman, Joseph A. Hibbard,
                 Dennis Pieprz, Jean Garbier, Kenneth Schwartz,
                 Kathryn Madden, Winston Hagen
Sub-consultants: Tampa Bay Engineering; GRG Vanderweil;
                 Anthony Blackett
Awards: American Society of Landscape
                 Architects' Merit Award in Urban Design, 1994

Academic core in the 1960s

Infill development to define new civic entry

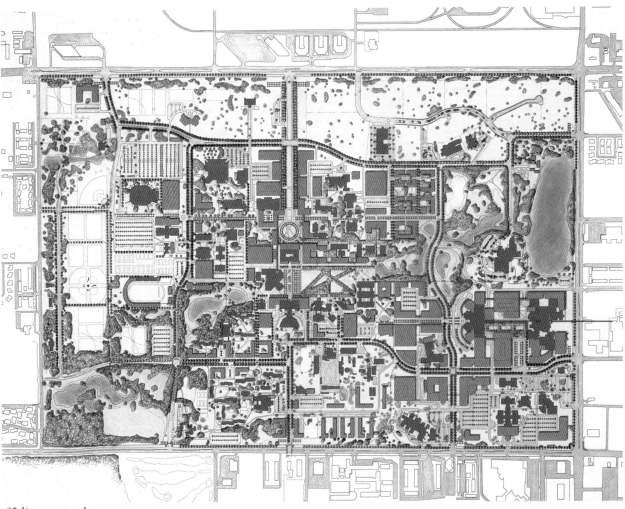
25-Year master plan

44

The University of South Florida at Tampa is a 1,000-acre campus that was originally developed on farmland in the 1950s. It was the first state university in the Florida system to be located in a major metropolitan area, making higher education available to a greater number of people. In 1993, Sasaki Associates was retained to prepare a master plan for the Tampa campus, following criteria set by the state university system to direct the planning and management of campus growth for schools in Florida.

Over four decades, the university had evolved to become a premier research institution with an enrollment of over 20,000 full-time students, making it one of the largest universities in the South. Enrollment was expected to grow by more than 40 percent, and the area occupied by buildings to double—to accommodate a required increase in floor space of more than four million square feet. The campus was sprawling, and lacked coherence and order. Surface parking for 11,000 vehicles dominated the open space.

Sasaki Associates' master plan redefines the character and density of the campus by accommodating the growth of the institution in an ordered way, linking disparate parts, and constructing a built environment suitable to the Florida climate.

The building program connects functional areas and unifies fragmented surface parking. To establish a coherent pattern of development, new buildings are located on infill sites, increasing campus density and forming an interconnected series of new quadrangles, courtyards, and arcades. A pedestrian circulation and spatial system builds on the original campus grid, and encourages walking and bicycling, reducing reliance on the automobile, and increasing communication and connection between campus districts. Parking structures are strategically located, and new systems of public transportation are provided.

The key open space is a greenway that traverses the campus with the University's central lawn as its focal point. It serves as a counterbalance to the increased campus density, and connects with natural open space and drainage areas at the campus perimeter. The greenway, which transforms the stormwater management system into an amenity, permits the restoration of a native sand hill landscape. The plan proposes the reclamation of native landscape as a unifying theme. It calls for the arrangement of buildings and open spaces in response to the climate—hot sun and intermittent downpours—and for sheltering arcades and breezeways.

The fundamental change made by the plan is the establishment of clear and animated connections between the academic, residential, and public areas of the university.

The firm's role in the design of the Martin Luther King Plaza on the central lawn demonstrates how trellises, shade trees, and fountains can be used in the pedestrian environment of the University.

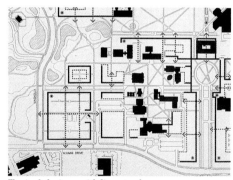

Typical design guidelines to shape open spaces and building zones

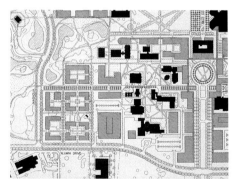

Illustration of building sites that follow the design guidelines

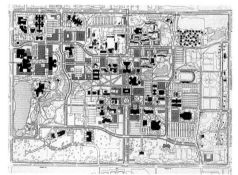

Illustration of open spaces and building sites for the entire campus

Palm walk at Martin Luther King Plaza

Shade trellis

Palm walk looking out to the central lawn

Martin Luther King Plaza reflecting pool

California State University, Monterey Bay Campus

Location: Seaside and Marina, California
Client: California State University, Monterey Bay
Project Dates: Ongoing (since March 1995)
Sasaki Staff: Robert Sabbatini, Julia Monteith,
                 Harry Akiyama, Patricia Sonnino,
                 M. Perry Chapman, Tim Deacon, Owen Lang,
                 Leo Ma, N. Scott Smith
Sub-Consultants: Adamson Associates; Bestor Engineers, Inc.;
                 California Polytechnic State University
                 Foundation; Economics Research Associates;
                 Fehr Engineering Company; Lee & Associates;
                 MGT of America, Inc.; Schaff & Wheeler;
                 TeleConsultants, Inc.; Terratech, Inc.;
                 Tomasi-Dubois & Associates;
                 URS Consultants, Inc.;
                 Wilbur Smith Associates;
                 Woodward Clyde Consultants

The color schemes of the renovated buildings announce the transformation of the campus

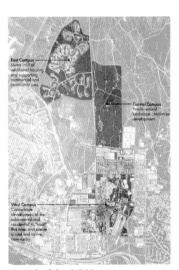

Aerial of the 1,300-acre campus indicating the land use for the East, Central, and West Campuses

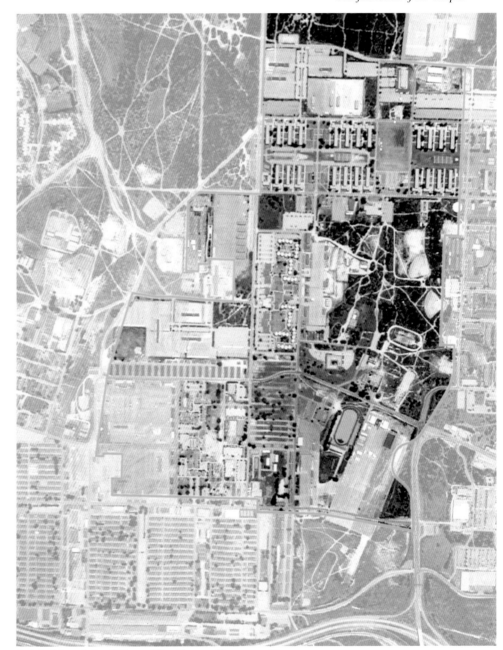

Aerial of the existing 615-acre West Campus illustrates military development over a 50-year period

California State University, Monterey Bay (CSUMB) is located on 1,300 acres of the former Fort Ord military base. To meet critical state and regional needs, CSUMB integrates resources within a curriculum and a variety of traditional and non-traditional learning experiences. As academic strategies evolve, the campus also will adapt and change. This evolution requires that the campus and its facilities incorporate flexibility, variety, and integration of uses.

Sasaki Associates' primary role was to develop a master plan that supports the university's educational mission. The plan addresses the essential elements of the campus and their relationship to regional, physical, social, economic, and political factors. Central to the campus' success as a community is its ability to offer a range of opportunities for residents and users. The goal of providing environmental leadership through sustainable development influenced the campus form, open space, land use, and circulation.

The master plan's framework encourages a dynamic educational, living, and working environment and envisions a campus community with a unique identity that will serve to frame its growth, evolution, and development. This framework is formed through an interconnected network of open spaces. These spines establish visual and physical links throughout the campus, integrating land uses and providing connections to the campus context. The spines share the role typically performed by streets while providing a new form of outdoor space. As the university and the surrounding communities grow, these spaces will become increasingly important. The campus is planned to promote pedestrian, bicycle, and public transit.

Another significant goal of the plan is to extend the campus community beyond its boundaries to the surrounding cities of Marina and Seaside. The plan creates a focus of educational uses in the center of the West Campus and wraps this use with residential neighborhoods which, in turn, create natural connections between the campus and adjacent mixed-use village developments. The West Campus includes stores, restaurants, commercial services, recreation, and wellness centers.

The proposed development patterns reflect the university's desire to maximize the use of existing buildings. Critical to the success of the architectural design on the campus is the response to climate and culture. Buildings organized around well defined courtyards offer a wind protected microclimate, while allowing solar penetration, and create outdoor spaces unavailable elsewhere on the campus. Climatic response go beyond the broad parameters of building design and are incorporated into more detailed development to meet the master plan's goal of sustainability.

Existing campus figure ground denotes grid of buildings, roads, and suburban development patterns

The master plan maximizes the use of existing buildings while aligning new development with the open space spine and street system

Open space is addressed within a hierarchy of public and private uses

The Ohio State University

Location: Columbus, Ohio
Client: The Ohio State University
Project Dates: 1995-1996
Sasaki Staff: M. Perry Chapman, Kenneth E. Bassett,
                  Kim Baur, Dennis Pieprz, William Colehower,
                  Ivana Sturm, Michael Regan
In Association
With: Michael Dennis & Associates:
                  Michael Dennis, Eric Thorkildsen,
                  Glen Knowles
Sub-consultants: Moody Nolan, Ltd., Inc.

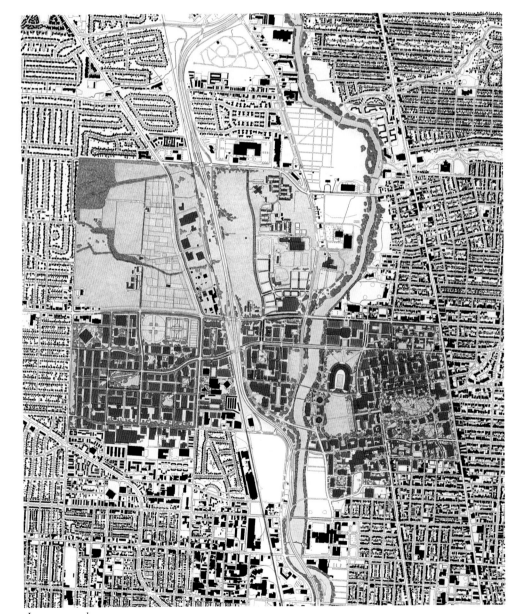

Long range plan

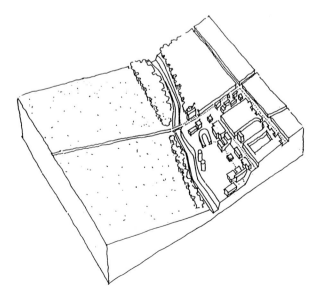

Diagram of the university's river corridor
and prairie environment

The Ohio State University is the flagship institution of Ohio's public higher education system. The 1,800-acre campus, traversed by the Olentangy River, consists of a built-up academic core east of the river and a largely open landscape of agricultural fields, parking, and dispersed building clusters to the west. The urban and rural environments of Ohio State are essential to the university's dual role, as an academic/research institution and as a premier public land grant campus. The urban core of the campus, which is organized around a memorable open space called the "Oval," provides a richly concentrated academic setting for learning, research, living and social functions. It is an integral part of the city fabric of Columbus. The western reach of the campus contains large areas for agricultural research that offer a broad spatial relief to surrounding urban areas.

The most recent generation of planning for the 50,000-student institution began in 1993 as an internal process which brought together academic, fiscal and physical planning constituencies of the university to define needs and establish principles for campus development. Sasaki Associates, in association with Michael Dennis & Associates, was engaged in 1995 to assist the university in defining a strategy for managing campus growth and change in the twenty-first century, and in establishing procedures for the enhancement of campus form and design.

Because of the size and complexity of the campus, planning was carried out at several levels. Priority was given to determining long-range capacity for growth, while preserving the university's land resources. A primary goal was to unify the development fabric of the campus while maintaining its "walking campus"

character by composing a variety of active open spaces for academic and social functions, in close proximity to one another. The maintenance of a diverse urban academic core called for well-defined design guidelines for campus architecture and site development.

A long-range plan was prepared for the campus as a whole, recommending policy measures to manage campus growth, preserve open space and strengthen the established urban texture. Among the most important planning policies adopted by the university was the decision to set aside a green reserve of critical open spaces consisting of the agricultural lands, recreation and athletic fields, arboreta, the space flanking the river corridor, and landmark spaces such as the "Oval."

Existing and future building sites in the academic core

Landscape fabric of the academic core

The natural beauty of the campus is reinforced by open spaces such as Mirror Lake Hollow

Memorable open spaces such as the Oval are key elements of the green reserve

Recreation fields south of the stadium framed by new buildings and landscape

The Oval

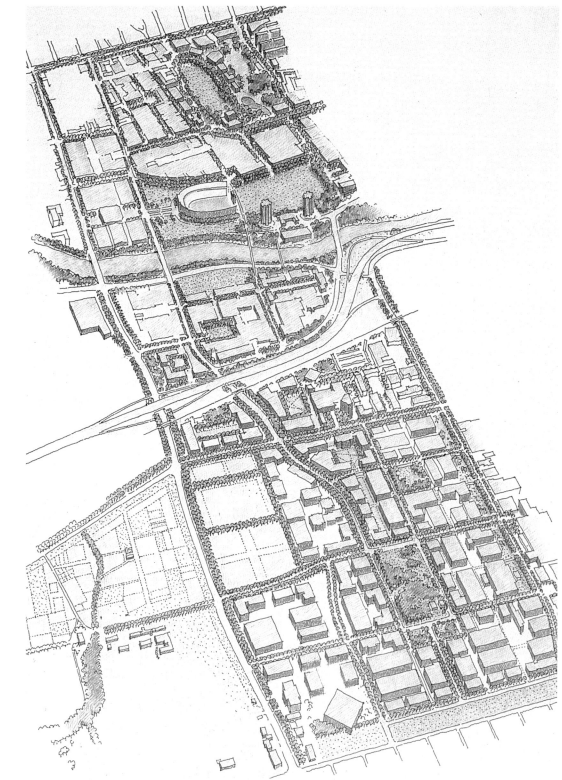

*Perspective of the University Master Plan with
West Campus research park site in the foreground*

The plan establishes minimum densities and land use priorities in development zones, to contain the spread of development. These zones include strategic infill sites in built-up areas. They provide for future growth in defined corridors, an "urban development area" that extends the core campus west, across the river, to lands designated for the growth of research facilities. A civic structure plan integrates circulation, open spaces, and areas for building development. The circulation system is centered on a "great academic boulevard" that links the areas east and west of the river, and a street system that is compatible in width and character with the grid of the academic core. It calls for the gradual redeployment of parking in structures in order to conserve land and reclaim open spaces for pedestrian activity.

The plan is reinforced with detailed plans for campus districts set up to create a rational framework for campus improvements. Specific site development criteria are included in these district plans. Sasaki Associates has prepared two district plans as prototypes—one for the "academic core" area and one for the West Campus, which includes the agricultural lands and University Research Park. The Sasaki team formulated a model process for the evaluation of possible locations for prospective facilities. Plans for the medical and athletic districts are underway.

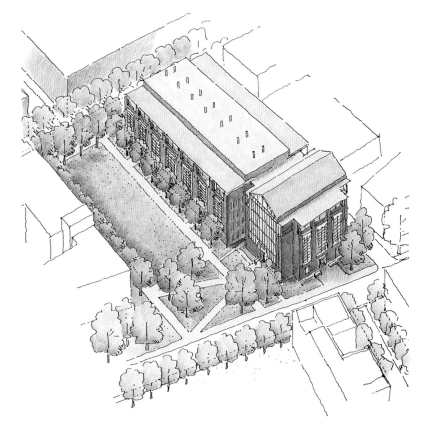

Study for siting an academic building

The Oletangy River corridor connects the university with the city

Study for integration of the stadium into the fabric of the campus

Urban Design

By Melanie Simo

When Stuart Dawson presented a paper at the Third International Conference on Tall Buildings, in 1986, he asked his audience to forget about tall buildings for a moment. "Too much attention to the skyline," he began. "Too much attention to net-to-gross; too much attention to unique fenestration. . . , security. . . , travertine; too much affection for the automobile and much too little concern for people on the street!"[1]

Dawson's topic on that occasion was the creation of great streets—specifically, Sasaki Associates' urban design master plan for the new Dallas Arts District, for which he was principal-in-charge. This project entailed the transformation of a "rather bleak stretch of pavement running through the center of the district" in northeast downtown Dallas into a grand, tree-lined boulevard, friendly to pedestrians and focused on the arts. The old name, "Flora Street," was retained, while several new low-rise structures helped to define and ennoble the street. They included a new concert hall by I.M. Pei, the new Dallas Museum of Art, by Edward L. Barnes, and new retail, entertainment, and restaurant uses, to be interspersed with office towers, schools, the historic Belo Mansion, and other structures. To explain the creation of this great street, Dawson gave ample legal, financial, horticultural, and architectural details that, when properly coordinated, would yield a grand space for the coexistence of pedestrians and automobiles, skyscrapers and small jewels of architecture. Dawson's final image, however, was drawn from the natural world. Quoting William H. Whyte, he said, "The street is the City's river of life. The best public places are those in which you don't know where the street ends and the place begins."[2]

In fact, the river is a recurring image in some forty years of urban design at Sasaki Associates. Suggesting movement, continuity, vitality, and a pace tempered by nature's own inclinations and rhythms, the river was one natural element, literal and metaphorical, that came to mind in the 1950s and early '60s, when Dawson, Kenneth DeMay, Richard Galehouse, Don Olson, and other now senior principals at Sasaki Associates were collaborating on urban design projects with the emerging leaders in the field. In 1959, for instance, the firm was working with Adams, Howard & Greeley; Anderson, Beckwith & Haible; and the independent consultants Kevin Lynch, John R. Myer, and Paul D. Spreiregen, to design the broad framework for several new structures to be built in Boston's new "Government Center." Conscious of the unfortunate tendency for urban renewal schemes to remain isolated from the fabric of the existing city, this group of consultants emphasized the integration of the old and the new, and the sequence of spaces that would be seen and experienced by people in motion. The consultants also proposed a chain of public open spaces that might "run like a river" down a valley, among low-rise buildings, eventually leading to the harbor. Later, in a moment of inspiration, someone referred to this sequence as a "walk to the sea." The concept was appealing, and the phrase lived on.[3]

Over the years, Sasaki's firm has taken on even more complex challenges, particularly in the decades since a myriad of regulations were put in place regarding environmental protection and the inclusion of the broad public into the planning process. Soon there were many more voices to be heard and factors to be considered. Often (as in the delicate negotiations over the recent "Cleveland Gateway" project), the firm was engaged to oversee the integration of the concerns of several interest groups, public and private, before the process traditionally known as urban planning and design could even begin. As Alan Ward, design principal for the Cleveland Gateway project, explained, "Two architectural firms were selected at the same time as we were: HOK Sport, for the ballpark, and Ellerbe Becket, for the sports arena. We were the party to coordinate the buildings on the site, to coordinate traffic and parking, and also to represent the public interest—to act as a neutral third party between the city, the development authority, and the public as well."[4]

Problems of urban design, like those of campus planning, tend to elicit from Sasaki Associates the kind of long-term collaborative effort that they find most satisfying; and, not surprisingly, it is in these projects that they tend to be most "competitive." The problems tend to be large, complex, one-of-a-kind, demanding skills and understanding that no single professional could offer alone. Rather, the architect, the landscape architect, the engineer, and the planner would each bring a particular understanding to bear on the problem, for which there is no obvious precedent.

And yet there is an historic precedent for the very fact of the firm's interest in, and suitability for, these projects. The precedent is not a single project, nor a unique moment in time; it is an evolving approach to solving complex problems, whereby no individual professional, no "master builder" or "caped hero" could be relied upon for the great formal solution. Instead, a group of differently trained, mutually respectful professionals had in common an earnest desire to work together, with individual egos held in check, to improve the urban environments in their midst. Of course, no individual or firm—or country—could claim a monopoly on such an approach. It appears, however, that this approach has developed in a few places where the ambitions and ideals of one forceful designer or group or school could be tempered by the ideals and values of another. One place this occurred was at Harvard in the 1950s.

When Josep Lluis Sert became Dean of the Graduate School of Design in 1953, an important change was made in the masters studio that Walter Gropius had previously offered to advanced students in architecture: it became multidisciplinary. Several of Hideo Sasaki's best students in landscape architecture and Reginald Isaacs' best students in city planning then joined advanced architecture students in exploring the more complex problems of architecture—essentially, those of urban design. This master's studio later became the model for the School's new Urban Design Program, established in 1960-1961 as an area of specialization for advanced students in architecture and landscape architecture. The program recruited students from all over the United States and abroad, and its graduates soon found jobs in design offices around Harvard Square and in the Boston area—notably, at the Sasaki office.

Because of the multidisciplinary nature of the office and its growing reputation for campus planning, urban renewal, and physical design, some of the Urban Design students at Harvard worked at the office, part-time, and a few were invited to join the firm. At that time, the planners in the office—including Richard Dober, John Adelberg, and Richard Galehouse—all had design backgrounds, mainly in architecture. These planners would work with early graduates of the Urban Design Program, such as Masao Kinoshita. In the process, the programmatic and physical elements of the new field of urban design were integrated, or fused. In addition, with the school as a theoretical base and the Sasaki office as a clinical center, the field of urban design was continually redefined as new problems arose.

Today, looking back over several decades of urban design at Sasaki Associates, in cities from Boston and Dallas to Potsdam and Taipei, one could trace a growing complexity of factors to be integrated and still recognize some continuities in broad vision and approach. The city is still viewed as a place in need of structure, patterns, contrasts, and a powerful, memorable image. The city is still a place where one tries to create sequences of spaces and views, to be experienced at human scale, on foot, as well as on the road or from the air. In 1963, when Hideo Sasaki sent Philadelphia city planner Edmund Bacon a series of suggestions for the improvement of that city's urban waterfront, along with quick, fluid sketches prepared by the office, he emphasized the river—the linear, continuous quality of the Schuylkill River. People could sit or stroll along a riverfront promenade, follow pedestrian overpasses above the railroads, or linger in quiet play areas and fields. In the background would be dense rows of trees that would give definition to both the riverfront and the urban fabric.[5]

Recently, some theories of urban design have focused attention on traditional neighborhood developments; the "New Urbanism." These are conscientious efforts, often driven by strong environmental and sociological purposes, to counter some of the tendencies of what was new some sixty or seventy years ago—that is, modernist approaches to urban design. To Alan Ward, an architect who studied landscape architecture and urban design at Harvard in the late 1970s before joining Sasaki Associates, there seem to be considerably more precedents for these recent urban design prototypes than current theory would suggest. "Each era wants to make a revolution and say 'We're starting over,'" he observed. "But actually there's a lot of continuity."

Recalling Frederick Law Olmsted's work with Calvert Vaux at Riverside, in Illinois (1869), and Sir Raymond Unwin's work with Barry Parker at, say, Letchworth, in Hertfordshire, England (1904), Ward detects an evolution of thinking about planning and urban design. He believes there is a thread that runs from the work of Olmsted, Unwin, and the early twentieth-century landscape architect/planners John Nolen, Elbert Peets, and others, to the late twentieth-century work of Sasaki Associates and their contemporaries in the design of new communities. The one dramatic break with this evolutionary development occurred within the modern movement, in the more revolutionary prototypes of Le Corbusier and others. But this movement was never so homogeneous as some now view it in hindsight; its solutions to the problems of urban design were varied. Even today, the successes and failings of modernist urban design are still being assessed.

In the meantime, Ward is more interested in the problems at hand—not the ideological ones but the concrete, pressing ones of the existing city, in America and elsewhere on the planet. "The real issue," he has come to believe, "is how to basically 'repair' the existing city. If you look at American urbanism as an experiment, it seems that we have had several hundred years, beginning with settling the frontier. Over the years, we have simply moved outward and extended the city, trying to improve on the past, rather than layering over it, as they have done in Europe over longer periods of time. I think it's time to draw some limits and say—'Let's refine the earlier, failed experiments and try to get it right.' So, you can try to reclaim and reconstruct the existing city, and try to reinforce a sense of community in the public environment. If you can make that environment more dense and urbanized, public space will become more important. That's part of our work ahead."

Ward pauses, as more issues and more opportunities come to mind—ecological, sociological, artistic. "My sense is, the fundamental issue ahead is how our culture relates to nature. I still think that remains the fundamental challenge that we face."[6]

The Dallas Arts District Urban Design Plan

Location: Dallas, Texas
Client: Dallas Arts District Consortium
Project Dates: 1982-1983
Sasaki Staff: Stuart O. Dawson, Daniel R.
                     Kenney, Alan L. Ward, David Bennett,
                     Jay Faber, Jean Gropp,
                     Randy Thueme, Stephen E. Hamwey
Sub-consultants: Halcyon Ltd.; LAN Engineering
Awards: First Place, Dallas Arts District
                     Competition; Honor Award, Planning
                     and Analysis, American Society
                     of Landscape Architects, 1984;
                     Honor Award, Boston Society
                     of Landscape Architects, 1st Professional
                     Awards Program, 1984

Arts District boundaries

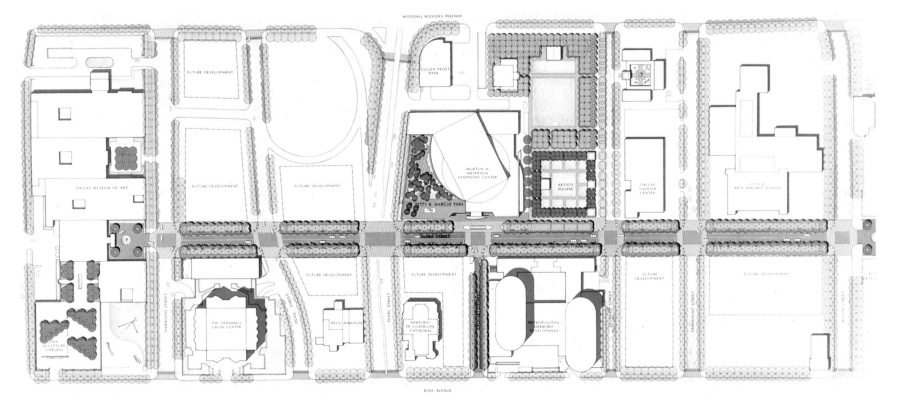

Master plan

The Dallas Arts District, a vibrant mixed-use district in the heart of downtown Dallas, was planned by Sasaki Associates to integrate arts institutions with private uses in an environment that would encourage pedestrian activity. The district is located in the northern sector of the central business district. It was an underutilized sector of the city and therefore represented a special opportunity to reestablish a pedestrian precinct in downtown Dallas. Recognizing the desirability of consolidating arts institutions in a new location, the Dallas City Council sought to establish a vision for the 17-block area by holding a national design competition.

Sasaki's award-winning design builds upon three fundamental principles: that public open space is an essential structuring element in the urban environment; that mixed use is important to the activation of urban places; and that public/private partnerships are a foundation for implementation.

The plan creates a "great street" for Dallas. Flora Street, the central spine that extends the length of the arts district, is envisioned as a pedestrian-oriented corridor along which arts institutions and development parcels front. Major institutions are situated at the ends and center of the 2,000-foot long street so that it will be animated by people during evenings and weekends. Flora Street is designed with a flush curb, a triple row of street trees on both sides, and special paving to encourage pedestrian activity. Closing the street to vehicular traffic allows it to function as a major space for public events. District identity is established by a uniform street tree palette, signage, and lighting.

To ensure that the district develops according to the master plan, a special district zoning ordinance was enacted. The Dallas Arts District Design Guidelines and Master Plan are part of that special district ordinance. An active pedestrian environment is encouraged by the design guidelines, which require all parking to be underground, and retail or arts-related uses to be at ground level; they establish minimum building frontage and maximum building height on Flora Street. Pedestrian connections to existing pedestrian corridors in downtown are also required.

The implementation plan establishes a public/private cost-sharing structure, a management organization, and a framework for public/private shared responsibility for maintenance of the public infrastructure. The Dallas Arts District management organization is responsible for scheduling and planning events in the district.

The Dallas Arts District is a living and evolving model of the translation of a vision—the potential of the public realm to transform the life of the city—into reality.

View toward art museum

New building according to guidelines

Flora Street and downtown

Shaded sidewalks

District signs and lighting

Outdoor seating

Street closed for outdoor museum event

Performance space

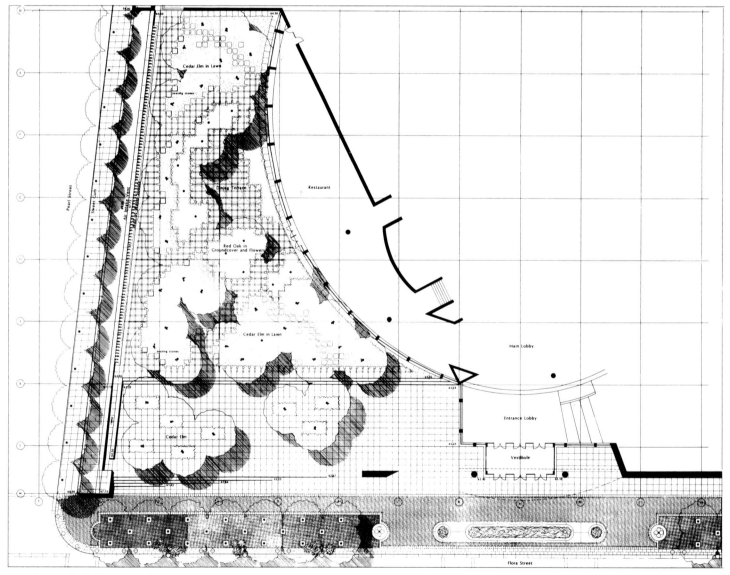

Betty Marcus Park illustrative plan

0   20 feet

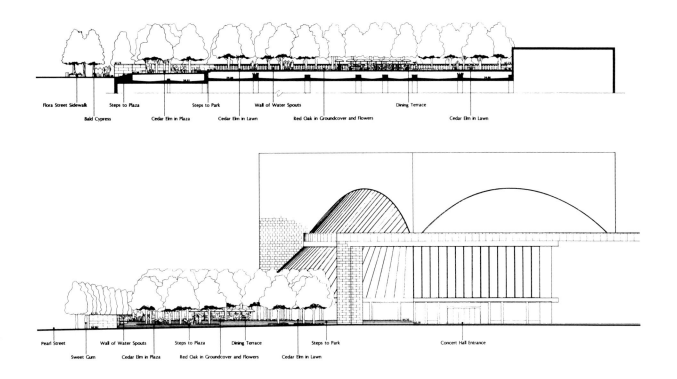

Flora Street Sidewalk Steps to Plaza Steps to Park Wall of Water Spouts Dining Terrace

Bald Cypress Cedar Elm in Plaza Cedar Elm in Lawn Red Oak in Groundcover and Flowers Cedar Elm in Lawn

Pearl Street Wall of Water Spouts Steps to Plaza Dining Terrace Steps to Park Concert Hall Entrance

Sweet Gum Cedar Elm in Plaza Red Oak in Groundcover and Flowers Cedar Elm in Lawn

Betty Marcus Park section and elevation

Sculpture in the park

Dining terrace adjacent to Concert Hall

Lobby connection to park

Concert Hall lobby

Planting and paving design extends building grid

Water wall

Taipei Terminal

Location:	*Taipei, Taiwan*
Client:	*Taipei Department of City Planning and the Federal Council for Economic Development*
Project Dates:	*1990*
Sasaki Staff:	*Alan L. Ward, Dennis Pieprz, Daniel R. Kenney, Ken Schwartz, Ya-Tien Chuan, George Bregianos, Pat Crowell*
Sub-consultants:	*ZHA, Inc.; Dr. Chin Pai; Professor Leon Huang; Dr. Edwin Lin; Asian Technical Consultants*
Awards:	*Merit Award in Urban Design, American Society of Landscape Architects, 1991*

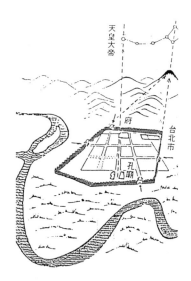

Original walled city related to sacred mountain and north star

Existing arterial to become boulevard

Existing North Gate

Plan showing new open space and planted boulevard along original walls

The City of Taipei is undergoing rapid and intense changes as it struggles with the urban and environmental issues of the late twentieth century. The Taipei Terminal urban design plan is a vision for a new, high-density district to be built in conjunction with major transportation improvements including an upgraded inter-city rail network and a new subway system.

The 46-hectare site is immediately north of the historic walled city. A new tunnel system carrying regional rail lines has replaced the surface rail yards that once occupied the site. The recently completed rail terminal serves as the central station for Taipei. The client recognized this as a rare opportunity to create a new district built around major investments in public transportation. A previous plan for the site, consisting of free-standing towers, did not respond to the culture and formal structure of the city. The challenge on this complex and extraordinary site was to create an integrated urban design plan rooted in the historic fabric of the city, yet adapted to contemporary building standards.

In a city desperately lacking open space, the plan creates Taipei's third major public space, adjacent to the original walled city. A sequence of public spaces, beginning at the north gateway to the city, extends through the district, connecting the riverfront to the terminal building and eventually to the area east of the project site. The plan considers the traditions of Taipei urbanism and the city's climate; streets are oriented north to south according to the principles of *Feng Shui*, and streets and open spaces are framed by arcaded buildings. A "grand arcade" is proposed, which would link the buildings on the north side of a series of new open spaces.

The North Gate, the last remnant of the historic city in this area, is enhanced by creating a boulevard, with a planted median, along the location of the original wall. Current city plans for an underground pedestrian system have been coordinated with a new network serving large numbers of people at street level, below ground, and on a second level connecting to the existing city in all directions. A vertical layering of uses typical of Taipei is extended into the site, with a continuous pattern of retail and, occasionally, cultural uses at lower levels and a mixed-use program above. Current public policy excludes housing from this district; however, the design plan is flexible enough to allow residential uses in the future.

A landmark tower, located at a strategic position where a new open space system and boulevard converge, is designed to symbolize the emergence of Taipei as an international commercial city. Buildings clearly frame and define streets and public spaces. Where important streets cross the site, plazas are formed, with taller buildings identifying their special position within the city. These buildings rest on articulated bases that relate new development to the existing neighboring context. Building heights range from 15 to 75 meters, thereby relating to building heights typical of three periods of growth in the City of Taipei.

The Taipei Terminal urban design plan represents a significant advance for Taipei. The planning process involved the integration of all key planning factors, including urban design, market, financial feasibility, traffic, parking and pedestrian circulation analysis, environmental concerns, and project implementation. Multiple meetings were conducted with public officials, city staff, advisors, and interested citizens in reviewing the plan as it developed. The plan was officially adopted by the planning commission and mayor in 1991.

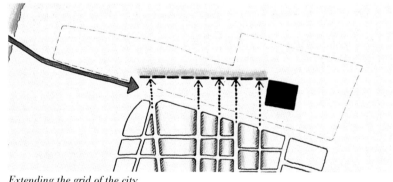

Extending the grid of the city

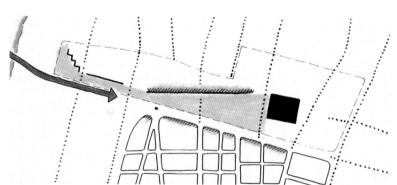

Defining a major space

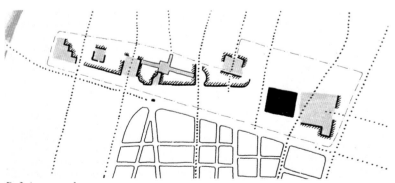

Defining secondary spaces

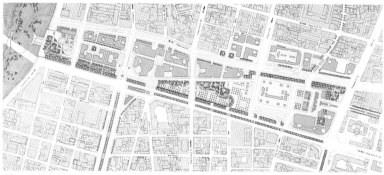

Master plan

Babelsberg Media City

Location: Potsdam, Germany
Client: CIP
Project Dates: 1993
Sasaki Staff: Alan L. Ward, Dennis Pieprz,
                  Anthony Mallows, Ivana Sturm,
                  Pat Doolin
In Association
With: Suter + Suter AG
Renderings: Jim Anderson

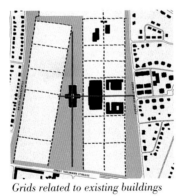

Grids related to existing buildings

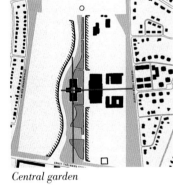

Central garden

Connections

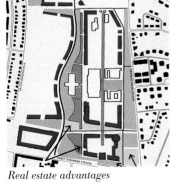

Real estate advantages

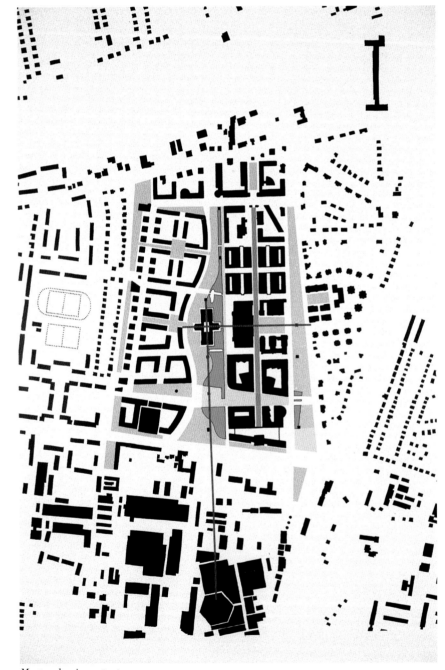

Master plan in context

Babelsberg Media City is located on the site of the former Babelsberg Film Studios in Potsdam, Germany. During the early 1900s, Babelsberg was a leading center of European filmmaking. Movies such as *Metropolis* and *The Blue Angel* were made at this site, and artists such as Billy Wilder and Marlene Dietrich worked on its sound stages. In the post-war era, the studio's importance was diminished, but with the unification of Germany in 1989, there was an opportunity to make a new media city on this once significant site.

The program includes audiovisual production facilities, a film university, retail and entertainment facilities, cinemas, two hotels and an exhibition center, offices, housing, a film museum, and community space.

The design is focused on a central garden inspired by the landscape tradition of the region. The garden sequence is revealed through a series of parallel rows of poplar trees, each defining a phase of development.

A number of historic structures are incorporated into the overall plan, with the original sound studios becoming a film museum, sited on the central garden. The grid pattern of the studio buildings is used to establish an urban order including a "Street of Dreams" axis, which is the public focus of the new studio district. A waterfront esplanade runs along the dynamic western edge of the space. The plan is a natural extension of the pattern of surrounding uses and green spaces, and is intended to make a new "great place" in the Potsdam tradition.

Numerous cinematic garden follies are designed to interpret the film history of the Babelsberg Studios. The follies contain cafes and restaurants as well as sculptural interpretations of studio history. "Star lights" along the waterfront esplanade will be etched with images of film industry personalities.

The site is organized into a number of urban districts, each bordering the central garden. The tourist/entertainment district is adjacent to the studios and connected to the rail station and bus arrival area. Directly connected by the "Street of Dreams" is the studio district, which includes audiovisual facilities and other related uses. The film university and radio station terminate the "Street of Dreams" and the central garden at the northern end.

The residential quarter to the northwest is focused on public spaces and quiet green courtyards. Key public facilities such as a church, school, and library serve the new development as well as the existing neighborhoods. The residential/mixed used district, with higher density focused on the central garden, is designed to accommodate a mix of uses.

The business/exhibition area, a highly visible site at the main entry, is connected to the activities of the tourist/entertainment district and studios by a plaza—the "meeting place"—a great urban space framed by hotels, cinemas, and shops. It traverses the water of the central garden and is framed on the west by an exhibition hall, hotel, and residences. Streets and pedestrian paths from each of the districts connect to the central garden.

Existing studio buildings

Cinematic follies in central garden

Central garden

Entertainment district, business/exhibition district, and residential quarter

Awards night in the entertainment district

Studio district and central garden

Oerlikon

Location: Zurich, Switzerland
Client: City of Zurich, Switzerland
Project Dates: 1991
Sasaki Staff: Alan L. Ward, Dennis Pieprz
In Association
With: Suter + Suter AG
Awards: Third Prize, Oerlikon 2011
                     Competition

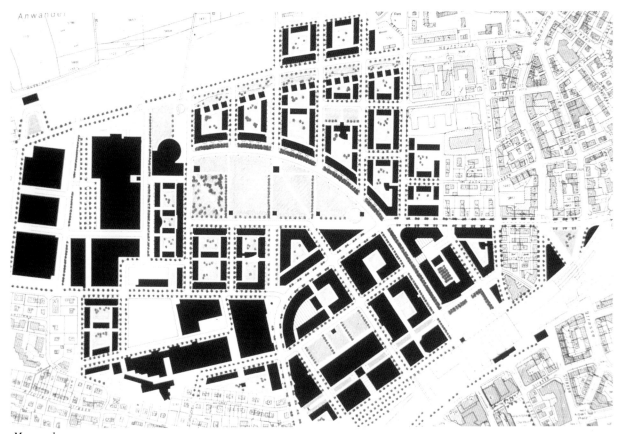

Master plan

Market square and train station
linked to the countryside

The Oerlikon neighborhood is located in the northwest part of the city of Zurich. A major rail line, which connects the city to the airport and the countryside beyond, passes through the community. Just west of the train station is an industrialized area now in decline. Oerlikon was no longer appropriate as a single-purpose district, and the City of Zurich sought to establish a vision for the 114-acre site by holding an international design competition, which was entered, and won, by Sasaki Associates. The Sasaki plan retained a number of industrial facilities, while new uses such as housing, office, hotel, education, and cultural functions were proposed.

In a single arcing gesture, disparate elements of the program were united to create a link between the existing market square and the countryside. A sequence of public spaces was proposed along a new boulevard extending from the train station to a new school, which is oriented to the farm fields beyond. A significant portion of the site is reserved for a community park, which will become a focus for the surrounding neighborhood. Most of the residential program frames the park, ensuring its viability as a lively place.

Loft apartments are integrated into office and commercial buildings near the enlarged railway station and its new commercial square. A mixed-use tower punctuates the skyline and marks the location of the station.

An educational and training college is proposed for an area adjacent to the station. Focused on an elongated quadrangle, and reusing a number of industrial buildings, this component of the plan will bring students from all parts of the city.

The design takes full advantage of the proximity of public transportation—train station, tram, and bus—and seeks to make this once isolated area a vital community.

Open space framework

Landmark buildings

Urban design framework

Existing site

Market Square

Existing buildings and view to countryside

Megaproyecto Puebla Plus

Location: Puebla, Mexico
Client: Government of the
                     State of Puebla, Mexico
Project Dates: 1992
Sasaki Staff: Alan L. Ward, Daniel R. Kenney,
                     Alan Fujimori, David McIntyre,
                     Paul Weathers

In Association
With: HKS, Architects
Awards: Honor Award, Texas Chapter,
                     American Society of
                     Landscape Architects, 1994

Urbanized area of Puebla and
surrounding towns

Projected urbanized area in twenty
years

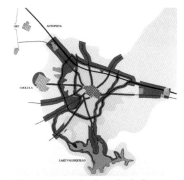

Planned growth along high density
transit corridors

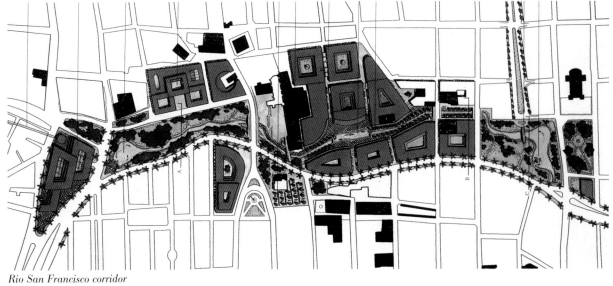

Rio San Francisco corridor

The City of Puebla, which was founded in 1519 along the Rio San Francisco in Mexico's central highlands, is a rapidly urbanizing community of 1.5 million people. Accelerated growth in the 1980s resulted in a 50 percent expansion of land area, creating a critical need to direct development toward a more sustainable future. Sasaki Associates' task was to prepare an overall plan for the 1,300-square-kilometer greater Puebla area—a coherent framework within which future development will occur.

A team of planners, urban designers, and engineers worked closely with municipal and state officials to develop a plan which would respond to issues of land use, transportation, infrastructure, and environmental impact and would outline strategies for implementation. The planning efforts focused on two areas: a major new industrial zone of 1,000 hectares to the northwest of the city, and the historic city center.

The complexity of the project required an approach that integrated technical studies of solid waste, public health, water supply, wastewater collection and treatment, transportation, land use, ecological systems, and historical/cultural surveys. Previous work was synthesized and a new land use and urban design strategy was developed. The plan calls for the concentration of high-density development along transit corridors, with a focus on exclusive, high-speed bus rights-of-way, a proven technology for mass transit. Environmentally regulated industrial zones with supporting commercial and residential uses are located along transit corridors parallel to the *autopista* or freeway.

The hub of Puebla is the historic city, defined by the Rio San Francisco. The existing river is in a culvert below an urban arterial street. The plan recommended that the city work with residents to acquire available land along the banks of the reclaimed river for development of a riverwalk, a cultural and entertainment district with restaurants and shops that would attract both international and domestic tourists to the city. The river corridor would provide open space connections for pedestrian and bicycle networks while incorporating large areas for urban runoff and stormwater management.

Traffic would be diverted to a loop road outside the historic city, making Puebla more inviting to pedestrians. Like spokes radiating from a wheel, transit corridors would radiate from the loop road into the surrounding countryside. High-speed bus rights-of-way would be incorporated in road design. Areas between transit corridors lying closest to the city would be developed for both residential and commercial use, allowing inhabitants to live in proximity to their workplaces and reducing automobile use. Further from the city, a greenbelt of reforested land would limit growth, preserve valuable agricultural land and historic towns, and create a strong edge between urban land uses and open space and agricultural land.

The plan also calls for the creation of protective zones and land use controls for existing and future groundwater resources, the extension of infrastructure networks in high-density corridors served by transit, and progressive measures to prevent the development of illegal settlements.

The issues of rapid urbanization and the uncontrolled growth of existing cities are global problems, particularly acute in the developing countries of the Americas and Africa. With some cities growing by as much as 10 percent each year, a realistic, effective plan requires public sector leadership and public/private investment. With the continuing support of the Mexican government, the efforts of the State of Puebla may prove a model for effective urban management.

Area surrounding Puebla

Buildings on Plaza Principal

Reclaimed Rio San Francisco

Plaza Principal and Cathedral

Teatro Principal and Barrio del Artista

New residential and employment zone along high speed bus corridor

Cleveland Gateway

Location: Cleveland, Ohio
Client: Gateway Economic Development Corporation
Project Dates: 1991-1994
Sasaki Staff: David H. Hirzel, Alan L. Ward,
                    Dennis Pieprz, James P. Doolin,
                    Robert Brooks, Edward Boiteau,
                    Richard F. Galehouse, Darrell Bird,
                    Thomas DiCicco, Elen Deming,
                    Neil J. Dean, Jeanne Lukenda,
                    Ivanna Sturm, Chuck Coronis,
                    David Oldman, John Barry
In Association
With: Ellerbe Beckett, HOK Sport,
                    Committee for Public Art
Sub-consultants: van Dijk, Johnson & Partners;
                    Polytech, Inc.; Richard Fleischman
                    Architects, Inc.; Amenta & Co.
Artists: Nancy Dwyer, R. M. Fischer, Red Grooms,
                    Angelica Pozo, Penny Rakoff
Awards: Honor Award in Urban Design,
                    American Institute of Architects, 1996;
                    Honor Award, American Society of
                    Landscape Architects, 1994;
                    Urban Design Citation Award,
                    Progressive Architecture, 1991

Downtown connections

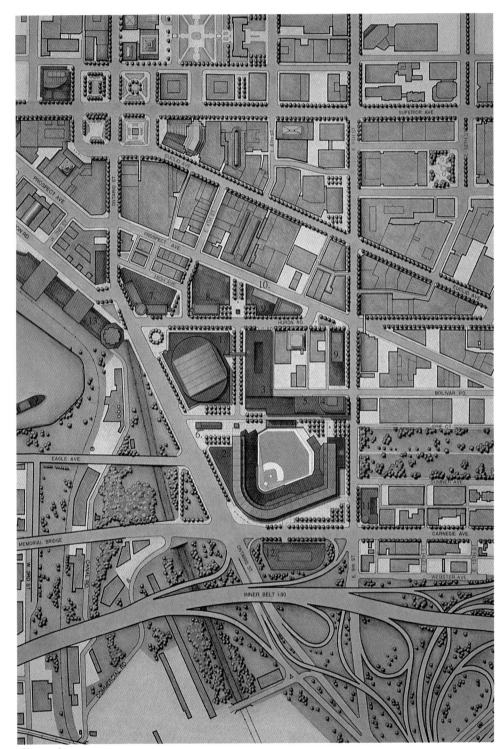

Master plan

Cleveland Gateway is a new downtown sports district, part of a well-developed and sophisticated strategy for the economic revitalization of the city. Gateway was realized with the cooperative efforts of the City of Cleveland Planning Department, the Gateway Economic Development Corporation, and two major league sports franchises.

The 28-acre site has a prominent location at a major point of entry to the downtown area. It is just two blocks from Public Square, and is served by regional highways and by a direct connection to public transportation at the landmark Terminal Tower.

Sasaki Associates' challenge at Gateway was to establish a master plan for a structure of civic quality; a new 42,000-seat baseball stadium, Jacobs Field, and the 20,000-seat Gund Arena. The complex had to take advantage of nearby transit facilities, to provide parking for 14,000 cars within a 20-minute walk, and to stimulate the revitalization of the adjacent district.

The urban design strategy has resulted in a radical transformation of the southern edge of Cleveland's downtown. The sports facilities are carefully positioned to form street edges, with urban sidewalks creating a seamless fit with the existing street and block pattern. By depressing the playing surface of each sports facility, the respective concourses are related directly to the sidewalk. This allows a building type which frames streets and open spaces, and avoids the multiple ramps and stairs which commonly surround such facilities.

Both building masses and open spaces are shaped to respond to views, connections, and sight lines. The various entries, positioned close to downtown, allow gathering crowds to flow naturally to restaurants, bars, and shops in the adjacent downtown area. The main entry to the stadium is part of a sequence extending from the nearby Cleveland arcades through a proposed new open space, along a new street aligned with the stadium. This relates Gateway Plaza's entry to views across the Cuyahoga River Valley and to the building towers and skyline of downtown.

These spaces, and Indians Square, accommodate a variety of civic functions. The significant service requirements of the complex are combined in an out-of-sight service area underneath Gateway Plaza, made possible by lowering the playing fields and by a careful coordination of service locations.

View of site from Terminal Tower

Relationship of Gateway to downtown

Building massing defines new streets and open spaces

New sidewalks define urban edges around Gund Arena

Light towers on Gateway Square by artist R. M. Fischer

New street between Jacobs Field and garage

Gateway Square between Gund Arena and Jacobs Field

Cleveland Gateway
(continued)

1 Gund Arena
2 Jacobs Field
3 Parking garage
4 Development site with temporary landscape
5 Gateway Square
6 View into Jacobs Field from Gateway Square
7 Indians Square

Jacobs Field and Gateway Square

*View from Jacobs Field to
downtown*

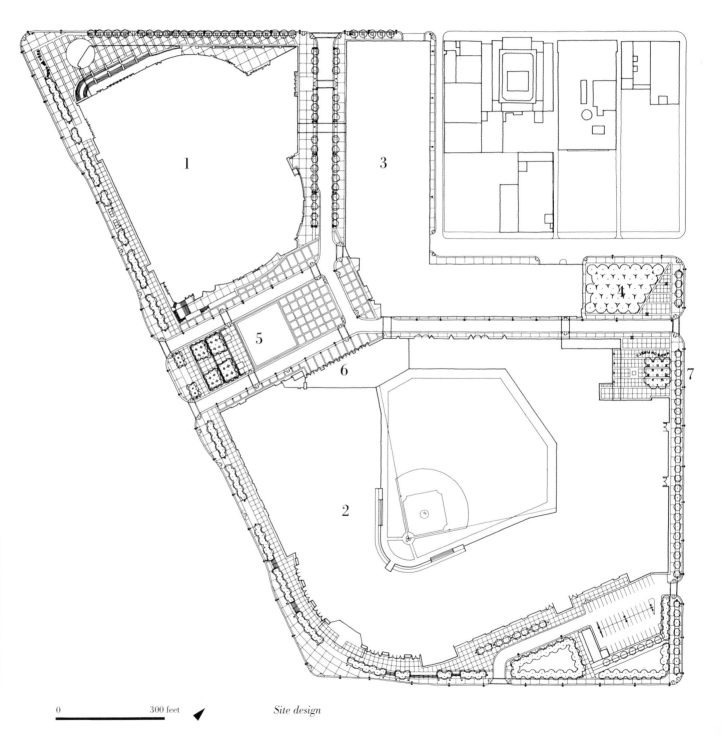

0   300 feet   *Site design*

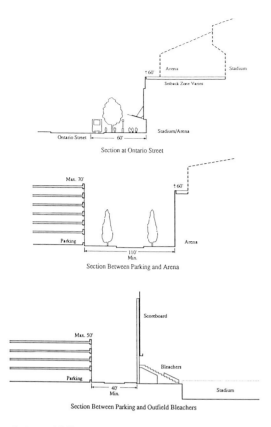

Section at Ontario Street

Section Between Parking and Arena

Section Between Parking and Outfield Bleachers

Urban design guidelines

The parking and traffic strategy is fundamental to the success of the plan. It was recognized that the adjacent downtown parking supply could easily accommodate the parking needs for sports events, which occur primarily on weekends and in the evening. This shared parking approach, in addition to a traffic management plan, satisfies event arrival and departure standards. A new on-site parking structure replaces the 3,000 spaces that covered the site before construction began.

Design guidelines were prepared to direct the facility architects. Important views, landmarks and edges were identified, so that the goals of the master plan would be met.

View to profile of Jacobs field

Gateway Square after baseball game

Honey locust grove at entry to Gateway Square

Public art by Cleveland artists

View into ballpark from pedestrian bridge

Site graphics and a row of gingko trees define edge of downtown

Sidewalk connections from downtown

Public art, "Who's on First" by Nancy Dwyer, in Indians Square

New Communities

By Melanie Simo

"Travel the Atlantic coast from Maine to Florida and you'll not find another place like this. Sandy beaches stretch uninterrupted for miles, and behind the dunes countless acres of salt marsh are laced by meandering creeks and shallow bays. . . .
To experience Virginia's Eastern Shore is to step back in time, to revisit a generation when lives were connected to the land, when families were sustained by the bounty of the soil and the sea."

–Curtis Badger, for
The Nature Conservancy

About five years ago, Sasaki Associates began to contribute to an ongoing series of planning efforts, begun by The Nature Conservancy, to maintain the traditional habitats of both human beings and the abundant wildlife on Virginia's Eastern Shore. These planning efforts for some 45,000 acres of barrier islands, salt marsh, and uplands along the Atlantic coast of the Delmarva Peninsula, are now under exceptional scrutiny; and not all of it comes from local citizens groups, planning commissions, business groups, tourist boards, housing trusts, and a local chapter of the NAACP. In 1979, the United Nations designated Virginia's Eastern Shore an "international biosphere reserve," essentially, a model of how human beings might live in harmony with nature. The Nature Conservancy has given this exceptional ecosystem its own designation, "a last great place," a phrase with hints of wonder, delight, and perhaps also of foreboding, even urgency.

In "The Virginia Coast Reserve," below, the contributions of Sasaki Associates to The Nature Conservancy's efforts are outlined in terms of strategies, prototypes, design guidelines, and so on. Unstated are the personal convictions of the senior principal involved, David Hirzel, who has played several administrative and professional roles since he first joined the firm in 1969. He was then a young architect with an M.B.A. degree from Harvard. Today he is one of Sasaki Associates' more outspoken principals on the subject of environmental sustainability. Speaking at the AIA Conference on Sustainability, in 1994, Hirzel emphasized the wide range of initiatives underway in The Nature Conservancy's programs along Virginia's Eastern Shore, from protecting the most fragile places, or "core areas," to promoting economic development through farming, fishing, arts and crafts, and small industry. "We learn that no single project can accomplish everything," he reminded his fellow architects. Still, each project offers an opportunity to take a step forward toward the goal of sustainability. "As professionals focused on the planning and design of the built environment," he concluded, "we must assume a leadership role in one of the critical issues of our time." [1]

Richard Galehouse, a fellow architect/planner at Sasaki Associates, would agree in principle yet express his convictions differently. "We're always searching for the environmental solution, the beautiful solution, but also the solution that makes economic sense. There has always been a concern for the quality of land, its inherent character, and the properties of the land as they would affect the economics of doing something." [2] Galehouse, who joined the firm in 1960, has a long perspective on the firm's involvement in the planning and design of new communities. For many years, as the head of planning at Sasaki Associates, he has frequently addressed the environmental aspects of planning these communities, speaking at conferences, writing for professional journals, or engaging a client in the subtleties of a new project. Typically, his starting point will be Sea Pines Plantation, a project that came into the office three or four years before he arrived. On the second phase of development at this new resort community, located on Hilton Head Island, off the coast of South Carolina, Galehouse served as planner.

"The development industry considers Sea Pines the country's first contemporary post-World War II destination resort and retirement community," Galehouse has observed. "The development standards that it established really set the standards for the entire industry."[3] Credit for this success is due not only to Hideo Sasaki and his associates—as planners, site designers, and architects for that new community, begun in the late 1950s—but also to the client, Charles Fraser, then a young graduate of Yale Law School with some exposure to the legal aspects of land use planning, including deed restrictions and covenants. Fraser has had an abiding interest in, and affection for, the island's natural landscape, including the flora and fauna. (As John McPhee has noted, the alligators and deer were later protected by Fraser's private police force.)[4] Nearly forty years after development began there, on some 4,500 acres, Fraser's vision of "harmony and cohesion" had largely been realized. "There are unspoiled beaches, sweeping water views, a continuous forest canopy overhead, and marshes curving out to the horizon," reported a journalist in 1990. "Despite intensive development over the past three decades, this serene landscape still dominates the character of Hilton Head."[5]

Galehouse has often served as planner in landscapes rich in natural amenities, such as coastal islands, high bluffs with river views, and relatively flat land with abundant watercourses. On occasion, as in his article on "Kingsmill on the James," a new community near Williamsburg, Virginia, Galehouse has emphasized ecological considerations that took precedence over other factors in the development process. "The ecological analysis of the Kingsmill site showed that the tidal marshes and the ravine systems with their fragile and easily eroded soils were the most sensitive natural environmental elements," he explained before outlining the main considerations of the master plan, completed in 1972. Technical details of earth-moving, tree-cutting, and sewage collection were worked out so as to minimize the environmental impacts while keeping the economic costs "competitive." Complicating the process still further were the remains of colonial plantations on future building sites. The developer's parent company, the Anheuser-Busch brewing company, agreed to sponsor an intensive archaeological program and to preserve the sites. The work sessions were long and sometimes tedious, Galehouse admitted, but in the end, the concerns of the developer, environmentalists, the National Park Service, Colonial Williamsburg, the Virginia Historic Landmarks Commission, and other interested parties were resolved in the master plan.[6]

It is this moderating, balanced tone that characterizes Galehouse's overviews of planning and design of new communities at Sasaki Associates. There is no single issue, no universally applied device, such as a street grid or a particular scale of development, that dominates his view of the firm's practice or his sense of what ought to be achieved. Regarding the form and structure of a new community, Galehouse remains open to the particular site and circumstances. "We've always tended to let the land have a big part in the decision," he explains. "At Kingsmill, you have this heavily variegated landscape of ridgetops and ravines; you can't force a grid on that landscape." At "The Hammocks," a 1,100-acre new community in Dade County, Florida, fourteen miles south of Miami, the firm introduced curvilinear forms into the county grid of arterial streets. An interior lake and park system was created. Small development parcels at neighborhood scale, fifteen to twenty-five acres each, were oriented toward the lakes. Community facilities such as schools, churches, a town common, and commercial services were clustered in three villages and a town center.

"Back in the '70s," Galehouse recalls, "The Hammocks" got planning approval only because of its town planning characteristics."[7]

Recently Galehouse has participated in some planning and design charrettes at Celebration, Florida, the new community now being built by the Disney Development Corporation. On one of those charrettes, he met with Charles Fraser, Jacquelin Robertson, Robert A.M. Stern, and a few Disney executives to discuss the design and marketing problems of housing. "Whenever Disney dealt with the focus groups—the people who were actually going to live in those places—people wanted to have nothing to do with the grid," Galehouse recalls. "That was their constant feed-back." The site, at any rate, is difficult to build on. Of a total of 10,000 acres, only about half is buildable; the rest is protected wetlands.[8]

In contrast, the site of Brambleton, discussed below, promises to be more compact, somewhat more urban in character; it is concentrated on 375 acres. Alan Ward, design principal for that project in rural Loudoun County, Virginia, considered the socioeconomic potential of the basic grid plan, which he and his colleagues adapted to the existing roads and topography of the relatively flat land. "I think it's easier and more palatable to introduce a wider spectrum of housing within a grid pattern than it is when you design exclusive neighborhoods or planned unit developments in which all the houses are marketed at a certain value," he said, speaking in a Landscape Architecture forum with George J. Pillorge, Robert C. Kettler, Sam Bass Warner, Jr., and Lewis D. Hopkins. "It's not just housing at different price ranges, it's also housing for the elderly," Ward continued. "The Brambleton plan has elderly housing near the main street within walking distance of the downtown center. . . . Now we can introduce [continuing care communities] on a block-by-block kind of scale, and it's much more acceptable than having them sit on the edges of exclusive residential pods."[9]

Ward and his colleagues in the forum eventually got around to talking about favorite places. "What we love about Annapolis [Maryland] is the scale of its streets, the density of the activity, the civic expression whereby certain streets terminate in beautiful, appropriately scaled civic buildings and grounds," Ward said, acknowledging that the need to design for the automobile complicates the urban designer's job today. "That pedestrian scale and tightness and compactness that make Annapolis so vibrant and vital are on another scale from the regional highway, and a transition is required from the regional highway to the boulevards and major roads. So we have to tame the car, get it into this urban fabric, and make it behave."[10]

There may be occasions when the principals must take a unanimous position at Sasaki Associates. In conversation, however, whether individually or in groups, what one tends to hear is a diversity of views, sometimes in sharp opposition, sometimes differing only subtly, as positions are refined or amended. Hirzel finds this quite normal in the spirit of collaboration and inclusion that the firm tries to maintain. "I really find that, with an inclusionary process of listening, responding to, and incorporating the multiple, conflicting points of view," he says, "you get better solutions. And when I look around this office, I look at Ken Bassett, Alan Ward, Dick Galehouse, Don Olson—I look at people who, by their disposition, have this kind of incorporating spirit in their approach to things. And that is fundamentally different from most other, or many other, firms in this business."[11]

Sea Pines Plantation and Harbourtown

Location:	*Hilton Head Island, South Carolina*
Client:	*Charles Frasier*
Project Dates:	*1964*
Sasaki Staff:	*Hideo Sasaki, Stuart O. Dawson, Kenneth DeMay, Frank James, Don Olson, George Conley*
Awards:	*Heritage Award for Excellence, Urban Land Institute, 1994; Top Honor Award, Classic Projects, the Waterfront Center, "Excellence on the Waterfront" Awards, 1987; Award of Excellence for Large-Scale Recreational Development, Urban Land Institute, 1985*

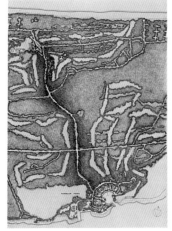

Master plan

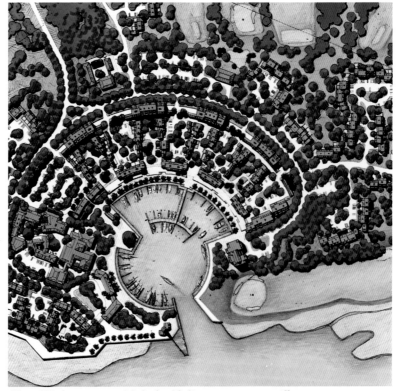

Plan of Harbourtown modeled after Mediterranean seaport village

Sea Pines Plantation, a 5,200-acre residential and resort community on Hilton Head Island, South Carolina, was designed by Sasaki Associates to be a self-sustaining community of individual homes, woodland parks, apartments, cultural facilities, churches, neighborhood shops, service facilities, and golf and recreational areas.

The natural character of the island has been retained by careful planning and attention to land use and architectural controls. The development preserves large amounts of open space and existing plant and animal life. Planning of waterfront properties was accomplished in a way that preserved the beach edge while it increased the number of residences sharing the frontage. This enhanced both marketability and land values. Similarly, internal lots are integrated with golf course planning to provide these sites with special advantages.

Sea Pines was the first destination resort built in the United States after World War II. The planning principles developed include the environmental design concept of fitting development into the natural landscape, the use of golf as a means of creating both amenity and real estate values in interior woodlands, and the creation of a harbor town as a destination and activity focus for residents. The wilderness beach character of over two miles of shoreline was preserved by building behind primary dunes. Design guidelines ensured that the scale, materials, and placement of residential blocks reflected the character of southern urban architecture, and preserved the natural landscape. A new style of architectural expression, known as the "island style," grew out of Sea Pines Plantation.

Sasaki Associates prepared the master plan for Harbourtown, a 100-acre village within the larger development, and provided architectural services for the phase one lighthouse, condominiums and shops. Harbourtown is the urban center and the visual symbol of Hilton Head Island. The lighthouse that defines the harbor's entrance to Calibogue Sound on the waterway is internationally recognized not only as the resort's landmark, but as a symbol for the island and for national events such as the Heritage Golf Classic which began at Harbourtown when the community opened in 1969.

Harbourtown fulfills the goals of both the developer and the community. At the broadest scale, it has become a landmark as well as a refuge along the inland waterway. The lighthouse is included on navigational charts for the area. It has become one of the best-known landmarks among resorts, regularly receiving unsolicited exposure in the press. The harbor provides slips for resident yachtsmen, fuel and facilities for transient yachtsmen, and a staging area for sightseeing cruises and fishing expeditions. On land, there are housing, restaurants, shops, golf, tennis, and special activities such as oyster roasts, live entertainment, and annual celebrations.

Harbourtown is a place for enjoyment, whether derived from participation in planned activities or simply from mingling with others—strolling, window-shopping, watching the comings and goings of yachts, or enjoying the sunset over Calibogue Sound.

There were once Native American settlements on Hilton Head Island, and later, cotton plantations thrived. The island played a key role in the blockade of Southern ports during the Civil War. The design of Harbourtown is sensitive to the island's heritage. A plantation cemetery is maintained, and two small historic buildings destined for demolition elsewhere on the island were preserved, floated to Harbourtown during its construction, and refurbished as part of the commercial area. By now, Harbourtown has begun to have a history of its own.

Finishing hole of the Heritage course

Promenade around marina

Tennis courts sited in existing woodland

Boardwalk to rice dikes and wetlands

View from clubhouse

The promenade as grand lobby

View from promenade to harbor

Bicycle connections to Harbourtown

73

The Landings

Location: Skidaway Island, Georgia
Client: The Branigar Corporation
(wholly-owned subsidiary
of Union Camp Corporation)
Project Dates: 1969-1986
Sasaki Staff: Hideo Sasaki, Don Olson,
Richard F. Galehouse,
Dick Magnuson, Joe Anglin
Sub-consultants: Thomas & Hutton,
Civil Engineering;
Hammer Siler George,
Economic Consultants

Awards: Award for Excellence for Large-Scale
Recreational Development, Urban Land
Institute, 1986; "Five Star Rating,"
World Class Resorts & Properties,
Real Estate Development and
Investment Institute, Winter 1984-1985;
Citation Winner for Land Use,
Environmental Monthly, 1975

Landings Way

Pattern of golf and housing carved out
of the forest at The Landings

The Landings is a planned residential community located on Skidaway Island, Georgia, in the chain known as Georgia's "golden isles." The island lies twelve miles southeast of downtown Savannah, and is surrounded by several resort communities, including Hilton Head Island. The Landings encompasses 3,900 acres of land planned to protect the unique environment of the Georgia coastline.

Skidaway Island is part of the complex system of marshes and hummocks characteristic of the coastal waters of Georgia and South Carolina. The island is bounded by marsh on the east, the Wilmington River on the north, the Intra-Coastal Waterway and the mainland on the west, with the Vernon River and other coastal islands to the south. These features, combined with the region's mild climate, provide for a dramatic year-round recreational environment.

When the development of The Landings began in 1971, the objective was to create a more relaxed and environmentally sensitive alternative to the busy resorts found on Hilton Head Island. Sasaki Associates' plan established strong environmental standards to protect the island's wooded perimeter, its salt marshes, pine forests, and historical assets. A significant amount of land was set aside as open space and wildlife reservation.

The master plan for The Landings includes naturally wooded home sites for both primary and secondary homes, and low-density, low-rise cluster villas and townhouse areas. The average density of the development is intended to reach 2.4 units per acre in the single-family residential areas and six to seven units per acre in the cluster villas and townhouse areas. Landing Village provides retail services, offices, restaurants, and civic facilities. Its design combines the traditional forms of main street and village green with contemporary access and parking. The style of the village is typical of the Georgia low country, with broad gabled roofs, and deep overhangs and porches for shade.

The design for Skidaway Island is intended to develop a "natural community" by preserving natural resources while providing a full complement of community and recreational facilities. The natural resources of the island include its virgin forest of live oak, pine and magnolia, the extended view across the sea marshes with their abundant wildlife, and immediate access to the Intra-Coastal Waterway and Atlantic Ocean via the Skidaway and Wilmington Rivers.

The entire perimeter of the island, including a necklace of small islands and hummocks on the western marsh approaches, will be preserved. The greenway system connects all community facilities and affords residents access to the state park, the rivers and canal at Priest Landing and Log Landing, the golf and community clubs, and the marina. Historic sites, such as the Civil War fortifications, monastery site and prehistoric shell ring, are accessible from this greenway.

Preserved forest

Tidal marsh

Golf course adjacent to the marsh at high tide

Central drainage lagoon

Pattern of golf fairways and housing with tidal marsh beyond

Golf and path system

Skidaway Village

1 Retail office building
2 Retail building
3 Market building
4 Parking
5 Pedestrian accessway
6 Covered pedestrian accessway
7 Light house
8 Pavilion
9 Fountain
10 Port-cochere

0   90 feet

Skidaway Village with traditional main street

A series of site design techniques was developed to address environmental and feasibility issues since drainage was a major consideration, existing sloughs and gum ponds were deepened, widened, and interconnected to form a highly effective system for stormwater collection. These lagoons provide visual and recreational enjoyment and add significantly to surrounding land values.

The marsh was of particular ecological sensitivity and was threatened by landowners' desires to clear trees for views, situate houses, and build docks. The plan prohibits private docks, and preserves a continuous, undisturbed 50- to 100-foot linear buffer along the marsh edge. This buffer protects the natural edge of the island and serves as an overland filter to rid stormwater runoff of pollutants from driveways and lawns.

Archaeologists assessed the significance of the island's various historical sites and incorporated them as destination points. Bike trails skirt ancient Indian shell middens and pass through "Oak Alley"; Civil War gun mounds rise up around the harbor; Delegal's grave and the masonry foundation of an old Benedictine monastery sit on permanent green space. An historic family cemetery has been preserved.

A new zoning ordinance, incorporating contemporary planning techniques for planned unit cluster development, was developed and approved by Chatham County. Clusters of four to six homes have been placed on private ways free of through traffic. Collector streets lead traffic away from these residential clusters. The relatively inexpensive construction of the narrow and curvilinear private ways, with their inverted crowns, responds to the presence of the woods of mature live oaks, as well as to the drainage requirement.

Golf view corridor from entrance road

Live oaks at Priest's Landing

Inverted street section for drainage

Guidelines define building materials and restrict lawns

Preservation of forest

Marsh overlook

Setting for typical single-family home on lagoon

Costa Smeralda

Location: *Sardinia, Italy*
Client: *Consortio Costa Smeralda*
Project Dates: *1968 to present*
Sasaki Staff: *Stuart O. Dawson, Morgan Wheelock,*
                    Jack Robinson, Frank James,
                    Paul Povlowski, Don Olson
Sub-consultants: *Economic Research Associates,*
                    Economic Programming; O'Donnal
                    Associates; Interplan Planning
                    Organization Co., Ltd. Planners

Topography

◼ Hotels and villages

◼ Village housing

◼ Villas

◻ Low density villas

◻ Golf

◻ Open space

▨ Natural areas and view protection

Original 1970 land use plan

In 1964, His Highness the Aga Khan, with other investors, purchased 3,000 hectares (7,500 acres) of scenic coastline in northeastern Sardinia, intending to build an exclusive resort destination. Four distinctly different hotel environments and a core village, Porto Cervo, were initiated. Soon there was a need for individual villas and small condominium clusters. In 1968 Sasaki Associates was engaged to lead a multidisciplinary team in defining a long-range vision for the resort, and to provide a phased program for its implementation. This resulted in the establishment of a permanent planning office within the Consortizio. Design controls were created, and a review and approval procedure was established to process applicant designs.

The master plan is based on a series of disbursed village centers. Lower density villas and recreational facilities were provided between these centers, their siting based on the topography and views. Generous open spaces were set aside, and environmental controls were established for the preservation of the scenic qualities of the rugged landscape of shoreline and mountain. The development of infrastructure, including roads and utilities, proceeded according to a phased hierarchy, to help balance investment and return. Amenities include 700 boat slips and moorings, yacht club, and a shipyard. There is a championship golf course with planned expansion for 54 additional holes. The village of Port Cervo has been completed, and includes more than 300,000 square meters of commercial space. Surface parking in this central harbor village has been

Density decreases moving up the hillsides

Marking the corners of a new villa for design review

Hotel Pitrizza

The arid vegetation unites the architecture with the land

Porto Cervo

Pevero Golf Center

Hotel Romazzino

Hotel Cala di Volpe

Costa Smeralda
(continued)

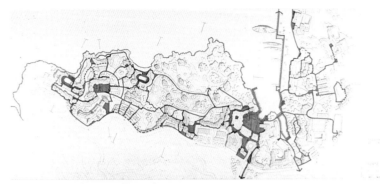

Pedestrian circulation at Porto Cervo

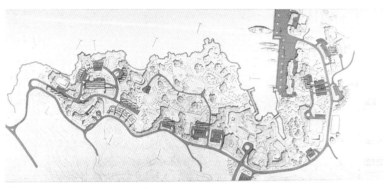

Vehicular circulation at Porto Cervo

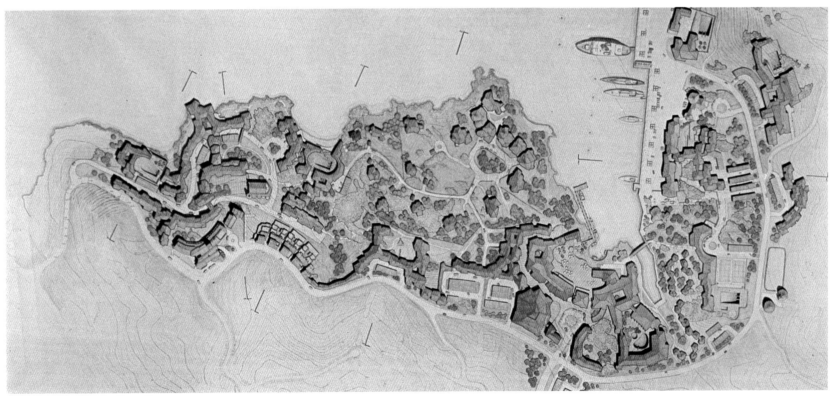

Concept Master Plan for Porto Cervo

reduced by significant amounts of underground parking to preserve visual quality. The next area of major expansion is in the vicinity of Cala di Volpe and Cala Razza di Giunco; a new harbor village, a sports and convention center, and a golf course are planned.

Sasaki Associates has played an active role in the planning of Costa Smeralda since the initial 1968 master planning effort. Services have included urban design, site design, and landscape architecture, in support of the Consortizio Planning Office. Sasaki's representation on the architectural review committee has also helped to provide design continuity over the years. Costa Smeralda remains a model of Mediterranean resort design.

Streetscape improvements, 1979

Porto Cervo Harbor

Cala di Volpe Hotel on lagoon

Cala di Volpe Hotel terrace

Lighting plan

Street at Porto Cervo

The Piazzetta at Porto Cervo

Bi-ways in Porto Cervo

Brambleton

Location: *Loudoun County, Virginia*
Client: *Kettler and Scott*
Project Dates: *1988*
Sasaki Staff: *Alan L. Ward, Dennis Pieprz,*
     Neil J. Dean, Kenneth DeMay,
     Greg Ault
Awards: *Citation for Urban Design*
     and Planning, Progressive
     Architecture, 1989

*Commercial street follows alignment
of the existing road*

*Residential square and adjacent
houses*

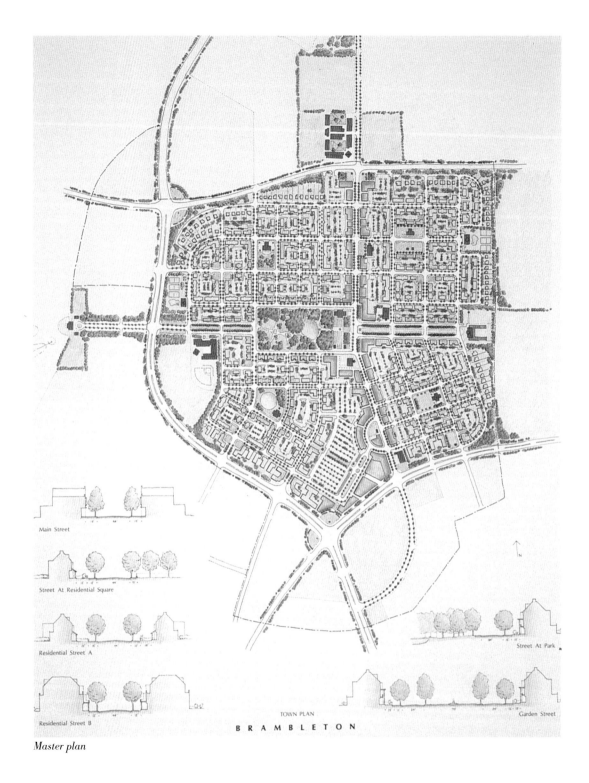

Master plan

A 1,200-acre rural site in Loudoun County, Virginia, at the western edge of suburban Washington, DC, is the setting for Brambelton, a new residential community designed for 12,000 people. It is located on unused agricultural land between Dulles Airport and Leesburg, Virginia, and offers convenient access to the expanding office and industrial zone to the southeast.

The challenge, on this relatively ordinary site, was to make a meaningful and beautiful setting for a community in the Virginia landscape. The plan for the 375-acre core area was informed by regional precedents in town planning, yet also accepts contemporary building requirements and the automobile culture. These regional precedents, as found in neighboring Leesburg, include the street as a commercial focus, an encompassing neighborhood grid linked to the main street, settings for institutions in green spaces, and the distinctive garden tradition of Virginia.

The concept for the site is a simple cross axis, with an urban commercial street extending north to south, contrasted with a series of green spaces extending east to west. This concept is an appropriate response to the natural and existing features of the site. The main street follows the alignment of the present country road. An existing gentle swale, with mature trees, slopes from west to east through the center of the site. The copse of trees is captured in the town park and extended to the east with town gardens to create the cross axis. The orthogonal geometry which organizes the neighborhoods is inspired by the pervasive American grid. It strives to be open and accessible; however, it is not without limits. There are clear boundaries, and distinctive focus in the town park and gardens as settings for civic institutions.

The framework of the plan is organized by streets and open spaces. The grids form a flexible pattern of blocks that can be developed incrementally. The organizing geometry is formal where appropriate: for example, where the town park and gardens meet the street, and at civic institutions. The neighborhood pattern is more relaxed and responsive to the land, and can adapt to several housing types. The town has a clear hierarchy of places, with the town park and gardens as a setting for the library and market. Residential squares are centrally located and create a focus for each neighborhood.

The town plan is compact and scaled for easy walking. Houses are never more than three blocks, along tree-lined sidewalks, from the neighborhood squares, where community facilities such as day care centers are located. Uses are overlapped; residential neighborhoods blend to meet the commercial spine. Office space is often located above retail stores on Main Street.

Existing site

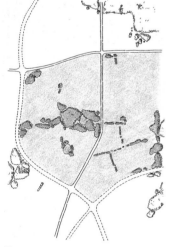

Existing site

Cross axis of commercial street and town park

Residential squares and public buildings

Street pattern

Sugarloaf/USA

Location: *Carrabassett Valley, Maine*
Client: *Sugarloaf Mountain*
Project Dates: *1986-1988*
Sasaki Staff: *John Ocrutt, Cindy Plank*
In Association
With: *On the Green Associates*
Sub-consultants: *Dutch Demshar*
Awards: *Honor Award, Commercial Design,*
     Boston Society of Landscape Architects,
     1988; Winner, Boston Society of Architects,
     Excellence in Housing Design Awards,
     1987; Project of the Year, Builder Magazine,
     Builder's Choice Design and Planning Awards, 1987

Sugarloaf ski area

Hotel, Sugarloaf/USA

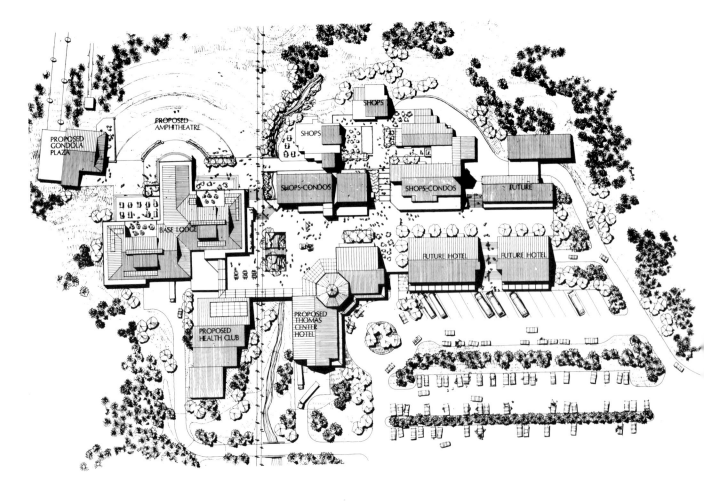

Site plan of Base Village

0   80 feet

Sasaki Associates' work at Sugarloaf/USA dates back to the early 1970s, when the firm prepared a master plan for the entire Carrabasset Valley area of western Maine. Further planning by Sasaki, in the early 1980s, responded to a program for the expansion of the ski area into a national year-round resort destination.

The 1980s planning proposed the creation of a village-like development at the base of the ski mountain. New buildings were to be clustered around existing buildings and connected by a pedestrian street linking retail shops and restaurants to a new base lodge. This base village concept was further reinforced by positioning and configuring a new hotel with a central, seven-story tower on the village pedestrian street, which is approached by a 20-foot wide stair connecting the hotel entrance to the village center.

The hotel is a 104,000 square foot, six-story structure with 102 rooms. It includes five meeting rooms and a 200-seat theater. The architectural character and detailing of the building recall the mills, commercial buildings, and other historic structures of western Maine, and at the same time the fine luxury resort hotels that flourished in the region in the 19th century.

Separate from the base village, but connected to the main Sugarloaf/USA mountain entry road, is the Village on the Green, the first luxury condominium development at the resort. Ninety townhouses are sited on 86 acres in and around a new 18-hole golf course. A large clearing forms a village green—an open mountain meadow with breathtaking views, which is the focal point of the community.

The condominium units are paired, and are connected by low sheds to a one-car garage at each residence, a form resembling the house-shed-barn arrangement common to the region. They incorporate the steeply pitched gables, low porches, and clapboard siding characteristic of the simple gothic farmhouses of northern Maine.

Hotel on village center

Resort course

Ski mountain from golf course

Base Village street

Village on the Green

Entries on the Green

Deck facing mountains

The Virginia Coast Reserve

Location:	*The Virginia Coast Reserve*
	Delmarva Peninsula, Virginia
Client:	*The Nature Conservancy*
Project Dates:	*1989-1993*
Sasaki Staff:	*David M. Hirzel, David L. McIntyre,*
	Andrew Weaver, Vladimir Gavrilovic
Awards:	*Boston Society of Architects,*
	Sustainable Design Awards Program, 1993

One of the most distinctive coastal ecosystems in North America, the Virginia Coast Reserve, occupies 45,000 acres of barrier islands along the Atlantic coast of the Delmarva Peninsula, the land between the Chesapeake Bay and the Atlantic. The Nature Conservancy has developed a replicable model for conservation and sustainable development. The model extends beyond the Conservancy's own land holdings because it was recognized that environmental organizations must be involved in land use management in areas that abut or "buffer" a critical protected area.

A comprehensive land management plan was a major component of the strategy. The plan integrates social, economic, technical, aesthetic and environmental goals. Planners and designers at Sasaki Associates played a key role in the development of the management plan.

New settlement clustered around a farm field

Delmarva Peninsula

Framework plan

Because the reserve is 60 miles long and the land buffering it is two or more miles wide, the first step in the planning process involved the selection of a smaller, prototypical study area. This area was selected to include representative built environments—towns, villages, and rural settlements—as well as unbuilt environments including farm land, forests, marshes, creeks, and coastal bays.

Analysis focused on three issues. The natural structure of the site was characterized by its soils, flood zones, and watersheds. Watersheds and the related impact on wildlife habitat proved to be the most critical of the natural landscape characteristics. The structure of the built environment focused on farms, roadways, and special features such as historic settlements and distinctive public places. The patterns of ownership, protection status, and identified threats also were identified, and demonstrated the urgency for action.

Several documents were prepared for the Conservancy's use. The first defined areas of land within which any anticipated activity should trigger a more comprehensive review to ensure that development actions not compromise larger goals or issues. The rationale used to determine these areas combined visual cohesiveness, land use, a common point of access, and a relationship to a watershed area.

The second document, design guidelines, provided a framework for the built environment. The guidelines set the historic context for settlement on the Virginia Eastern Shore. Two extremes of settlement—plantations and towns—formed the basic physical structure of the area. The "in between" consisted of small farms and mercantile villages or small clusters of roadside houses. The design guidelines discussed prototypical details for each of the settlement patterns.

The guidelines also prescribed forms for new development drawing directly from the historic land use and architectural forms that give the region its character. They recommend that new development follow historic village patterns and require buildings of an architectural character reminiscent of existing structures.

The third document, the concept master plan, gave focus to the goals and actions most critical to achieving the physical and visual dimensions of a sustainable community. The plan addressed the built and natural structure of the environment, reinforcing the existing towns and villages as centers for community and cultural resources. The rural settlement clusters were reinforced by concentrating new development around existing settlements and/or by encouraging compatible infill. Since new development could be outside existing settlements, the plan called for siting this development in a

way that echoes traditional settlements and protects critical environments and viewsheds. The roadway corridors and the sequence of open, wooded and settled areas were identified for protection to avoid monotonous strips of development.

Landscape protection recommendations called for watershed protection which is critical to protecting environmental quality as well as the economic viability of the working waterfront. Retention of farmland and the open space structure was necessary to protect the character of the landscape while maintaining the economic viability of the working farms. The woodlands were identified for protection for environmental and visual reasons and can continue to be a viable source of income for farmers.

Virginia Coast Reserve waterways

Woodland/marsh edge

View from The Nature Conservancy Headquarters

Brownsville Marsh

Willis Wharf

A resident heron

Lowry Development Plan

Location: Denver and Aurora, Colorado
Client: Lowry Redevelopment Authority
Project Dates: 1994-1997
Sasaki Staff: Daniel R. Kenney, Alan L. Ward,
Alan Fujimori, James Maloney,
Lisa Gaffey
Sub-consultants: BRW, Inc.
Awards: Texas Society of Landscape
Architects Award of Excellence, 1996

View toward downtown Denver and Front Range

Educational campus and open space connection

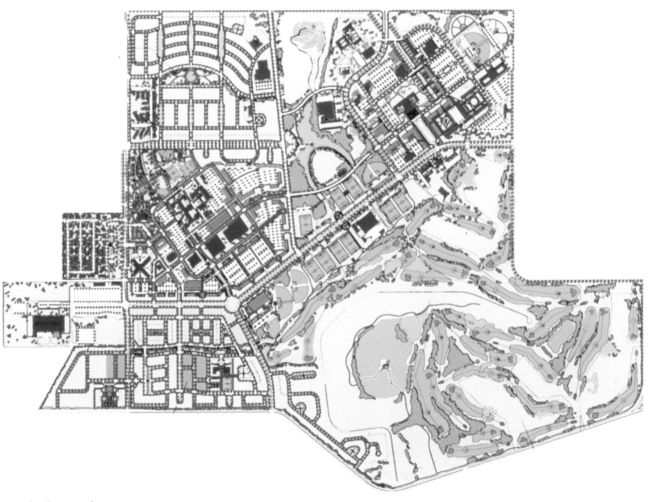

Lowry development plan

Lowry, an urban infill community planned for the 1,866 acre site of the former Lowry Air Force Base, was designed so that the four major program elements—residential neighborhoods, an education campus, an employment center, and recreation and open space—would be integrated into the surrounding Denver neighborhoods by careful design and detailed design controls. Traditional features of the neighboring older areas, including the street and block structure, parkways, neighborhood parks, street tree plantings, and house architecture, are included in the design. This knits the development into the fabric of the community, replacing what was once a separated and secured enclave in the middle of the city.

Lowry is the first significant new development in Denver in over 50 years, providing housing, employment opportunities, and significant new open space not previously available within the city. The planning principles developed there include the establishment of a strong urban design framework in the public realm; the creation of an open space focus for the community; the integration of natural systems such as drainage into the open space system; and the establishment of a sense of community and neighborhood.

The streets of Lowry form the basic framework for development, and are the connections that join the community together. The treatment of these streets establishes the character of the community. Major streets, such as Lowry Boulevard, 6th Avenue, and Yosemite Street, are parkways or boulevards. All other roads are landscaped with rows of street trees set in eight-foot tree lawns to define blocks and development parcels. New streets connect with existing streets to weave the new and old neighborhoods together.

The open space system, which covers more than thirty percent of the land, follows the natural drainage corridor along the center of the property and forms a "spine" within the community. It is tied into the adjacent development areas by "green fingers" that serve as pedestrian and bicycle access corridors and drainage ways. The environmental sustainability of the development is promoted by such techniques as the orientation of houses, the location of deciduous trees, and by covenants and restrictions that require environmentally responsible design, materials, and equipment.

Just as most existing Denver neighborhoods have convenient retail centers within walking distance, Lowry's town center provides retail stores and services within a ten-minute walk of new residential development. The central green is a civic focus for Lowry and the surrounding neighborhoods. To reinforce the pedestrian character of the town center, and to enliven its open spaces, housing for the elderly and higher density residential uses are located within and immediately surrounding it. Three existing bus lines will be rerouted to an integrated transit transfer point there, providing convenient transit access for the approximately 5,000 residents who will live within a ten-minute walk of the center.

To enhance the sense of community in the residential neighborhoods, streets are narrow, garages are accessed from alleys, and architectural guidelines require houses to maintain the scale and character of the surrounding older Denver and Aurora neighborhoods. Small parks and parkways establish visual landmarks and create a sense of neighborhood identity.

Lowry will become a model of how urban infill can promote sustainable development and a vibrant part of the city—a place where people can live, learn, work, and play.

600-acre central open space

Residential boulevard

Higher education and advanced technology campus in reused buildings

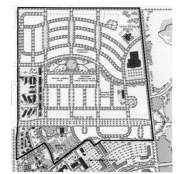

Plan for new residential neighborhood around a park

Existing buildings to be reused

Views to Front Range

The San Nicolas Master Plan

Location: *San Nicolas, Aruba*

Client: *Government of Aruba,*
     Ministry of Economic Affairs

Project Dates: *1994 to date*

Sasaki Staff: *Kenneth E. Bassett, Anthony Mallows,*
     Alan L. Ward, Steve Garbier,
     John Massauro, Gregory Havens,
     Dan Boudreau, William Colehower

Sub-consultants: Arthur Consulting Group International

Circumferential bicycle path and historic/cultural site

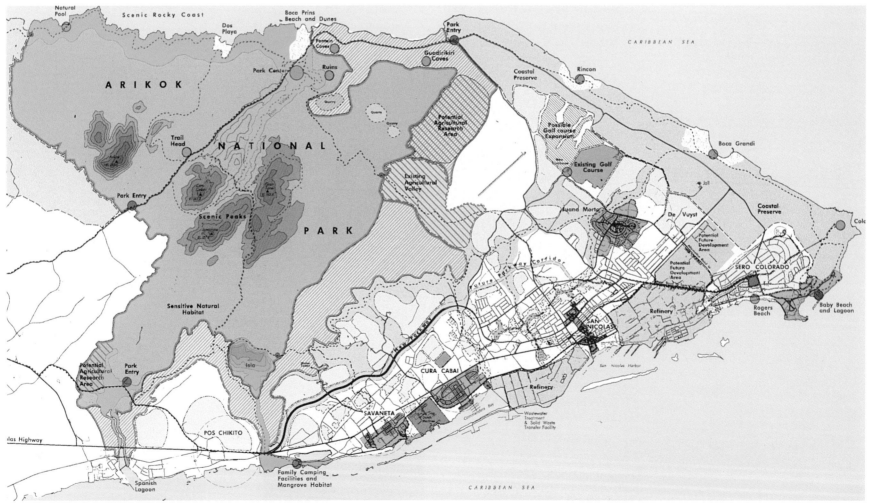

San Nicolas land use and circulation plan

In the mid-1980s, a planning initiative developed by Sasaki Associates established a land use and roadway framework for visitor-related development in the northwestern portion of the Caribbean island nation of Aruba. The goal was to stimulate and guide the development of hotels, interval ownership (time-share condominiums), restaurants, casinos, and similar amenities, while assuring that the resulting increase in tourism did not overwhelm the natural setting. That plan was completed and successfully implemented. With a current tourism market of approximately one million visitors each year, the government has recently directed its attention to the next stage of planning, focusing on the San Nicolas area, in the southeastern part of the island.

Sasaki Associates' San Nicolas Master Plan is a development plan for communities located in the project study area, which is made up of Arikok National Park and the villages and towns of San Nicolas, Savaneta, Cura Cabai and Seroe Colorado. San Nicolas is the primary population and economic center in the study area, and lends its name to the master plan. The plan differs from the tourism plan of the 1980s in its clearly stated goal, which is the establishment of a development framework for reinforcing the authentic character of the San Nicolas area. The framework can guide development by establishing a pattern of streets and circulation paths, open spaces, and public amenities, that will organize public and private land uses. Within this framework, opportunities for the participation of local residents in the tourism sector of the economy are noted.

The plan identifies business opportunities in the San Nicolas area; it describes how access to a broad range of sports and recreation activities can be provided, and how tourism in this part of Aruba can be increased. It identifies natural and historic resources throughout the island, so that they may be preserved, and interpretive programs provided for them. The attractiveness of the physical environment in the San Nicolas area is considered, and suggestions are made for its enhancement. Necessary transportation improvements are noted. The plan emphasizes that it is important that land for housing and other uses be identified, that the natural environment be protected, and that the basic infrastructure for necessary transportation, wastewater treatment, recycling and solid waste management be established.

Framework plans, including land use and circulation development concepts, were developed for the three communities of the study area: San Nicolas, Savaneta, and Seroe Colorado, for the Arikok National Park area, and for the eastern and northern coastlines.

A new civic center is proposed for San Nicolas, to be made up of public buildings and places for community activity. It is referred to as the "civic spine." The plan suggests the renovation and expansion of the existing Lago Sports Complex, and the construction of several new markets and a shade park.

It identifies development sites for cultural organizations and businesses, and suggests the eventual connection of the center of San Nicolas with the Caribbean Sea, by way of a waterfront park. Currently, the buildings and towers of the Lago Oil Refinery, which is no longer in operation, separate the community from the water.

The village of Savaneta has historical significance as the site of the first settlement on Aruba, and the island's best agricultural lands are found there. The plan provides for the preservation of the scale of the village and its position on Commander's Bay. Open space to be preserved, fields that allow for sports and recreation, and the locations for possible new housing are identified. The fundamental organizing form is the Savaneta Village Spine, which connects a new recreation facility with existing schools, civic institutions, new housing sites, refurbished sports fields and, again, a new waterfront park.

Coastal landscape of new Arikok National Park

Desert landscape of the park

Cave paintings in the park

Preserved fishing fleets

Tierra del Sol, desert course

Sero Colorado, once the residential enclave for middle and upper managers of the Lago Oil Company, but now partially abandoned, is transformed in the plan into a residential community of approximately 700 houses. The community is enhanced by new facilities which include schools, a village center, a church and a transit stop. In support of the Aruban government's intention to introduce a limited amount of tourism, a small visitor destination area, integral to the community, is planned for the southern end of the town. It would include a conference center, a spa, and small inn, on a site overlooking Baby Lagoon and its beach. The inn and several planned bed-and-breakfast facilities will accommodate travelers who seek a Caribbean experience somewhat more authentic than that provided by the big hotels at the other end of the island. This will diversify the tourist market and encourage longer stays on the island.

At Arikok National Park, the scenic beauty, unspoiled natural habitat, and diverse terrain can provide a unique program of recreational and educational activities to both residents and visitors. The park is also an essential resource for the preservation and study of Aruba's fragile ecosystem. The plan focuses on strategic site and facility improvements designed to enhance visitor interpretation, education, and recreation. Measures include the upgrading and expansion of the existing network of trails for pedestrians and bicycles; the improvement of existing roads and signs; and the development of facilities for environmental preservation and agricultural research.

The northern and eastern coastlines of the island are to be protected and preserved. A setback of 200 meters beyond the escarpment line is proposed to protect coastal land and visual resources. Development within the setback is prohibited, with the exception of recreational and cultural attractions.

Several transportation improvements, both island-wide and local, are suggested, including a new parkway to mitigate traffic congestion on the island's major east-west highway. Extensions of this parkway, providing convenient access to communities located in the outlying northern and eastern parts of the study area, are proposed. An island-wide system of informational signs, to help tourists to find their way to the San Nicolas area, and to find their way around once there, is also part of the plan—it would serve to link major natural, historic and cultural sites, and communities throughout the island. Similarly, a system of bicycle paths is planned, to link natural, historic, and cultural sites, and the island communities. Improvements in the public transport system are recommended.

Two new wastewater treatment facilities are proposed, to meet existing and projected needs. They are: a municipal facility in Cura Cabai, to treat wastewater from the communities of San Nicolas, Savaneta and Cura Cabai, and a second facility for Sero Colorado. The plan also recommends the establishment of a comprehensive solid waste collection system.

The San Nicolas Master Plan offers a vision for the future of eastern Aruba. It focuses on improving the economic, social and environmental quality of life for residents, while maintaining the area's unique natural, historic, and cultural resources. The planning process was enriched by suggestions and contributions from local residents and community groups.

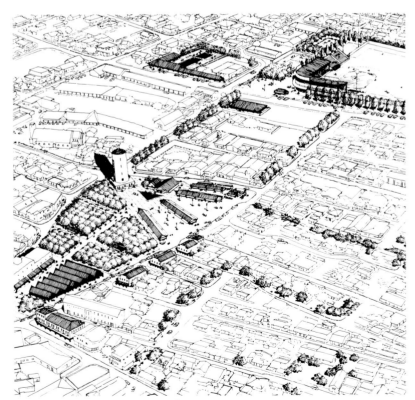

San Nicolas civic spine showing market square, shade park, and artisan market

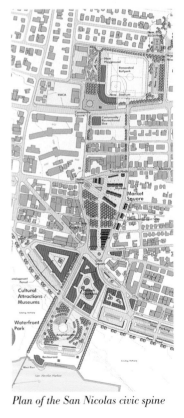

Plan of the San Nicolas civic spine

Existing San Nicolas center

Lago oil refinery

Dialogues

Mr. Hunter Morrison
Planning Director
Cleveland, Ohio

The Honorable Joseph P. Riley, Jr.
Mayor
Charleston, South Carolina

By David Dillon

Hope Memorial Bridge entry to downtown Cleveland

View of downtown Cleveland from Jacobs Field

Sasaki Associates has been working in Cleveland and Charleston for thirty years, wearing many hats—as planner, landscape architect, urban designer, engineer, public advocate—and supplying both a broad planning vision and the specific guidelines to carry it out.

Thirty years ago multi-disciplinary firms were rare, and even today, when most large offices employ engineers and landscape architects and everyone calls himself a planner, few keep to the collaborative path as steadfastly as Sasaki. Long associations, like long marriages, contain peaks and valleys. Some projects succeed, others flop. Some mayors encourage good design, others couldn't care less. The expectation, nevertheless, is that a shared history, seasoned by good will and alertness to one another's strengths and limitations, will ultimately produce better work than an expedient alliance of strangers. That has been the case for Sasaki in Charleston and Cleveland.

The firm's involvement in downtown Cleveland began in the late 1970s with the redesign of Public Square, a formal civic space dating from the city's founding, and continued through the planning of Gateway Center and North Coast Harbor in the 1980s and 1990s. Connect the dots and you have a map of the current Cleveland renaissance.

The 1970s were a dark decade for Cleveland, when its politics were chaotic and its finances nightmarish. Desperate to appear progressive on some front, a coalition of private groups led by the Garden Club of Cleveland and the Downtown Cleveland Corporation selected Sasaki to renovate Public Square. A conservative city with a streak of Yankee pragmatism, Cleveland scorned trendy design. It wanted simplicity and restraint, and that's what Sasaki delivered. The firm made a few modest changes to each of the square's quadrants, adding fountains, flowering trees, and seating, providing more lawn in one area, more paving in another. Ultimately, the project was less about urban design details than about wresting a grand public space from the technocrats and returning it to the people. With help from the city's engineering department and regional transit agency, Sasaki narrowed streets, shortened crosswalks, eliminated unnecessary bus stops and generally gave the pedestrian a fighting chance in the historic heart of Cleveland. "The renovation of Public Square showed that Sasaki understood the tenor of the town," says Cleveland's planning director Hunter Morrison. "They delivered a critical project at a time when that was not easy to do, and they did it without losing their temper."

That precedent proved invaluable a decade later when Sasaki became the master planner for Gateway Center, a $400 million redevelopment of the southern fringe of downtown. Anchored by new homes for the Cleveland Indians and the Cleveland Cavaliers, Gateway represented a struggling city's huge gamble on its beleaguered downtown. Mayor Michael White said bluntly that unless Gateway amounted to more than a stadium and an arena it wouldn't receive a dime of public money. It had to energize the entire downtown and generate economic benefits that everyone could share.

Sasaki's mandate was to tame the ballpark and arena so that they fit seamlessly into downtown. Its other charge, more social than architectural, was to be ombudsman, grievance committee, and cop for the various participants. The firm had to articulate the public agenda as forcefully as the Indians and Cavaliers were articulating the private one. "Sasaki had a sense of the scale of the challenge, which other firms did not," adds Mr. Morrison. "They framed the question broadly instead of thinking only as architects interested in designing the buildings. They understood that we needed a framework within which to place the architecture as much as we needed the architecture itself." This framework consisted of a master plan for the 28-acre site, and a set of design guidelines that enabled the city to say to the teams, and to prospective developers, "This is good," and "This is not so good."

Sasaki's opening move was to rotate the ballpark to the north, toward downtown and the historic street grid. The Jacobs family, owners of the Indians and shrewd retailers, knew the value of showcasing the product, which in this case was the Indians *and* the downtown skyline that they had helped to develop. Using downtown as a backdrop for baseball projected an image of urban sophistication for a city that was notorious for burning rivers and mayors who set their hair on fire. At the same time, Sasaki persuaded the ballpark architects, HOK Sports Facilities Group, to lower the seating bowl to make the main concourse an extension of the sidewalk. This eliminated the swirling ramps and clunky stair towers that disfigure many stadiums, while producing a crisp urban edge along Ontario Street. In the master plan, as well as in the firm's history, edges and linkages are as important as buildings.

Within the site, Sasaki delineated a series of plazas—more social than ceremonial—and landscaped boulevards, to funnel the golden flow of visitors back and forth between Gateway and downtown, the way malls shuttle shoppers between their anchor stores. The corners of the ballpark were left open so that passersby can look in, and fans can look out to the city.

Sasaki's intentions were as much poetic as pragmatic. "We wanted to create a memorable series of spaces as you approach the park," explained design principal Alan Ward. "You see the screen, you hear the crack of the bat, maybe a home run bounces at your feet. We wanted people to see, hear, and feel the park even if they weren't going to the game."

Gateway's big urban design ideas depend on hundreds of small urban design ideas about views, materials, dimensions, entrances, and exits. Playing off the city's romantic but conceptually mushy idea of, "a field of green, a field of dreams," Sasaki devised guidelines that covered everything from tree grates to public art to parking. Some were subtle, such as the proper location of police barricades after a game, while others have changed downtown significantly. Sasaki's parking plan restricted on-site parking to 3200 spaces in two garages, with everyone else being accommodated in existing lots and garages. The Indians and Cavaliers wanted more, but since the goal of the plan was to invigorate downtown, not pave it, the city and Sasaki wouldn't budge. Using existing lots and garages forces fans to walk the streets, to window shop and walk together, and in the process rediscover downtown. "We don't think of the ballpark and the arena as quick fixes," explains Hunter Morrison. "They are part of a long-term strategy to re-establish downtown. By tying the park into the fabric of the city, we believe that people will be more inclined to flow through it instead of rushing to their cars, and to empty their wallets along the way."

Nearly two dozen new restaurants and clubs have opened around the park and the adjacent Flats, a historic warehouse district along the Cuyahoga River that is now connected to Gateway and North Coast Harbor—site of the Rock and Roll Hall of Fame and Museum—by a light rail line planned and designed by Sasaki. Several hotels are in the works, and half a dozen old office buildings are being converted to housing. Most hadn't been touched for 50 years. Without Gateway they might have moldered for another 50. The project has changed the public's perception of downtown. Suddenly, it's the place to be. "The biggest bang for the buck at Gateway was the parking and traffic plan," says assistant planning director Linda Hendrickson. "If that failed, everything else would have failed too. Getting two sports teams, two owners and all those egos to agree was phenomenal."

Sasaki's introduction to Charleston was its 1957 master plan for Sea Pines Plantation on Hilton Head Island, which included the site for Harbourtown. Charleston was the model for Harbourtown, and developer Charles Fraser insisted that anyone who worked on it had to understand the original. So Ken DeMay, Don Olson, and others became intermittent squatters in Charleston, surveying its history and landscape, photographing its buildings, and generally storing up impressions for use in some future project. As principal Stu Dawson noted ironically later, the firm "had established roots in South Carolina before it had roots in New England."

The "future project" arrived in 1979, when Sasaki won a competition to design Charleston's new 7-acre Waterfront Park. By this time the city's waterfront had been reduced to a string of rotting piers, derelict warehouses, and unpaved parking lots, interspersed with gated apartment buildings that provided a bleak commentary on the neighborhood's decline.

Mayor Joseph Riley vowed to change all that by creating a park that would renew the waterfront and adjacent neighborhoods. Not a gentrified park for commodores and vacationing CEOs, but a public space with a fishing pier, gardens, and fountains that encouraged Charlestonians to reestablish an intimate connection with the sea. The mayor knew Sasaki's work in Newburyport and Boston, two historic port cities with decaying waterfronts. And he appreciated their distaste for making grand architectural statements at their client's expense. "They were a big firm with a big reputation," the mayor said, "yet they displayed real sensitivity to what we had here. Not much ego there at all." But as in Cleveland, Sasaki was hired finally because of its comprehensive grasp of Charleston's urban problem. "They understood that we weren't doing just a park, we were redeveloping a whole edge of the city," said Mayor Riley.

Waterfront Park, stretching 1300 feet along the Cooper River, took 11 years to complete, and much of that time was spent in the preparation of the site. Sasaki's architects and engineers took the lead. First they designed two parking garages to accommodate the cars that would be displaced by the new park. That consumed three years. Then they had to compact the mucky soil—"black mayonnaise" to Charlestonians—by covering it with nine feet of sand. That took another two years, during which the sand pile was christened "Riley's mountain" and became the butt of jokes by his political opponents. Even when compacted, the soil couldn't support fountains, plazas, and piers without an elaborate substructure of pilings and platforms. Fifty percent of the park's cost is under ground, invisible to the public. Building new bulkheads disturbed the tidal marsh, which Sasaki had to restore, along with historic Adger's Wharf, to the south. Only a tightly integrated firm accustomed to working across disciplines could have solved these technical problems and still produced an attractive and coherent design.

Mayor Riley proved a surprisingly patient politician, and an enthusiastic collaborator. He participated in numerous charrettes, drawing lines and choosing colors—the green on the downtown parking garages is his—and always reminding the designers of their larger social responsibilities. "So many cities turn the work over to a junior person and you never see the mayor again," recalled Stu Dawson. "That's the rule. The exception was Joe Riley. He attended every public meeting. He introduced us, served as our host, saw that we talked to the right people. He ran the whole project like a symphony conductor."

The completed park combines classical formality with a vernacular ease typical of Charleston. Decisions about the major features—esplanade, fountains, lawn panels, oak grove, the transition from hard paving on the north end to a softer landscape on the south—came quickly. The details took forever. The mayor and the architects collected fifty gravel samples before choosing a mix for the walkways. The height of the seating wall around the lawn and the location of the palmettos were debated with Jesuitical intensity. The brick paths on the western edge had to be reconstructed because the herringbone pattern ran in the wrong direction. If only good engineers could have devised the park's substructure, only landscape architects who had studied the Low Country could have got the hundreds of little details right. The brick paths link eight small gardens reminiscent of the private gardens found throughout Charleston—the anterooms of the grand public space. Mayor Riley required that they be uniform on the outside yet sufficiently different within that "a gentleman who proposes to his sweetheart in one of them will remember it for the rest of his life." A program in a sentence.

To tie the park to the city, Sasaki preserved views back to the streets and alleys of the adjacent historic district, so that the street grid seems to flow through the park to the water. One axis terminates at the public fishing pier that Mayor Riley insisted on building, despite the initial objections of his architects. The signature pineapple fountain sits between two other axes. "We kept telling him that the pier would be an ideal place to tie up yachts," Dawson recalls. "He said that Charleston needed a place for people who didn't *have* yachts. He had a way of bringing humanity to the lines we drew."

Since opening in 1990, Waterfront Park has become Charleston's most popular public space. It has spurred development of other waterfront projects, including the Maritime Center—also designed by Sasaki's architects—that provides a home for Charleston's struggling shrimp fishermen. A Low Country vernacular structure of exposed studs and corrugated metal siding, the center contains a packing room, retail store and gift shop, plus a broad arc of lawn for community gatherings. Like the fishing pier at Waterfront Park, the Maritime Center is more a cultural statement than an economic one. "I wanted to make sure that an industry that was important to our culture and our sense of ourselves was kept," Mayor Riley explained. The mayor considers the Maritime Center another key piece in an eight-mile waterfront promenade that eventually will include an aquarium, a ballpark, and housing, as well as Waterfront Park. "Every town needs a place of beauty and inspiration," he says, "where you can feel a sense of ownership. The greatest cities are measured by the degree to which they create beautiful places in the public domain."

Charleston waterfront promenade on the edge of a replanted salt marsh

Pineapple Fountain in Waterfront Park

Portfolio

Design

Design

By Melanie Simo

Alan Resnick, a principal at Sasaki Associates and head of the firm's architecture discipline in Watertown, is exceedingly pleased by the talented, energetic young people who have recently joined the firm. "They arrive with fresh ideas and terrific enthusiasm" he observes. "They may not be fully aware of the firm's history, but they sense that Sasaki Associates is a special place. All they want to do is great work with good people." [1]

Similar comments are heard among designers in the other disciplines of the firm. The emphasis is on the work—its complexity, its diversity, its many challenges—and on the people, who thrive on the challenges and opportunities. Over time, these people learn something of the firm's illustrious past and of the culture that has evolved through the collaborative process and the multidisciplinary interactions. But the history remains a remote territory, further distanced by a refrain heard not only within the firm but in the larger environment. The early postwar years? "It's not the same place." "It's not the same world." "There may be a thread somewhere. . . ."

In fact there are some threads that bring together the work and the people at Sasaki Associates, from the early 1950s to the present. The willingness to work on teams, to suspend (at least temporarily) the individual ego, to listen, and to sift through a range of factors, priorities, and possibilities in the search for the best solution to a problem—in short, to work through the collaborative process—is a common thread. The interest in, even the zest for, integrating one's own skills and insights with those of others, who are differently trained in a range of planning and design disciplines, is a common thread. There is a consistency among the project types that the firm has worked on for nearly 45 years—particularly campus planning and design, new communities, and large-scale corporate and commercial landscapes, rural and urban. Stuart Dawson, Don Olson, Richard Galehouse, and their colleagues have enjoyed relationships with long-standing clients, who have continued to request the firm's services for a series of projects over long periods of time. This continuity represents a thread, as does the delicate balance of functional and pragmatic concerns, expressive qualities, and cultural significance. But beyond these and other threads is the question of the fabric that they yield when woven together with great skill—the synthesis known as "design."

On this issue, too, one hears many voices in harmony—not necessarily in unison. Joseph Hibbard, a principal and head of the landscape architecture discipline, has adapted an approach to design that he absorbed from his two mentors, Hideo Sasaki (who retired shortly after Hibbard was hired) and Don Olson. That is, "Solve the functional problem first; worry about expression and composition later. Don't forget about them, but don't give them high-tide visibility on day one." Hibbard has also recognized subtle differences in the way he and Olson approach a design problem. Olson will begin with a kind of "scientific objectivity," yet never abandon his intuitions; he has very strong intuitions about composition and about what works, Hibbard observes. Olson likes to examine a problem in its broadest possible context, open up the analysis, and consider many precedents and possibilities before determining the direction of a particular design. Hibbard does likewise, with somewhat less research and analysis. "I have a deductive method, but I enjoy getting to the quick, very soon," he explains. In the end, like many of his colleagues, he will determine which of several variables or factors is critical, then move on to conceive of a structural foundation for solving the particular problem of design.

This approach to design is able to accommodate—indeed it welcomes—contributions from several colleagues and collaborators. The solution may be richer, more generally satisfying, as insights from different disciplines are brought to bear on the problem. And yet the process of arriving at a solution, a true design synthesis in physical form, remains something of a mystery—a mental process unique to each designer or principal-in-charge. For Hibbard, it is a question of several activities occurring simultaneously. "Landscape architecture deals with style, form, aesthetics and sensory quality, and at the same time it deals with function and utility," he observes. "You have to get both kinds of things going at the same time, on the same wave length, in order to solve the problem well."[2]

Scott Smith, an architect and principal who heads the San Francisco office of Sasaki Associates, recalls that he was first drawn to the firm because of its collaborative practice. "But I really didn't know how strongly I would feel about it until I was there a while," he observes. In the early 1980s, on one of his first projects in the firm—the expansion of Western Wyoming College—he worked with Galehouse, Hibbard, John Orcutt (then head of the firm's architecture discipline), Sasaki (who was brought in as a consultant), and others in the firm, as well as with associated architectural firms. In particular, for a few insights that had a profound effect on the siting and form of the building expansion, Smith credits Hibbard. "If an architect went out there on his or her own volition," he remarks, "I don't think the building would be what it is today. That's one of the things I treasure about our practice—this collaboration."

As for the design process itself, Smith prefers to address the broad context first. "Architecture is a social art," he affirms. "It is shaped by the cultures we live in and by the people themselves. Of course, there is a time in the process when the professional must give this piece of work the inspiration; buildings are not designed by a democracy! There is a leader who designs the building. But the success of a building depends on how well that leader absorbs a great number of things, from site visits, the public meetings, the in-house process, and so on. We spend a lot of time and energy with focus groups. We ask questions. The really challenging part of the creative process is to listen well."[3]

The willingness to listen is one of the strongest threads in the nearly forty-five years of Sasaki Associates' practice. But the nature of the listening has changed somewhat over the years. Stuart Dawson's perspective on this reaches back to the late 1950s, when, as a young graduate in landscape architecture, he joined the then small firm of landscape architects, architects and planners. Now a senior principal in the firm, Dawson has emphasized the range of voices that, increasingly, must be heard, particularly on urban projects: the redevelopment agencies, the planning boards and commissions, the community organizations and various interest groups, the marketing people, sometimes arts administrators and collaborating artists, as well as one's own colleagues, in the office and in associated firms. Dawson is particularly attuned to the voice of the client. "There's plenty of room for creative listening," he has observed. "It takes a more mature professional to help lead the client's dream a little bit into your own vision. I think that's exciting. We've done things that, when we first talked with the client, we didn't think were possible. But gradually, everyone involved

became convinced that there is a better way."[4]

In the 1950s and '60s, if the client was an architect, Dawson sometimes found that he was listening more to his own colleagues in the office than to that architect. Eero Saarinen, for instance, showed considerable concern for the landscape setting for his building—early on. "It was interesting. He cared at the model stage," Dawson recalled. "But after we'd given him our vision—what it would be like, what colors, roughly what textures, some details, not too many—then you were left alone, and you were expected to do a good job. And that was also true of Kevin Roche. He was most involved in the early stage of a project—in the vision." Working on the Deere headquarters, in Moline, Illinois, then, Dawson listened when Sasaki offered critiques of his work and recommended a certain way of planting—grouping the hawthornes together in a single mass, for instance, and grouping the maples and the oaks in the same manner—as large drifts, sweeping over the undulating landscape. Out of that design process, Saarinen's building was given a noble, yet understated, setting. Dawson saw the entire process through, from conceptual design through the trials and hard-won successes of landscape installation. Satisfied, both Saarinen and Deere & Company continued to seek out the services of Sasaki's office over the years.

For Dawson, the design process has evolved along with changing conditions. "I think the issues were simpler in the '50s," he reflected. "The client we were listening to had a fairly simple agenda. It gave you a lot of space for innovation. Today people are much more sophisticated. They ask a lot more of you. And they tell you a lot more, if you listen." Looking back on the early years inevitably calls to mind anecdotes and the conditions of practice that were simply circumstantial—a function of the size of the office and the youth of the personnel. "I think we were a lot more informal in the early years," Dawson remarks. "We would work all night, then go out and play if we were overworked." He pauses, as if allowing a crowd of memories to sort themselves out. "We had a great time. We made full-scale models, all kinds of things. We made a light fixture design—full-scale. We did everything in an exploratory way."[5]

Layered over the youthful high spirits and optimism of the early postwar years was also a pervasive sense of expansion, derived in part from a buoyant national economy and the pressing need to rebuild and build anew—not only in the United States but abroad as well. There was also an expanding base of the kinds of knowledge and understanding deemed essential, or at least relevant, to planning and design. Studies in sociology, urbanism, anthropology, the aesthetics and psychology of design, and the technological issues of heating, lighting, ventilating, solar orientation, and other environmental controls were increasingly being integrated within the professional curriculum.

As noted earlier, Sasaki's office had long maintained strong ties to educational institutions, particularly to the design schools at Harvard and MIT, led by Josep Lluis Sert and Pietro Belluschi. These ties not only brought commissions into Sasaki's office—for Sert and Belluschi remained close collaborators with the office for many years—but they also ensured that the new forms of knowledge and understanding would inform the work of the firm. Some of the early partners and associates were teaching on a part-time basis as well as practicing. For these designers and their colleagues, both at the school and at the office, the learning continued. A seminar, a book-in-progress, or a problem in studio might yield a new theory or even a simple hypothesis, which could then be tested in practice, on a project. Some projects might be small, isolated in space and time. Others, on a campus or within a city, might be interrelated within a larger context, where more factors had to be considered over long periods of time. Sometimes a series of commissions would be brought into the firm for the same large context, or for similar contexts. In this case, a sequence of design solutions could be tested, and designers could develop a cumulative understanding of the larger problem.

From these larger, more complex problems there emerged a vision of something greater than the sum of the parts. There evolved a sense of wholeness, difficult to articulate in words yet recognizable when it was achieved. In time it became apparent to some designers that this wholeness was not ensured simply by bold geometries or forceful personalities, nor by consistency of material, style, or scale. More subtle and elusive, this quality of wholeness remained intangible, nearly inexpressible, and rare. One simply felt it in certain environments where the people, the built forms and spaces, and the natural elements seemed to have reached an equilibrium.

For Kenneth DeMay, one of the first architects that Sasaki hired, a sense of wholeness in the built work came, in part, from the nature of the way the architectural practice evolved at Sasaki Associates. At first, the small office was absorbed in projects of master planning and site planning and design. Commissions came in from architects such as Sert, Belluschi, Skidmore, Owings and Merrill, I. M. Pei, Ernest Kump, William Wurster—people who liked to work with Sasaki and his firm. (Everyone worked "very, very hard, long hours," DeMay recalls. "We worked so hard, so diligently, that it became ingrained in all of us.") Beginning by helping out in a variety of ways, DeMay soon focused on the development of institutional master plans—which often led to a commission for a building. Essentially, he and his colleagues shaped the whole first, looking at a campus from an overall point of view. Then they would work their way down to a smaller scale—to design the building. [6]

If Sasaki Associates' architectural practice can be said to have grown out of planning, the same is true of several other areas of their practice. As Galehouse has explained, the urban design practice grew out of the planning discipline, as did the environmental services and the graphics capabilities. That these developments occurred quite naturally, in an evolutionary way, can be traced to the fact that "planning" at Sasaki Associates has always been understood to be physical planning. The ultimate product of the firm's planners—many of whom have degrees in architecture as well—is usually a built work or series of spaces and structures. "Planners succeed [in this firm] only if they have the ability to really feel the physical dimension," David Hirzel recently observed. Policy skills, for instance, although useful, would not be sufficient. Similarly, Hirzel has noted that "the architects who survive here are those who can live in a contextural world." [7]

Smith would agree, noting that "context" involves more than the architectural and natural environment of a project. He would emphasize that the program, the region, the climate, even the particular architectural technology used, all contribute to what he understands as "context." He can point to a long list of buildings and landscapes designed by Sasaki Associates that remain eminently suited to their context, in the broad sense of the word. And yet he is aware of certain limitations that such work entails. "Sasaki Associates has no 'signature' architecture," he observes. "You look at our buildings and you don't know necessarily how they came about or who did them." Rather, the design of the building is informed by a number of factors, often a distinctive natural landscape or an urban or institutional setting that has been built up and refined over long periods of time.

This lack of signature—a form of anonymity that landscape architects have known and often struggled with for many years—has other implications as well. In the continuing tradition of collaboration with associated architectural firms as well as with one's own colleagues, the contribution of the firm to a particular building often goes unheralded. In many states, the building will be generally known, both officially and informally, as the work of the in-state architect or firm—the "architects of record." Today, as in the 1950s and '60s, much of the firm's architectural work is a collaborative effort with other architects, for which Sasaki Associates provides design services. Whether the firm receives public recognition for this work may be left to any number of factors, some beyond the control of the designer or the firm. Smith does, however, derive great personal satisfaction in the working relationships that are formed in the process—both within the firm and on the outside. A client or a colleague will become a good friend. And sometimes a building will emerge as a kind of "signature," not of the designer or of the firm, but within its own context. "The building is the signature of the campus," Smith says with pride.

To speak of signature is to raise questions of identity, both individual and collective. Some designers at Sasaki Associates, mature and confident of their own abilities, have spent their entire professional lives in the collaborative, multidisciplinary environment of this firm; they have known no other form of practice. Some have worked elsewhere but find that they prefer the collaborative to other modes of practice, in part because of the intriguing types and wide range of problems to be solved and the successes realized. After many years, some remain intrigued by the very idea of collaboration, a powerful ideal which one strives daily to achieve in concert with others. Ironically, in the outside world, both design professionals and the broader public tend to think of Sasaki Associates as a planning firm or an environmental planning and design firm, or a landscape architectural firm, an architectural firm, or an engineering firm. "We're known for our parts," Galehouse explains. "The central message of the collaborative idea just doesn't come across." [8]

"Well, we are what it is we've done for our clients," Hirzel point out. To explain in detail would involve a more comprehensive and historical overview, in both words and images, than is possible in these pages. Here, at any rate, the retrospective glimpses, along with the recent work and thought of professionals at Sasaki Associates can offer a sense of the firm's collective identity.

Observations by relative newcomers are also illuminating. For Nancy Harrod, a principal and head of the interiors discipline (which grew out of the architectural discipline), the time frames in which a project must go from initial meetings, programming and conceptual design, through installation, have been dramatically shortened since she first arrived at Sasaki Associates in 1987. Deadlines are tighter, resources are more limited, and the demands are greater. "It takes more and more energy every year," she admits, noting that the faster pace can also be exhilarating. Teams working more quickly and efficiently can see the results of their work (and learn from them) faster. [9] Another development is in the programming phase, where, as in other disciplines, some of the greatest opportunities for creativity now lie. Clients look to Harrod and her team, as they look to Smith, Hibbard, Bassett, Galehouse, and others in the various disciplines, for help in defining the problem, given an increasingly complex assortment of needs, desires, and constraints.

One development that may have profound implications for the design process itself is the introduction of new technologies, particularly computers and other electronic equipment. At Sasaki Associates, enthusiasm for computer-aided design, or CAD systems, and related technologies varies from one professional to another. Most designers view them as design tools, perhaps ultimately indispensable ones. New technologies also represent an increasingly large component of the design problems to be solved, as computers and other electronic media are being introduced into campuses, corporate offices, financial institutions, and elsewhere, on a vast scale. As mentioned earlier, Perry Chapman has found that campus administrators are increasingly emphasizing the need to integrate the new apparatus into existing spaces as well as to create or redesign places where students can mingle and socialize, face-to-face, after spending many hours before a computer monitor.

While some writers theorize about the decreasing need for physical public space, in view of the electronic meeting places that are bound to emerge in virtual space, Alan Ward is more cautious. "I'd agree that [electronic media] fundamentally affects how we work and view the world, and how we do our work. It changes that. And the media has distanced us from the places where we live, from our sense of community. But I don't believe the physical world is going to become a virtual world. I would rather look in the other direction. Rather than say that this physical world around us is dissolving, so let's move on to something else—I'd rather try to reclaim what is fundamentally human." [10]

This, too, is what Sasaki Associates have done for their clients. To reclaim, redesign, and build anew physical places that are fundamentally human have been significant pursuits in the past, and they continue to be major goals of this collaborative practice. In time these places, too, may form part of the firm's collective identity.

Deere & Company Administrative Center

Deere & Company Administrative Center

TRW Corporate Headquarters

Frito-Lay Corporate Headquarters

Western Wyoming College

Boston College

College of the Holy Cross

Recreation and Aquatics Center, University of California, Santa Barbara

Boston College

College of the Holy Cross

113

College of the Holy Cross

The University of New Hampshire

Greenacre Park

Christian Science Center

Pennsylvania Avenue

Reston Town Center

Boston Waterfront

Charleston Waterfront

Charleston Waterfront

Deere & Company
Administrative Center

Location: *Moline, Illinois*
Client: *Deere & Company*
Project Dates: *1959 with continuing consultation to the present*
Sasaki Staff: *Stuart O. Dawson, Neil J. Dean, John Emerson, Hideo Sasaki*
In Association With: *Eero Saarinen Associates; Kevin Roche–John Dinkeloo & Associates*
Awards: *25-Year Award, The American Institute of Architects, 1993; Classic Award, American Society of Landscape Architects, 1991; Honor Award, Boston Society of Landscape Architects, 1st Professional Awards Program, 1984; Honor Award, American Society of Landscape Architects, 81st Professional Awards Program, 1981*

In the late 1950s, Sasaki Associates was retained by Eero Saarinen Associates to develop a site plan for John Deere and Company's new administrative center. Out of the collaboration between Sasaki and Saarinen came the shared conviction that the architecture and landscape of the center should be part of one another, to capitalize on the natural beauty of the 1,200-acre site and to express Deere's Midwestern prairie roots. The property encompassed a natural ravine adjacent to the floodplain of the Rock River, and, as was characteristic of such Midwestern landscapes, the predominant tree was the American elm.

The design which emerged consists of a main office building which bridges the valley floor; an auditorium and product display building connected to the middle floor of the office building by glass-enclosed bridges; and a parking lot located on a plateau so that it is not visible from anywhere inside the buildings.

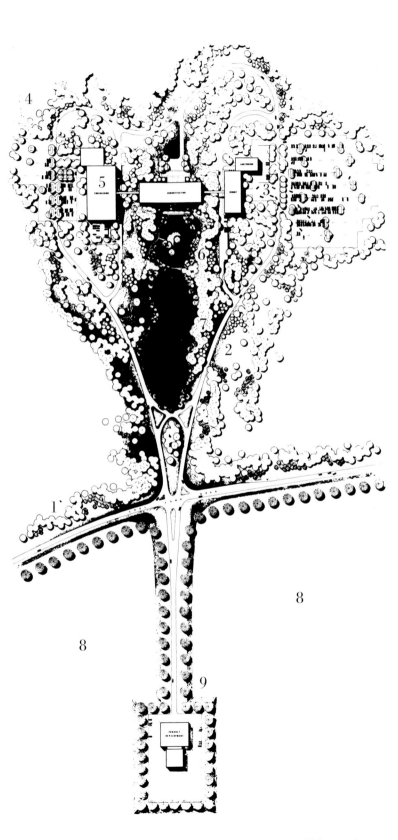

Original site plan

0   400 feet

Deere Center in context

1   John Deere Road
2   Entrance road
3   Main entrance
4   Parking terrace
5   Later addition
6   Upper pond with Henry Moore
7   Lower pond
8   Floodplain fields
9   Product development building (deferred)

Lake reflects building which bridges valley floor

Road leading to exhibits building

Two lakes were created, one to serve as a reservoir for flash-flood storms, and the other to provide a focal point for the central volume of the building. The larger lake also acts as a heat exchange medium for the air conditioning system. A small island in the upper lake is the focal point of the composition when viewed from within the office building. Grades were adjusted so that guests at the tables in the executive dining room look out across the lake at tabletop height to the island which serves as a nesting habitat for the swans and geese that inhabit the lakes. The result is animation in the landscape and entertainment for employees who stroll along the crushed traprock paths and feed the fish and waterfowl during their lunch hours.

In marrying the building with the land, Sasaki and Saarinen selected construction and plant materials that would underscore the natural elements of the site, and developed a road and parking system which would have minimal impact on the surroundings. Each solution, while not the least expensive, was always the least disturbing to the existing landscape, particularly to the mature oak trees. The color and texture of the Cor-ten steel chosen for the building, bridges, and other site elements, co-exist harmoniously with those of the coarse grained trees and grasses of the site.

The placement of the roads and attendant drainage is a good example of the way in which the designers retained the best of what existed. Drainage is in swales designed to resist erosion and maximize the availability of rain and snow for irrigation. Because the native soil is a heavy clay, which typically holds too much water and drowns new plants, almost all new plant materials had to be given underdrainage.

Hard site materials were kept to a minimum, with asphalt used to pave streets and parking areas, and dark exposed aggregate concrete used for pedestrian areas. A combination of sod/seed, natural meadow grass and forest undercover blankets the balance of the land. Over 1,000 trees were added to complement the existing hardwood forest and to replace some 500 elm trees which died of Dutch elm disease prior to and during construction. (The original design concept called for a preponderance of native woodlands, with the exception of 40 tended acres adjacent to the upper lake and the area around the buildings. Over 400 acres are now maintained as lawn, a consequence of Deere's entry into the domestic mower market.)

Subsequent consultations to Deere included the 1974 placement of the Henry Moore bronze sculpture "Hill Arches." After placement of the sculpture—via helicopter—on the chosen site in the upper lake, the shape of the earthwork proposed around the sculpture was mocked up with string, which was adjusted until suitable contours were agreed upon.

In 1975, Sasaki was asked to create a setting for five stones purchased in Kyoto by Deere's chairman, William Hewitt. A site close to the building was selected in order to relate the stones to the structure, and make the garden visible to people inside. Spring highlights the Kyoto stones; the bright colors of the dogwood, Japanese maple and rhododendron *yakusimanum* planted in the garden contrast with the dark colors of the stones and the raked gravel base upon which they are set.

Subsequent consultations, such as the landscape design for the west office building and the John Deere Insurance Company building, have continued the close working relationship between Deere, its architect, landscape architect and landscape contractor. Sasaki's consultation, including the selection of all plant materials in the nurseries and the staking of plant locations at the site, continues on an annual basis today, as it has for over 30 years.

View from executive dining room

Henry Moore "Hill Arches"

"Hill Arches" and south terrace

Upper and lower lakes

Lower lake and Administration Center

Lower lake willows

Main entrance road, hawthorne drift

South terrace

TRW Corporate Headquarters

Location: Lyndhurst, Ohio
Client: TRW Inc.
Project Dates: 1989
Sasaki Staff: Stuart O. Dawson, Mark O. Dawson, Robert Fager, Alison Richardson, Thomas R. Ryan

In Association
With: Lohan Associates, Architect; William Bevins, Civil Engineer

Awards: Merit Award, American Society of Landscape Architects, Professional Awards of Excellence, 1987; Honor Award, Boston Society of Landscape Architects, 2nd Professional Awards Program, 1985

1 Entrance drive
2 New bridge
3 Pool and falls
4 Entry court
5 Central atrium
6 Garage entrance
7 Pond garden
8 English cottage garden
9 Japanese park
10 Bolton house
11 French garden
12 Terrace
13 Trails
14 Minoru Niizuma sculpture

Site plan

0   200 feet

Technology giant TRW Inc. planned to build new headquarters on the venerable Bolton Estate outside Cleveland. Many of TRW's top managers were being asked to relocate, so the company felt it was important to create an extremely attractive work environment. TRW invited three leading architects to participate in a design competition for the facility. Among them was Dirk Lohan who, in turn, asked Sasaki Associates to join his team because of the earlier success of the two firms' collaborative ventures for the McDonald's Corporation in Oak Brook, Illinois, and Frito-Lay in Plano, Texas.

The competition was masterfully managed by TRW, who asked for two models—one to address the design of the site, and the other to show the design of the building. The Lohan/Sasaki team won the competition largely because their solution achieved an equal balance of program, architecture, and the landscape. The team also proposed that all parking be underground to preserve the extraordinary site.

A horticultural survey provided the basis for an extensive pre-construction preservation effort. Numerous trees, shrubs, and ground covers were moved from areas prior to construction; large expanses of woodland were pruned, fertilized, and sprayed. "Yield to the trees" was the watchword throughout the construction process. Decals bearing the phrase were put on workers' hard-hats to indicate that all members of the construction crew had watched a film about erosion control and protection of the woodlands during construction.

The gardens between the wings of the headquarters building include a circular garden with perennial plantings in the English style, and a pond garden with aquatic plants. A park in the Japanese style features a split stone bridge, a symbolic ground-cover stream, and Japanese maples, pagoda trees, and weeping cherries. At the former estate mansion, which had been converted to a guest house, a neglected formal French garden was restored. A creek that traverses the property was impounded to form a series of small waterfalls that enliven the view along the entry road.

A three-story central atrium, which connects directly to the parking beneath the building, features a tropical garden with pools and waterfalls, palm trees, aquatic plants, and an informal seating area in a grove of fig trees.

Landscape/building interface

Headquarters in natural setting

Entry road

Minoru Niizuma sculpture

New bridge

Terraced creek

Restored formal garden

Tree preservation

Frito-Lay Corporate Headquarters

Location: Plano, Texas
Client: Frito-Lay, Inc.
Project Dates: 1987
Sasaki Staff: Stuart O. Dawson, Jay B. Faber,
                 Varoujan Hagopian, Edward B. Boiteau,
                 Thomas R. Ryan, Maurice Freedman

In Association
With: Lohan Associates, Architect;
                 Howard Garrett, Landscape
                 Consultant; David Carsen,
                 Structural Engineer
Awards: Citation, Boston Society
                 of Landscape Architects, 1989

Entrance road

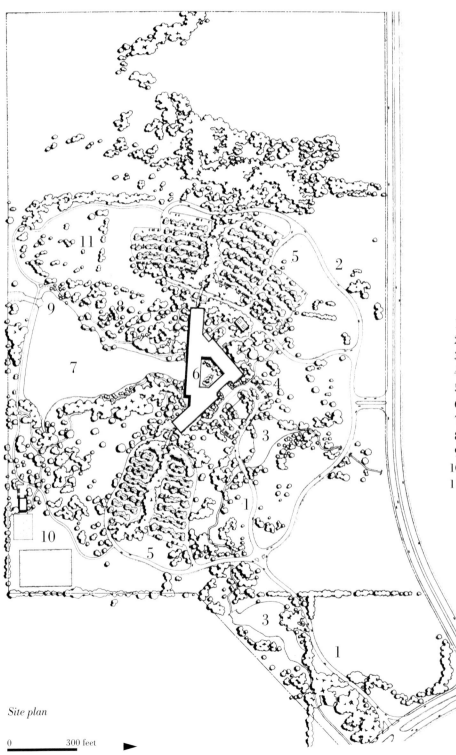

1 Entrance road
2 Loop road
3 Upper pools
4 Entrance/visitor parking
5 Parking gardens
6 Courtyard and falls
7 Lower pool
8 Native woodland
9 New wier
10 Service and recreation
11 Building expansion

Site plan

0   300 feet

The design team of Lohan Associates and Sasaki Associates was chosen by Frito-Lay to help select a site and to design and construct a new national headquarters. The two offices had just completed the McDonald's Corporate Headquarters in Oak Brook, Illinois, and were well established as an interdisciplinary team. The selected site, twenty miles north of Dallas, was on the 2,600-acre property owned by Ross Perot's EDS, for which Sasaki had completed a master plan in 1983. Frito-Lay became the first corporate facility built there. The site's 218 acres of open fields, topography, stands of mature oak, pecan, elm and persimmon trees, farm ponds and eroded limestone streams, unusual in the arid north Texas prairie, presented an opportunity to create an exceptional work setting for Frito-Lay's employees.

Inspired by this extraordinary property, Frito-Lay's management, Lohan's architects and Sasaki's landscape architects, environmentalists and civil engineers agreed on four primary goals: to preserve the trees; to minimize the impact of buildings, roads and parking; to limit grounds maintenance; and to make the most of the limestone outcroppings and flowing surface water that distinguish the site.

Many alternatives for the form and location of the 500,000 square-foot program were explored. The selected alternative placed the three-sided, four-story headquarters building low, bridging the stream and floodplain, with two parking gardens sited on adjacent hilltops.

An open-air courtyard, overlooked by offices and the main dining area, is at the heart of both the building and the natural water system. Water from the existing upper pond cascades over naturalistically placed layers of Texas limestone into the courtyard pool, then flows into the 10-acre lower lake. Native flowers and other plantings bring the natural landscape into the courtyard and a recirculating pump carries water from the lower lake to the top of the falls to assure a refreshing flow through the courtyard even in dry times.

To draw visitors into the landscape, the entry roadway winds through open vistas of wildflower meadows and stands of shade trees. Visitors cross the stream and upper pond to arrive at the entry porte-cochére, and then proceed to a walled and heavily landscaped visitor parking lot or to the executive parking garage within the building. Employees reach the parking gardens via perimeter roads. Pedestrian bridges that pass over the internal loop road lead people from their cars into the mid-level of the building, eliminating all vehicular/pedestrian conflicts and making for very pleasant access to the workplace.

Sasaki's landscape design establishes three broad-scale tiers of landscape development to simplify maintenance and limit the need for irrigation. Expanses of low-maintenance meadows of natural pasture, grasses and wildflowers are preserved and augmented at the periphery, while transitional "rough areas" are planted with native grasses that require less intensive maintenance and irrigation. The irrigated lawns adjacent to the building and lake edges are kept to a minimum.

The landscape at Frito-Lay exemplifies Sasaki's characteristic interdisciplinary approach to problem solving. The issues to be resolved ranged from landscape architectural and civil engineering design to flood control (involving the replacement of the lower lake weir) and stringent environmental permitting, including construction phase services for all site-related elements.

Lower pond seen from building

Entry road, upper pond

Courtyard from lobby

Upper pond flowing through building into courtyard

Path from lower pond

Path through cedar elms

Detail of courtyard

Wildflower meadow

GTE Telops Headquarters

Location: *Los Colinas, Texas*
Client: *GTE Telephone Operations Division*
Project Dates: *1989-1991*
Sasaki Staff: *Stephen E. Hamvey, Alan Fujimori,*
                 Mark O. Dawson, Roger Degan, Jay Marsh,
                 Paul Weathers, Jim Sandlin
In Association
With: *HKS Architects;*
                 Staffelbach Designs and Associates;
                 HC Beck Company and GTE Realty
Awards: *Excellence in Planning and*
                 Development Award, City of Irving
                 Planning and Zoning
                 Commission, 1991

1 Waterfall
2 Rotunda
3 Terraced walls
4 Building entry
5 Retention ponds

Site plan

0   400 feet

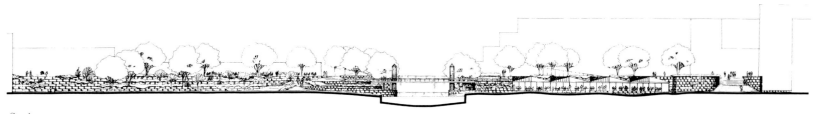

Section

The GTE Telephone Operations Division's state-of-the-art headquarters facility is an example of an efficient working environment designed to meet the challenges of the new and rapidly changing telecommunications industry.

Strategically located between downtown Dallas and Dallas/Fort Worth Airport, the 100-acre site is part of a large, planned, mixed-use development known as Los Colinas, and is home to a number of Fortune 500 companies. Highway 114 is located to the north, and Los Colinas Golf Course and the historic Carpenter Ranch Homestead form the other boundaries, delimiting an impressive setting for the new corporate headquarters.

Sasaki Associates was selected as the site planners, site engineers and landscape architects to participate in a multidisciplinary team effort to fast-track the construction of 1,200,000 square feet of office facilities and a 3,500-car underground parking structure. Working in association with architects, interior designers, contractors, and with GTE Realty, who managed the program design and construction process, a two-building scheme was developed to minimize the negative impact that a single footprint would have on the site. The rolling North Texas topography forms a series of ridgelines and valleys which are used to organize the buildings and site elements. Buildings are located on a major ridgeline to take advantage of the views to the Dallas skyline, the adjacent golf course and nearby ponds. Existing stands of mesquite, cedar, elm, and live oak trees have been preserved to unify the site.

Buildings were limited to four stories to promote better employee interaction. Underground parking below the buildings allow efficient pedestrian connections into the building cores and, again, minimize the impact on the site.

The planning and project delivery of the new facility was designed to reflect GTE's corporate philosophy; the principle of business efficiency in a quality and environmentally sensitive workplace prevailed in the design. A key objective called "22+2" represented the goal of delivery of the project in 22 months for the east building, and two months later for the west building, including all site improvements. This objective was attained on time and within budget.

View from rotunda

Pond and landscape

Waterfall along connector

Informal pond edge and pathways

View from inside connector

Exterior garden space

Terraced stone wall

Pedestrian bridge

Western Wyoming College

Location: *Rock Springs, Wyoming*
Client: *Western Wyoming College*
Project Dates: *1981-1988*
Sasaki Staff: *Hideo Sasaki, Richard F. Galehouse,*
    N. Scott Smith, M. Perry Chapman,
    John Orcutt, Joseph A. Hibbard,
    David Mittelstadt, David French,
    John Hawes, Anne Casey

In Association
With: *Anderson Mason Dale and the*
    BKLH Group

Awards: *Honor Award, Western States*
Regional Awards Program,
American Institute of Architects,
1988; Exports Award, Boston
Society of Architects, 1988; Design
Award, Colorado Chapter of the
American Institute of Architects,
1985; Citation Award, American
School & University, Architectural
Portfolio, 1983

1   Entry drive
2   Performing arts
3   Sciences
4   Commons
5   Trades
6   Recreation
7   Academic
8   Arts
9   Housing

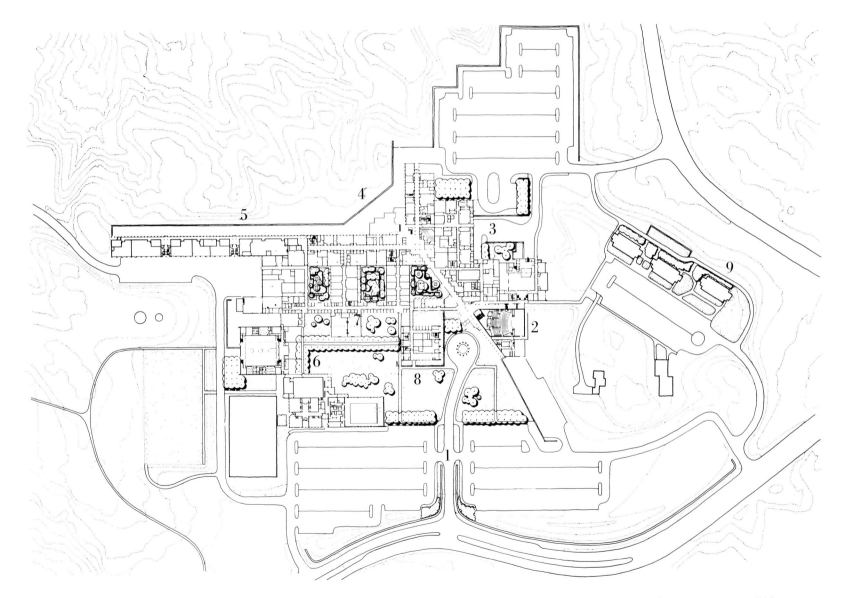

Site plan

0   300 feet ▶

Western Wyoming College occupies the top of a bluff above the town of Rock Springs, with sweeping views of the Wind River Mountains and desert terrain. The original campus, constructed in the 1960s, consisted of single story buildings lacking any visual or symbolic relationship to the dramatic setting. In 1981, the voters of Sweetwater County passed a major bond issue to double the size of the college to serve population growth in the energy-rich region, and in the following year Sasaki Associates became part of the team retained to prepare the master plan, building program, and architectural design for the expanded college.

The assignment presented both a need and an opportunity to embark on campus planning and architectural design as a seamless process. Several challenges were addressed. The existing buildings needed to be integrated into the expanded complex, and it was necessary for the site and interior planning to respond to the hostile, high desert climate, with its constant winds and extreme seasonal temperature shifts. At the same time, the project demanded a solution that would dramatize the location of the college on the bluff as a powerful cultural symbol for the community.

The plan for the 280,000 square-foot expansion surrounds the original buildings with new structures in a compact, interconnected ensemble that covers less than ten percent of the 268-acre site. The layout provides protection from the weather and preserves the sensitive sagebrush landscape. A network of interior "streets" joining parts of the campus is animated by public and student service functions. Public spaces are bathed in natural daylight controlled by a continuous system of overhead light monitors.

The streets are anchored by a performing arts complex, a gymnasium, and other general facilities, and they converge at the Commons, a great atrium "living room" with breathtaking views of the mountains on the horizon. Exterior landscaped courtyards and niches are interspersed throughout the complex, offering an intimate sense of the traditional outdoor campus while being protected from the wind conditions. The small scale of the outdoor spaces concentrates the green zones into compact areas, so different from the surrounding desert gullies, limiting the amount of irrigation required.

The design of the Western Wyoming campus is an expression of its rugged mesa setting. Seen from afar, the building mass appears to grow out of the site. The rhythm of the rooftop light monitors, reminiscent of the coal tipples on early mine sheds, reminds the observer of the region's robust history as a natural resource economy. The transparency of the Commons complements the solid masses that flank it on either side. Facade colors and textures are composed in strata that emulate the reds, browns and terra cottas of the native soil and the sage-green of the local desert plants. The physical form of Western Wyoming College functions as a kind of metaphor for its natural and cultural environment, a landmark in the region.

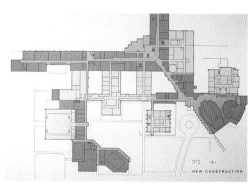

Existing buildings and new construction

Context plan

Classroom wing

Desert landscape

View from commons

The commons

143

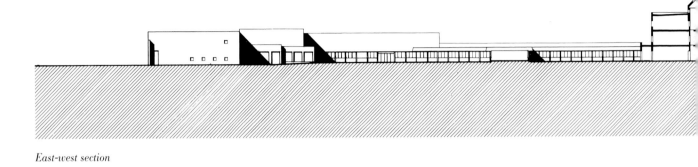

East-west section

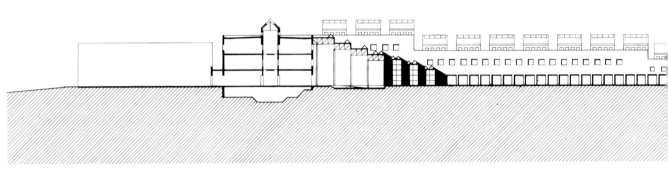

North-south section

The Commons

Commons and academic wing

Light monitors along pedestrian spine

The building design respects the contours of the land

Desert foreground

The building uses rich colors of the landscape

Boston College: Sports Facilities, Theater, Dormitories, and Entry

Location: Chestnut Hill, Massachusetts
Client: Boston College
Project Dates: 1979-1989
Sasaki Staff:
Parking Garage
Stadium:
Phase I: John Orcutt, James Edwards,
Robert Livermore
Phase II: Roy Viklund, Ernie Marsh,
Richard Farrington,
Paul Berkowitz, Paul DiBona, T. Meyer
Theater: John Orcutt, Roy Viklund, Stan Fink,
Susan Robers, Skip Jacobs
Sports Facilities: Roy Viklund, Ralph Wolfe,
James Edwards, Rich Farrington,
Patricia Birch, Paul Berkowitz,
Mani Farhadi, Mark Finneral,
Paul DiBona
Student Housing: Roy Viklund, Steve Oppenheimer,
Paul DiBona, John Hollywood,
Richard Farmington,
Deborah Collins, Edith Calzadilla
Campus Entry: Roy Viklund, Gary Hilderbrand,
Edith Calzadilla, Les Stucka

Sub-consultants:
Parking Garage
Stadium: LeMessurier Consultants;
C.A. Crowley Associates
Theater: Souza and True, Inc.;
C.A. Crowley Engineering, Inc.;
McCarron, Jufnagle & Vegkley;
Bolt Beranek & Newman, Inc.
Sports Facilities: Weidlinger Associates;
Karl Beitin Associates
Student Housing: Foley & Buhl Engineering;
Richard J. Comeau,
Johnson and Stover, Inc.;
AM-Tech Engineers, Inc.
Awards: Citation Award, American School
and University, Architectural Portfolio,
1990; Facilities of Merit Award,
Athletic Business Conference,
1990 (Silvio Conte Forum)

In the 1980s, Boston College evolved from a regional institution to one with a strong national presence. Driven by the vision of its president, J. Donald Monan, S.J., and the enthusiastic support of its alumni, BC undertook a number of projects with Sasaki Associates to enhance the quality of the institution's programs and physical environment. These projects made the most of limited land resources and contributed coherence to the so-called "lower campus," down the hill from the older, collegiate-gothic, academic core. The area lacked any guiding plan, having been created, in part, when an adjacent reservoir was filled.

Sasaki's first assignment was to design a home for BC's performing arts program. The Robsham Theater Arts Center, intended for both teaching and performance, is a simple, direct response to the constraints of the small corner site, a limited budget and a tight design and construction schedule. The sky-lit glass, brick and tile entrance lobby leads to a

Main campus entrance with spires of Gasson Hall in the background.

Aerial view of Boston College campus with the City of Boston in the background

600-seat proscenium theater and a smaller studio theater, and at the same time leads visitors to other spaces in the building. The building's exterior, of earth-toned tile and brick, complements the materials of neighboring campus buildings. The diagonal entrance facade opens to a landscaped plaza and the main campus drive.

Anticipating future lower campus development for sports, housing and other uses, Sasaki carried out some basic campus planning exercises to help define a structure within which such individual projects could be organized.

In the design of two student apartment buildings on Commonwealth Avenue, the public edge of the campus, Sasaki's architects were faced with a steep slope and zoning setbacks, which combined to allow construction of the buildings on only a very narrow swath of land parallel to the street. The six-story buildings are set into the slope so that only three floors extend above the level of Commonwealth Avenue, minimizing the

visual impact on the street, and maximizing acceptance by homeowners in the adjacent upper middle class neighborhood. The public entrances facing Commonwealth Avenue occur two levels above the primary student entrances that face into the campus on the other side. Familiar residential forms—dormers, bays and sloping roofs—break down the building scale and relate to the scale and texture of nearby private houses. These forms, as well as the masonry and trim colors and materials, recall the collegiate gothic character of the inner campus. The four-person apartments have bedrooms and bathrooms, living/dining rooms and full kitchens.

The multiphase athletic facilities program that Sasaki designed for BC produced an integrated complex that includes the multipurpose Conte Forum, additional spectator seating for Alumni Stadium—which had been relocated from the middle campus some years earlier—and parking facilities for sports events and commuting

students. The four-level 850-car parking garage, built in two phases on the east side of Alumni Stadium, was designed with stadium bleacher seats at the top level, and private boxes, concessions and rest rooms. Conte Forum seats 8,500 for basketball, 7,500 for hockey, and accommodates university-wide events such as concerts and convocations. The building consolidates facilities for over 30 varsity sports for men and women, including offices, support spaces, a separate 1,000-seat gymnasium, a weight room and a sports medicine complex. Integrated into the east facade are an additional 5,600 stadium bleacher seats for Alumni Stadium and a multi-level press box. VIP boxes look out on both the stadium and into the arena, expanding the potential for revenue generation for three major varsity sports. The diamond truss roof structure of the arena, with its translucent skylights, has allowed the University to save energy by the use of natural light—luminous, glare-free and shadowless.

As with the other BC projects, Sasaki was confronted with site constraints for the forum, which needed to be fitted tightly between Alumni Stadium and a 40-foot hill that runs the length of the campus. As a result, the forum has two entrances: the south entrance is formal and public, while the north entrance, on the interior, campus side, is informal and student-oriented.

Finally, Sasaki designed a new, entrance to the campus from Commonwealth Avenue. A sea of asphalt was replaced by an information/control gatehouse and a garden. An allee of linden trees frames the classic vista from Commonwealth Avenue toward the spires of Gasson Hall and the middle campus.

Robsham Theater

Main entrance to Conte Forum

Conte Forum Arena

Commonwealth Avenue apartments

Parking garage/stadium

Conte Forum and parking garage/stadium

College of the Holy Cross:
Edith Stein Hall

Location: Worcester, Massachusetts
Client: College of the Holy Cross
Project Dates: 1986-1988
Sasaki Staff: Larry R. Young, N. Scott Smith,
John Hawes, James Mellowes,
Robert Paladino, Edith Calzadilla,
Cynthia Plank, John Jennings,
Henry Ricciuti, John D. Hollywood
Sub-consultants: Weidlinger, R. G. Vanderweil

Awards: Honor Award, San Francisco Chapter,
American Institute of Architects
"Beyond the Bay" Awards, 1993;
Built Environment Award,
Boston Society of Architects/American
Institute of Architects, 1990;
Special Mention, New England
Regional Council/American Institute
of Architects, 1988

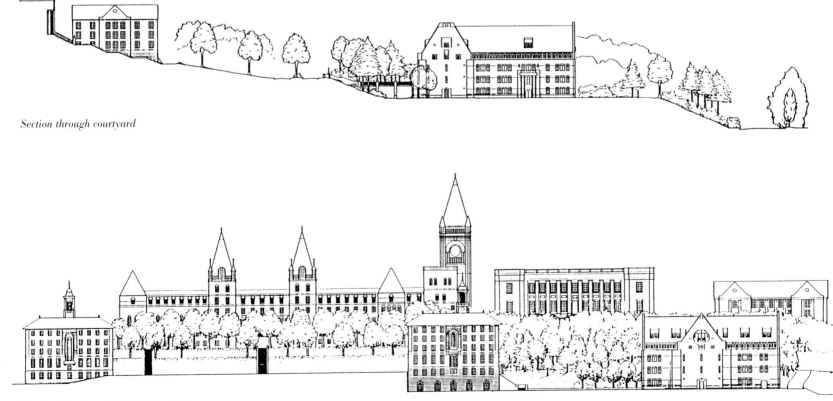

Section through courtyard

Section showing relationship to existing campus

The College of the Holy Cross sits apart from the adjacent city of Worcester, providing a view of slender spires and trees against a hillside. Occupying steeply sloping and heavily terraced terrain, the campus is organized around a series of quadrangles. Edith Stein Hall, a classroom building on the lower edge of the campus, is a striking form in the foreground.

The building is a reinterpretation of the traditional collegiate gothic type; however, while the rhythm and proportions are traditional, it clearly expresses its own strong identity. It is set into a sharp grade adjacent to the college's main boulevard, and is constructed of pre-cast concrete and brick, materials used in existing campus structures. Its "T" shape allows the building to face the older campus, creating a relationship with adjacent buildings, and forming a courtyard system, that relates to the quadrangle pattern of the old buildings

further up the hill. Campus circulation patterns and terrain are maintained or enhanced by the building's position.

The principal entrance to the building is located at the upper part of the "T", facing the entry road, and is reached by passing through a grove of pine trees and crossing an elevated footbridge. This entry form, seen elsewhere on the campus, results from pushing the building back from the street in order to preserve the trees lining it. The footbridge entry leads to a second-level lobby in the classroom building. Below are two quiet courtyards, formed by the configuration of the building. This entry on the second level, with progression to the inviting courtyards, binds the building to the upper and lower parts of the campus and encourages circulation between these areas.

Lower entry from courtyard

Upper entry

New building defining courtyard

Bridge entry

College Hill context

Pattern of campus courtyards extended

Relationship to existing buildings

Athletic fields

The University of New Hampshire: Student Housing, Arena and Recreation Center

Location: Durham, New Hampshire
Client: University of New Hampshire
Sasaki Staff:
The Gables: 1991
                 Roy V. Viklund, N. Scott
                 Smith, Joseph A. Hibbard,
                 John D. Hollywood,
                 Jonathan Austin, Jeffrey Wogan,
                 Timothy Whitney, John Amato
Whittemore Center: 1995
                 Roy V. Viklund, Jonathan Austin,
                 Richard Friedson, Joseph Lafo,
                 Lawrence Schwirian, Jerry Chao,
                 Bill Winkler, Robert Bell,
                 Thomas Mullane, Brad McCord,
                 Paul Berkowitz, Laurie Lebbon,
                 John D. Hollywood, John Amato,
                 Kevin MacNeill

Sub-consultants:
The Gables: Foley and Buhl, Inc.; R.G.
                   Vanderweil Engineers, Inc.
Whittemore Center: R.G. Vanderweil Engineers, Inc.;
                   LeMessurier Associates, Inc.;
                   Cavanaugh Tocci Associates, Inc.
Awards: Merit Award, Boston Society of
                   Landscape Architects, 1994
                   (the Gables); Honorable Mention,
                   Boston Society of Architects,
                   Housing Design Awards, 1992;
                   Merit Award, Boston Society of
                   Architects, Honor Awards, 1992
                   (the Gables)

The site allotted for the Gables, which is remote from the older, main campus, lies on a small granite hill in a heavily forested area. Protecting the character of the surrounding area was fundamental to the design solution. During design, every tree on and adjacent to the site was surveyed according to species, location, and state of health. Necessary roads were cut along a former equestrian path, minimizing tree removal. A protection program for specimen trees and forest edges was carried out during construction. Careful siting preserved features such as an old stone wall. Residents walk through an opening in the wall to reach the parking area, which is located in a meadow away from the building.

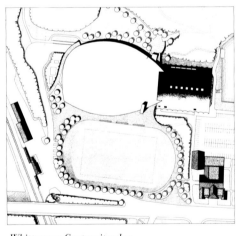

Whittemore Center site plan

0   240 feet ▶

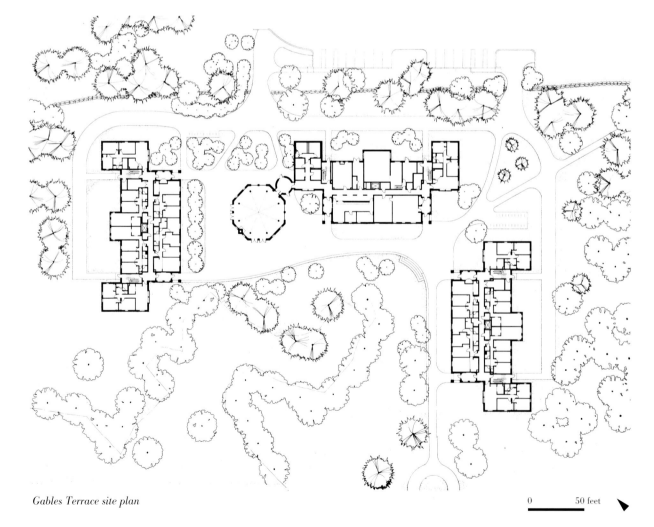

Gables Terrace site plan

0   50 feet ▶

In order to impinge as little as possible on the forested area, the housing takes the form of a compound of multi-story buildings. A terrace was built to avoid cutting into the granite hill that forms the site. This plane, which acts as a connecting element for the buildings, creates an area for community life and provides a variety of places to sit at the edge of the woods. It also provides a comfortable means of access to the buildings for the physically challenged.

While located apart from the main campus, the new student housing buildings are tied visually to the older campus by the use of traditional red brick and stone. Steep, gabled roofs, entry arches, wall detailing, and brick coursing are echoed in the new compound. The roofs, seen from the old campus, strengthen the connection; steep gables, like spires, rise above the trees. The residence buildings provide housing for 600 undergraduate students in apartment-style suites.

The community building is the focal space of the complex intended for social gatherings, study, and meetings. The building takes its octagonal shape from traditional barns in the area. The sheltering form, exposed wood, ornamented brick, high ceilings, and broad fireplace create a warm and ceremonial space.

The Whittemore Center has a dual personality. It is the university hockey arena—a very public building with 6,000 seats and an Olympic-sized rink—and a recreational sports center providing a wide variety of activity and workout spaces. An adaptive reuse of the university's old ice rink, Snively Arena, it is a long span, wood arched structure clad in wooden shingles. The bold design of the new concrete and steel arena compliments Snively's closed vaulted form with curved glass walls and a sweeping roof. The design emphasizes the contrast between these structures, creating a unique, contemporary building that is well fitted to its central location on the university's historic campus.

The impetus for the project grew out of a desire to enlarge the seating capacity of Snively Arena. Snively's arched construction severely limited options for expansion as an arena. However, with 60 feet clear height to the underside of the arches, there was considerable potential to insert new steel-framed floors inside to accommodate the activity spaces of the recreational sports program. The final design inserted three floors, many of which have natural light from openings cut into the smooth vaulted roof-form. A large gymnasium level was inserted under the apex of the arch and a series of double- and single-height spaces at the lower levels are circled by a jogging track.

The challenge was to add to Snively without making a "caboose-like" addition that would devalue the presence of both buildings. Study of the arena plan found that, while the seating bowl was relatively determined, the perimeter walls could be configured to form a sensuous curve in

plan, as a counterpoint to Snively's vaulted form. The arena's cantilevered roof reinforces the wall's curve, overlapping Snively without a break, and effectively establishing both buildings as one unified composition.

The arena is designed to be a very accessible building and a campus landmark. The exterior grade was raised around much of the building to allow easy access directly onto the concourse that surrounds the seating bowl and rink. This grade change, at the same time, completed another bowl outdoors, surrounding the university's historic Memorial Field with grassy banks for casual seating. The arena design emphasizes the building's public accessibility. At night, the sports lighting inside illuminates the curtain wall glazing, and a back-lit glass block tower at the building's entrance becomes an alluring beacon on campus.

The Gables at the edge of the woodland

Community building interior

Arena entry

Fitness center

Gables terrace

Living room interior

Arena interior

Multi-purpose courts

University of California, Santa Barbara: Recreation and Aquatics Center

Location:	*Santa Barbara, California*
Client:	*University of Santa Barbara*
Project Dates:	*1993-1995*
Sasaki Staff:	*N. Scott Smith, Patricia Sonnino, Clint Fuller, Eric Lassen, Ralph Wolfe, Pauline Chin, Tim Deacon, Harry Akiyama, Joanna Fong, Owen Lang*
Awards:	*Outstanding Sports Facility, National Intramural-Recreational Sports Association, 1996; Athletic Business Facility of Merit, 1995*

View across the savannah

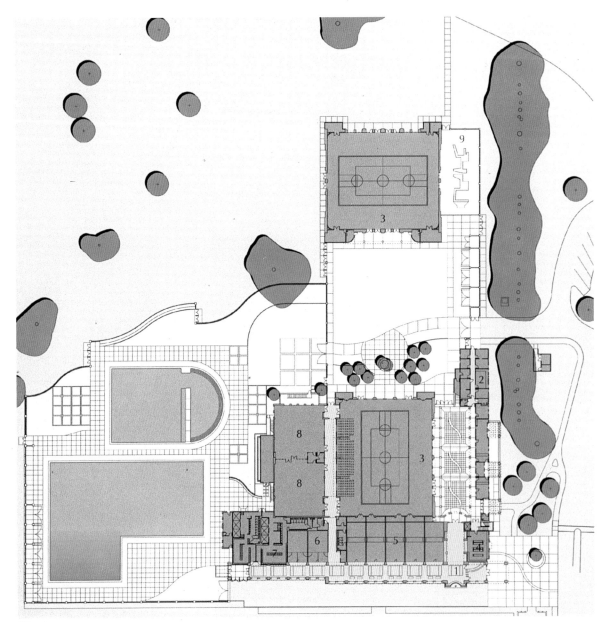

Site plan

This center for recreational activity and team sports is a social focus and a significant visual landmark at the northern edge of the Santa Barbara campus, establishing its formal presence far beyond its building walls. The center provides a tranquil backdrop for vigorous physical activity.

Generally flat and open, the site lies between two eucalyptus windrows. An earthquake fault runs through the site, which is near a protected species habitat containing California live oaks. The Santa Ynez mountain range forms a backdrop.

In a plan based on regional vernacular forms, the complex is an assemblage of integrated indoor and outdoor "rooms," complementary in form and use. Organizational elements providing circulation, structure and access-control include an internal gallery and two courtyards. The form modulates light and the flow of space; the complex has an expansive, serene character.

The gallery, a transparent seam between playing fields and indoor recreation, is the major connector between exterior and interior spaces. This light-bathed space, with its warm materials, gracious proportions and lofty ceilings, welcomes many activities. It is a generous entry and passageway leading from the street edge, a social focus, and a place for viewing activities on the glass-walled racquet courts. Colors here, as elsewhere in the compound, relate to the trees, water and mountain views outside.

The campus community asked Sasaki Associates for views and natural light wherever possible. Outside, the two pools are sited for views of the mountain range to the north and playing-fields to the south. Even the gymnasium, traditionally a monolithic enclosure, is an expansive space; a continuous clerestory provides natural day-lighting. A wood ceiling floats above the clerestory, and a wide overhang extends the ceiling plane beyond the walls. Banks of doors open to courtyards and to views of the mountains.

The two courtyards are highly active outdoor rooms with distinct characters. The paved lobby courtyard is an extension of the lobby, gymnasium and offices that enclose it. It serves as a transition to the larger activity courtyard, a grassy outdoor room providing space for large gatherings such as picnics and ball games.

Existing California live oaks are preserved by the plan. The use of native plant materials links the complex to its context of oak savanna and eucalyptus windrow.

North gymnasium

North gymnasium and savannah

View to activity courtyard

Entry

East garden entry

Lobby courtyard

Building skyline

Gallery

Interlochen Center for the Arts

Location: Interlochen, Michigan
Client: Interlochen Center for the Arts
Project Dates: 1991-present
Sasaki Staff: Kenneth E. Bassett, Kim Baur,
                          Ralph Wolfe, Jonathan Austin,
                          Gary Hilderbrand, N. Scott
                          Smith, Patricia Sonnino,
                          Maureen O'Leary, Tim Deacon,
                          Joanna Fong, Diana Kissil,
                          Vitas Viskanta,
                          Anne-Sophie Divenyi

In Association
With: Clark Walter Sirrine Travis
Sub-consultants: ARTEC Consultants, Inc.;
                          Hanscomb Associates, Inc.;
                          Fishbeck, Thompson,
                          Carr & Huber; John
                          McCaffrey; Grenier, Inc.

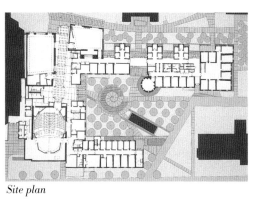

Site plan

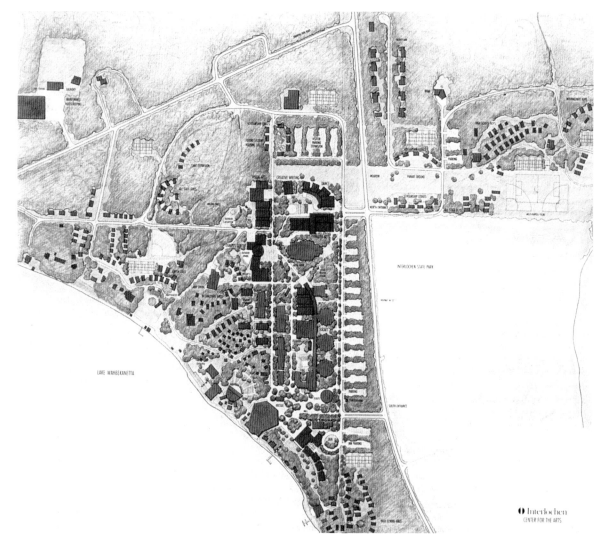

Master plan

Existing stone practice building

East elevation

Courtyard entry

East entry

Interlochen Center for the Arts is a nationally-known institution providing sophisticated training in music, dance, theater and the visual arts. It occupies 1,200 heavily-forested acres on Michigan's lower peninsula along the sandy shores of a lake. The center consists of Interlochen Arts Academy, a high school and college preparatory program with 400 boarding students, and Interlochen Arts Camp, a summer program that accommodates up to 5,000 students, faculty, staff and guests, who often include world-famous musicians. Interlochen began as a summer music camp, and consists of an assortment of small wood and fieldstone structures arranged in an informal pattern.

Sasaki Associates' ongoing relationship with Interlochen began in 1991, when the firm was asked for an assessment of existing facilities and program accommodations, recommendations for space reorganization and re-use, and proposals for new buildings and campus amenities. A campus master plan and landscape master plan developed by Sasaki directs the center's long-term growth and enhancement.

The music building is a product of those plans, and will consolidate the music program under one roof. The 100,000-square-foot building is large by campus standards. Practice and rehearsal spaces have been designed to strict specifications in order to provide superior acoustics. The character of the building draws on the form and materials of the best of Interlochen's architectural foundation. Examples include the small stone practice and classroom buildings completed early in the school's history. These buildings represent Interlochen tenets; they are functional, elegant and simple. Their pitched roofs and natural materials suit the climate and the site.

Stone, wood and slate are the major materials in the music building. Stone is used in the band rehearsal room, the chorus/lecture hall, and through the gallery, defining public entries and public passages through the building and on the lower portions of the wings. Wood used on the upper portions of the buildings and in the gables, as in the older Interlochen structures, is dyed in greens and yellow-greens like the foliage of tree canopies. Roofs are slate; a variety of broad and steep pitches articulate different program elements.

To respect the scale of the campus, the program is articulated in a series of simple, shed-like structures. The sheds are assembled to form outdoor courtyards and passageways. The larger sheds, housing the recital hall and large practice spaces, are grouped near Corson Hall, a 1970s brutalist-style performance hall. Smaller elements of the program fall away to the scale of the classrooms and dormitory structures. A two-story gallery space links entries, maintaining circulation through the site. A colonnaded porch defines the building entry on the public arrival side. A new courtyard, anchored by a small fieldstone practice building, shapes an entry from one of the main campus walkways.

Greenacre Park

Location:	*New York City, New York*
Client:	*Greenacre Foundation*
Project Dates:	*1971*
Sasaki Staff:	*Hideo Sasaki, Maseo Kinoshita, Thomas Wirth, Russell Burditt*
In Association With:	*Goldstone & Heinz, Architect*
Awards:	*Merit Award, Boston Society of Landscape Architects, 3rd Professional Awards Program, 1986*

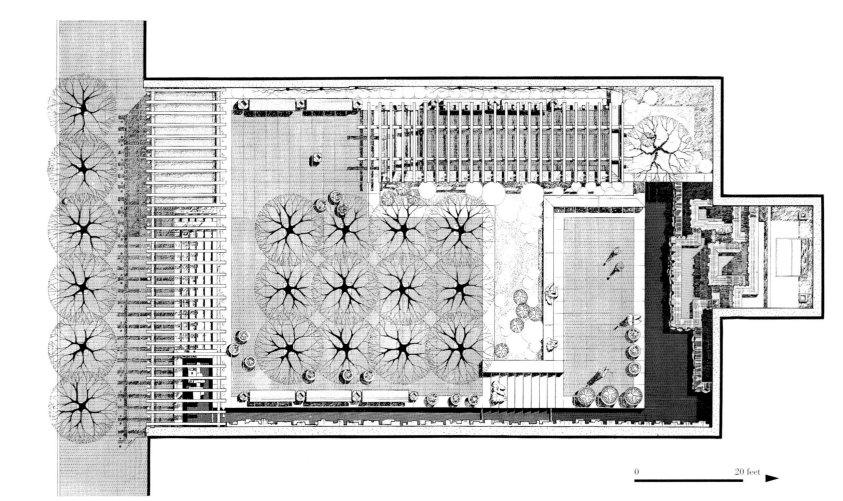

Site plan

0   20 feet ▶

The "vest-pocket" park is a form of urban open space which has evolved only relatively recently. Constrained by the high cost of center city land, high intensity of use and the need to secure the park after hours, these parks are small, dominated by hard surfaces and secured by gates. Such parks frequently are provided to the public by private donor foundations to enhance the quality of city life.

Greenacre Park is one of the most intensely used parks in New York City, with over 10,000 visitors a week. Measuring sixty feet along the street and 120 feet deep, it is the size of a tennis court. The design of the park is based on multi-level sitting areas, integrated with planting and water display. The central sitting area is slightly elevated above sidewalk level and is approached by steps passing under the trellis which articulates the entry to the park. The walls of a small snack bar form one edge of the entry, and a water sculpture on the outer side serves as an invitation to enter the park.

The main sitting area accommodates informal groupings of tables and chairs. Honey locust trees allow sunlight to penetrate while creating a protective veil to screen out adjacent buildings. The entire length of one wall consists of a relief sculpture. Water trickles over its surface into a runnel at its base which leads, in turn, to the focal water display at the end of the park.

Ten thousand gallons of water cascade over the granite fountain, creating a strong visual focus as well as a soundscreen against traffic noise outside. The lower level sitting area at the base of the water display provides visitors a more immediate sense of contact with the water. Along the adjacent wall, a raised terrace allows an overview of the whole park and an elevated view of the water display. This terrace is roofed with a trellis and acrylic domes, and is equipped with lighting and radiant heating for evening and cold weather use.

Moveable chairs and tables invite park users to relax. Ample seating walls and broad steps provide additional places to sit during peak times such as lunch hours. The built-in food bar offers snacks and coffee throughout the day. Visitors may choose the dappled shade of the central honeylocust grove, open sun by the fountain, the enclosure of trellises at the entrance, or a rain-protective canopy along the side. The landscape materials provide a soft contrast to the granite, brick and steel. Evergreens—rhododendron, azalea, Japanese holly and andromeda—are planted amid a pachysandra ground cover. A star magnolia, azaleas and rhododendron provide early spring blossoms. Seasonal flowers fill urns which are placed informally about the park, and Boston ivy on the brick walls turns a brilliant red color in early fall.

Section through park

Water cascade

Central seating area under honey locust grove

Street entrance

Movable chairs

Christian Science Center

Location: *Boston, Massachusetts*
Client: *First Church of Christ, Scientist*
Project Date: *1973*
Sasaki Staff: *Stuart O. Dawson, Peter Pollack*
In Association
With: *I.M. Pei and Partners, Architect*
Araldo Cossutta, Principal-in-Charge
Awards: *Honor Award, Mature Projects,*
Boston Society of Landscape
Architects, 1988; Honor Award,
American Society of Landscape
Architects, Professional Awards
of Excellence, 1987

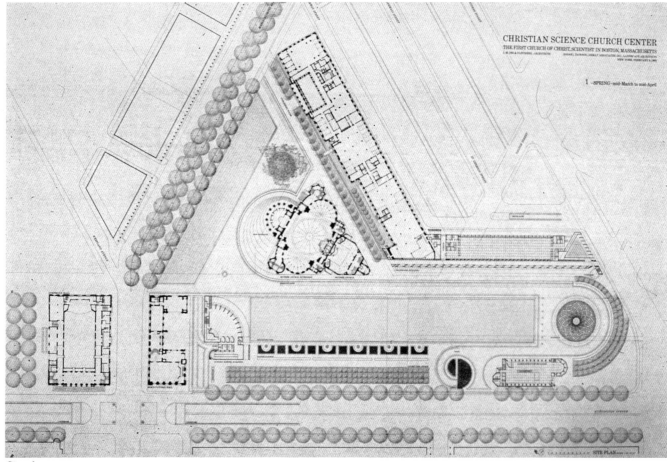

Site plan

The headquarters for the First Church of Christ, Scientist is located in Boston's historic Back Bay. The original Mother Church (built in 1894) and the domed extension (1905) were followed by the Christian Science Publishing Society building (1934). The Christian Science campus was set tightly into the surrounding grid of streets, with a small park along Huntington Avenue linking that thoroughfare to the Mother Church. By the 1960s, the immediate neighborhood had seriously decayed and was far from an appropriate setting for this small but important religious center. At the same time, the church had reached a point where additional space was essential to its continued growth.

The church hired architect Araldo Cossutta of I.M. Pei and Partners, and, working in cooperation with the Boston Redevelopment Authority, developed a master plan of immense scale. Several city streets were closed, and over 25 acres of land were acquired and developed as a setting for both new and existing buildings. New facilities called for in the master plan included an entrance portico for the Mother Church, a colonnaded office building, a 28-story administration building, and a quarter-round Sunday school building. The design for the great plaza incorporated a spray fountain 80 feet in diameter, and a 700-foot-long reflecting pool with a 600-car parking garage beneath it. Other buildings were designed and developed around the edges of the Christian Science Center to guarantee a controlled setting, providing opportunities for private investment.

The church was determined to create a public place comparable to Europe's classic urban church spaces, both as an appropriate context for its own buildings and as a benefit to the surrounding community. Sasaki Associates was engaged as landscape architect for the project by Araldo Cossutta of I.M. Pei Associates in the mid-1960s. The firm worked closely "on the boards" with Cossutta, whose office was in New York, to determine the best possible arrangement and details of the central open space and adjoining areas. The final design addressed the great rectangular reflecting pool, the circular fountain, the flower gardens, linden grove, paving, walls, and lawn panels, and included the reuse of existing plant material from the original garden on Huntington Avenue.

Almost 200 linden trees, selected four years in advance from a nursery in northern Illinois, form a distinctive arching grove that parallels Huntington Avenue, making the connection from the administration building to the Sunday school, and continuing around the fountain to the new arcade building. Thirty linden and several magnolia trees, which had been removed from the old Huntington Avenue garden to an off-site nursery, were brought back to line the pedestrian pathway along the long facade of the historic publishing house and connect Massachusetts Avenue with the new reflecting pool and plaza. A simple plane of grass forms the foreground for the Mother Church's new portico, which faces Massachusetts Avenue.

The landscape architects gave special attention to seasonal floral displays in large waist-high raised beds, with flower colors ranging from pink and white in the spring to a cooler palette in the summer, and shifting to orange and rust in the fall. Massive plantings of holly fill the beds during the winter months.

700- foot long reflecting pool

Plaza at new entrance portico

Lindens and reflecting pool

Seat wall

Linden grove

Seasonal planting

Relocated lindens

Circular fountain

Pennsylvania Avenue

Location:	Washington, DC
Client:	Pennsylvania Avenue Development Corporation
Project Dates:	1976-1986
Sasaki Staff:	Hideo Sasaki, Don Olson, Skip Burck, Joseph A. Hibbard, George Burr
In Association With:	Grenald Associates, Ltd., Lighting; Tippetts-Abbett-McCatrhy-Stratton, Engineering; Herbert S. Levinson, Traffic Engineering
Awards:	Federal Design Achievement, Presidential Design Award, 1988

Pennsylvania Avenue

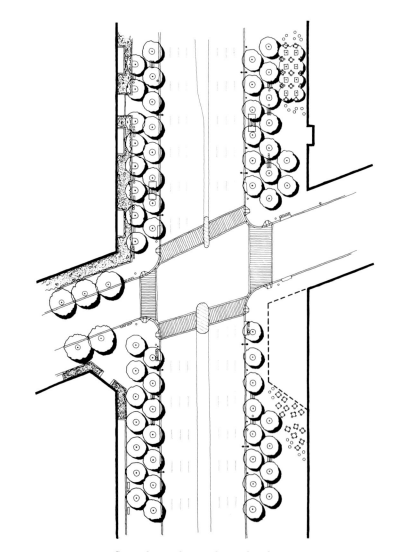

Street design showing hierarchy of tree planting, street lighting, and crosswalks

Recipient of the prestigious Presidential Award in 1988, the redevelopment of the Pennsylvania Avenue corridor from the White House to the Capitol illustrates the power of public improvement design in leveraging private investment. The strategic allocation of $130 million for urban design and public improvements has resulted in over $1.3 billion in private sector construction and renovation. More importantly, the main street of the nation has been restored, in an expression of national and civic pride.

Following the presidential election of 1960, a series of studies were initiated, resulting, in 1972, in the creation of the Pennsylvania Avenue Development Corporation, charged with the revitalization of this important corridor. Sasaki Associates, together with specialists in lighting and engineering, was engaged in 1976 to implement a new vision for the avenue.

The assignment involved the establishment of an urban design framework for the avenue as a whole, as well as a vocabulary of specific materials, details and design guidelines, for public improvements, to be followed by all developers and designers engaged in implementation. The design process involved active participation from the Commission on Fine Arts, the National Capital Planning Commission, and other agencies on a regular basis prior to review. This included on-site review of design mock-ups of all major elements and materials. The National Parks Service and the Department of Public Works, who are responsible for the avenue's upkeep, were also regularly involved in initial design decisions.

The design for Pennsylvania Avenue balanced three major goals. First, the overall vision should be subservient to, and yet enhance, the primary vistas of the Capitol and the Treasury buildings which define the corridor's axis. Second, the various sector plans should strive to mend encroachments on L'Enfant's 1792 design for the Capitol, which had been compromised by construction of the Federal Triangle in the 1920s and 1930s, and subsequent changes throughout the post–World War II period. Third, the plan should create a hospitable pedestrian environment linking the avenue's many destinations for both residents and visitors.

To reestablish a simple visual frame for Pennsylvania Avenue's symbolic vistas, multiple rows of willow oak trees were planted, with a supportive pattern of both decorative and concealed lighting. These robust trees now minimize the impact of the divergent architectural forms which in scale, style and setback define the avenue. Urban design concepts for architecture, land use and open space at the western terminus and central "market square" areas have now erased the residual fragments of streets left behind by the imposition of the Federal Triangle, which additionally eliminated commercial street life from the south side of the avenue. Reduction in the traffic way, expansion of walkways and inclusion of pedestrian amenities, together with the encouragement of restaurants, cafes, retail activity, monuments and art have further enhanced the public environment both by day and by night. Through an unusually cooperative and mutually supportive effort between public sector agencies, private sector developers, and design professionals, an historically significant and emotionally important work of urban design has been revitalized for future generations.

Capitol vista at night with new street lights

Shaded walks

Market Square and Eighth Street axis

Capitol vista during the day with new street trees

Crosswalks help to unite both sides of the avenue

Retail in the old Post Office Building enlivens the avenue

Reston Town Center

Location: Reston, Virginia
Client: Reston Land Corporation,
                   Himmel MKDG
Project Dates: 1987-1992
Sasaki Staff: Kenneth E. Bassett, Alan L. Ward,
                   George Burr, Joseph Hibbard,
                   Duncan Alford, Darrell Bird,
                   Mike Sobczak
Sub-consultants: Urban Engineering
Awards: Urban Design Award,
                   American Institute of Architects, 1992;
                   Award for Projects Outside the
                   BSLA Chapter Area, Boston Society
                   of Landscape Architects, 1992;
                   Certificate of Excellence,
                   National Association of
                   Industrial & Office Parks, 1990

New park on Market Street

Market Street

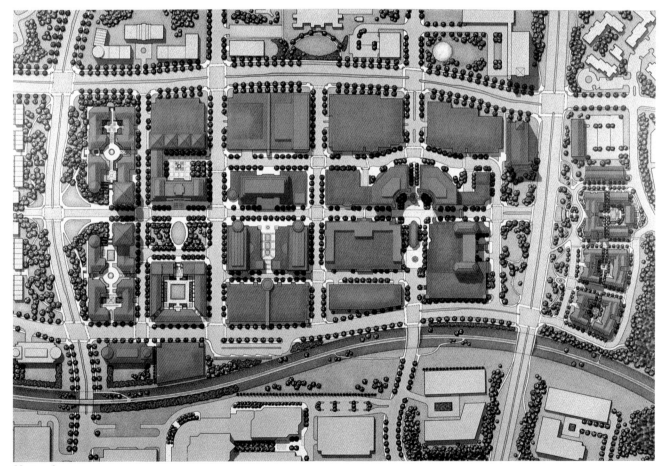

Master plan

The design of Reston Town Center creates a dense and walkable urban environment that is an alternative to typical suburban development. Reston, 15 miles from Washington, DC, is a new community, first planned in 1964, which had matured to a population of 50,000 by the mid-1980s. Sasaki Associates' plan makes the town center a focus for the Reston community, and a new downtown in the suburbs. While adjacent suburban development is in large, single-use parcels best served by the automobile, Reston Town Center is composed of a series of mixed-use blocks, urban streets, parks and plazas that create an environment designed for the pedestrian.

The central organizing element of the town center is Market Street, which functions like Main Street in a typical American small town. The street, with cars and curbside parking, extends eight blocks from a high-density commercial area at the east end to intown residential blocks at the west end. Along Market Street, con-tinuous retail businesses, including restaurants and cinemas, open onto tree-lined sidewalks. Hotels and offices are located above street-level retail in the commercial area. To the west, Market Street slopes gently downhill to a residential district. High-density urban residential blocks form courtyards in the downtown core area. The street continues westward to a neighborhood of townhouses and three-story apartments.

A sequence of open spaces, each of distinctly different design, is located at two-block intervals along Market Street. At the east end, along Reston Avenue, there is a park with shady paths, where mature hardwood trees are preserved and new understory planting has been introduced, as an entry to the town center. The symbolic center and focus of Reston community events is Fountain Square. It is a small, intimately scaled, paved plaza and fountain, framed by symmetrical twelve-story buildings. Grids of trees give shade to tables and chairs in the plaza. An urban park that is less formal than Fountain Square, and much greener, is the focus in phase two of the town center, where a transition to residential uses occurs. This park is similar in scale to other American residential squares, like Johnson Square in Savannah, or Grammercy Park in New York.

Reston Town Center has become a new urban destination in the suburbs surrounding the nation's capital. Retail stores make it a shopping destination, and the eating and drinking establishments have so flourished that it has become a vibrant place in the evenings, when significant pedestrian activity and outdoor dining energize the streets and plazas.

View to Fountain Square from entry

Community event in multi-use pavilion

Casual seating in Fountain Square

Market Street retail

Grid of trees in Fountain Square framed by buildings

Outdoor dining in one of twelve restaurants

Center of community at Fountain and Market Street

Retail and cinema lobby oriented toward street

Lima Downtown Civic Center

Location: *Lima, Ohio*
Client: *Veterans Memorial Civic and Convention Center Board of Trustees*
Project Dates: *1976-1984*
Sasaki Staff: *John R. Orcutt, Kenneth E. Bassett, Richard Galehouse Robert Livermore, III, Stan Fink, Lori Rohr*

In Association With: *James H. Bassett, Inc.; Cosentini Associates, Inc.; LeMessurier Associates/SCI, Bolt, Beranek & Newman, Inc.; V. Piacentini/PA*

The civic, cultural, and business communities of Lima and of Allen County wanted a new facility that would serve both as a performing arts center and a public gathering place, and would act as a catalyst for the economic and spiritual revitalization of downtown Lima, a city of 50,000 in northwestern Ohio. The community supports its own symphony orchestra and many local and touring musical, dance, and theatrical groups, but existing facilities were inadequate and renovation was determined to be impractical. In addition, over recent decades, Lima's central business district had declined as local businesses closed or relocated to suburban shopping malls.

Sasaki Associates prepared an urban design plan for revitalizing the city's core area. An economic assessment of Lima, a market analysis of the central business district, and an evaluation of public attitudes about that district were performed in the first phase of the project. An analysis of the potential for a new performing arts facility also was completed. The second phase focused on the preparation of a plan for the central business district, with particular emphasis on a strategy for initial rehabilitation, and its relationship to subsequent development of both new and rehabilitated structures. A key element of the plan was an analysis of the off-street parking supply and a determination of additional parking necessary to support the retail, office, residential, and civic center uses which were being evaluated.

Following careful analysis, the design team outlined a program calling for an 1,800-seat auditorium equipped with a stage that would accommodate all types of performances and presentations, from symphony, to dance, to opera, to Broadway musicals, to speeches and panel discussions. Careful attention would be given to the facility's acoustics. Convention space would function separately or in combination with the auditorium, offering greater flexibility for large

trade shows and small business meetings. The design of the facility—inviting yet dignified—would be compatible with the surrounding 19th century commercial buildings, while establishing a strong presence on the town square. Finally, construction costs should be kept to a minimum. More than 65 percent of the cost of the civic center was raised from local businesses and individuals.

The new structure needed to be more than a theater, with images of marquees and bright lights, and more than a convention center, typically a massive, anonymous structure. A new building typology was needed to convey the building's public status.

The product of this process of analysis and design is a steel-framed, concrete structure with red brick facing. It includes a three-story glass lobby—a pivotal space that creates an attractive introduction to the auditorium and prevents the large volume of the building from overwhelming surrounding structures. Indoor and outdoor spaces flow together. Bridges and galleries surround the glassed-in atrium space and provide access to the upper level of the theater and the second floor of a multipurpose wing. A large skylight separates the galleries from the brick theater structure, admitting natural light to the interior. The resulting balance of indoor and outdoor light makes the glass of the lobby "invisible," and allows activities in the interior space to be seen clearly from the square both day and night.

The plaza outside the building is an extension of the town square. Concrete brick pavers flow from the plaza into the carpeted lobbies. Casement doors along the entire lobby edge can be kept open to facilitate movement in and out of the building during events that use both indoor and outdoor spaces, strengthening the "city room" concept.

Downtown Lima design plan

Public Square facade

Lobby atrium

Scudder Stevens & Clark

Location: *Norwell, Massachusetts*
Client: *Scudder Stevens & Clark*
Project Dates: *1993-1994 (design)*
1994-1995 (construction)
Sasaki Staff: *Alan Resnick,*
Robert Titus,
Elizabeth Meek,
Rita Ruskin,
Stacy Chambers,
Marc Mazzarelli,
Brian Pearce,
Maurice Freedman
Sub-Consultants: *R.G. Vanderweil*
Engineers, Inc.;
Bradford & Saivetz &
Associates, Inc.; Schweppe
Lighting Design; Mead
Consulting, Inc.;
Engineers Design Group

In 1993, Scudder Stevens & Clark asked Sasaki Associates to help them evaluate several sites and existing buildings to accommodate Scudder's growing Shareholder Service Center operations. Located approximately 25 miles south of its principal offices in downtown Boston, the service center provides telephone contact and account management functions for clients throughout the country. The highest priority was to create a comfortable and well-ordered environment for their associates. While efficiency and technology systems were important, special emphasis was placed on creating group gathering spaces, indoor and terrace dining areas, views of the natural landscape, daylight, indoor environmental controls, and outdoor recreation amenities.

Concurrent with the early site development concept formulation, Sasaki prepared a detailed space program for the new facility. Additional design goals included flexibility, allowing Scudder to reconfigure its working groups in response to clients' ever-changing needs and to encourage communications among associates throughout the building.

The resulting design is comprised of approximately 110,000 square feet. The cafeteria, training center, and other fixed operations are located on the ground floor. The general, more flexible open office areas are located on the upper two floors. The 33,000 square feet. floor plates are organized around a central atrium which penetrates all three floors and terminates in a clerestory to allow natural daylight into the central portion of the building and to provide a visual orientation element which is visible from all parts of the office floors. A gracious open stair and elevator located in the atrium encourage inter-floor communication. The curved floor plate configuration mediates the otherwise relatively large floor areas, zoning the building into east and west components. The shape of the building also allows the front door to be visible from the site entry point as well as providing afternoon daylight at the building entry. The dining terrace is nestled among the natural woodlands to the south and protected from the highway by the curved shape of the building. On each of the office floors, several groups of fixed wall offices and conference rooms form focal points for the various working groups located in open work stations. Uninterrupted glazing around the entire perimeter of the building maximizes views to the natural surrounding landscape. All associates are located within 35 feet of the perimeter with ample access to daylight. The interior color palette was developed to enhance the connection between the interior environment and the natural surroundings of the building. Deep greens, earth tones, natural wood veneers, and selected architectural stone recall the region's seasonal color spectrum.

The material selection reflects Scudder Stevens & Clark's traditional commitment to a set of values which includes performance, dignity, integrity, and responsibility while pointing an eye to the future through innovation, responsiveness to change, and client service. The building is clad in stone-colored precast concrete with subtly varying shades of green vision and spandrel glass. Vertical columns and horizontal mullions are crafted from mill-finished aluminum which captures the setting sun, giving a gentle sparkle to the facade.

Completing the dialogue between interior and exterior spaces, an oval garden is situated on axis with the front entry, creating a distinctive welcome for visitors as well as associates.

Entry and oval garden

Work spaces from open lobby

Reception area

The DART Transitway Mall

Location: *Dallas, Texas*
Client: *The Dallas Area Rapid Transit Authority*
Project Dates: *1988-1996*
Sasaki Staff: *Stephen E. Hamwey, Alan Fujimori, Nancy Armstrong, Paul Weathers*
Sub-consultants: *Arredondo, Brunz & Associates; Barton-Aschman, Inc.; Berryhill-Loyd Associates; Campos Engineering; Brad Goldberg, Inc.; Haywood, Jordan, McCowan, Inc.; H.M. Brandston, Inc.; Huitt-Zollars, Inc.; Leonard Technical Services*

In 1988, the Dallas Area Rapid Transit Authority initiated the design and construction of a 20-mile light rail system to help reduce traffic congestion in the downtown area and increase the number of transit riders. In addition to assisting DART in the location of the rail corridor and stations throughout the downtown area, Sasaki Associates developed the conceptual and final design for the transitway mall, a 26-foot-wide trackway with four at-grade stations and associated streetscape improvements.

The transit mall, which is one mile long, passes through districts of varying character, ranging from historic brick warehouses to modern office towers, with many surface parking lots and garages in between. Within this context, Sasaki's design uses a simple but powerful strategy for creating consistency in the public realm, making this corridor a city-scale urban design element that extends through the downtown area of Dallas. The project provides a strong sense of continuity through the use of common forms and elements, while allowing for variations in materials, color, and detail.

The orange brick trackway extends continuously through the project, recalling a period in the city's history when such brick was commonly used for paving streets. Sidewalks and access lanes are paved with larger dark gray concrete pavers. Custom poles integrate both street lighting and catenary wires; variations in the poles use interchangeable light fixtures and pole bases. All poles are capped with reflective ball finials and are set close to the trackway, further defining its edge.

Each of the four at-grade stations features a covered waiting area, benches, information displays, and access for mobility-impaired users. The principal feature of each station platform is the shelter canopy, consisting of curved steel plates which arch above the passenger platform. This is consistent with curved shelter forms at all the other stations in the transit system. Each of the four stations can be identified by its distinctive color, materials, and detailing. Artists from the Dallas area were commissioned to provide identifying features for each station, such as the station clocks, each of which is unique.

The transit mall brings the convenience of mass transit by light rail to the central business district. The reemergence of trackway and trains in downtown Dallas, imaginatively effected, transforms the street-life there into an environment which is vibrant, colorful, inviting, and safe. People are attracted to this place, not necessarily the transit mall itself, but by the myriad urban options that it makes accessible to the transit user. Its construction has stimulated new retail, residential and business development. New restaurants have opened and adjacent hotels and office buildings have been refurbished.

Station area

Station area art program

Transit corridor

San Francisco Waterfront

Location: San Francisco, California
Client: City and County of San Francisco
Project Dates: 1991 to present
Sasaki Staff: Owen Lang, Joanna Fong
Sub-consultants: AGS, Inc.;
Cambridge Systematics;
Don Todd Associates;
Helene Fried Associates;
Keilani Tom Design;
Levy Design Partners;
Anna Murch;
Michael Smiley

The San Francisco waterfront, with its magnificent views of the bay, is being revitalized as a major urban destination. Historically, maritime activities along the waterfront were a vital part of the city. Construction of a double-decker Embarcadero Freeway along the waterfront in the late 1950s isolated the waterfront from the rest of the city. However, in the 1980s, the City of San Francisco began to reclaim its waterfront. The goals were to improve physical and visual access to the bay, to accommodate multiple modes of transportation service, to link together distinct neighborhoods along the Embarcadero, and to bring new public and private investment to the area. Planning began for a new Embarcadero roadway, which would transform asphalt travel lanes and abandoned rail tracks into a world-class urban boulevard. The 1989 Loma Prieta earthquake resulted in the demolition of the Embarcadero Freeway and created additional opportunities for reconnecting downtown with the waterfront. Today, the San Francisco waterfront corridor consists of a palm-lined boulevard and a pedestrian promenade, enriched by public art projects, that extends from Fisherman's Wharf to King Street (near the site of the proposed Giants Stadium). When the roadway project is complete, a light rail transit system will run along the Embarcadero and connect the waterfront to the rest of the city.

Since 1991, Sasaki Associates has been providing the City of San Francisco with urban design consulting services for the 2.5-mile long Embarcadero Roadway. The project consists of three components: North Embarcadero, South Embarcadero, and King Street; the Muni Metro Extension (MMX) Transit Shelters; and the Mid-Embarcadero Open Space and Roadway. The variety of land uses and ownership patterns, the multi-jurisdictional interfaces, the transit operations, and the historical and contemporary maritime activities along the waterfront corridor make this project unique.

The scope of work for the North and South Embarcadero and King Street improvements encompasses detailed design review of all streetscape elements, coordination of public art projects, and recommendations for street tree selection. The design review process implemented by Sasaki has included establishing a set of design principles upon which future design decisions can be evaluated.

Another component of the project is the MMX Transit Shelters along South Embarcadero and King Street. Sasaki collaborated with artist Anna Murch in developing a design for shelters. The community wanted a design that was distinctive to the waterfront and, at the same time, would not interfere with the magnificent views of the bay. The curvilinear form of the shelters was inspired by the waves of the bay; the extensive use of glass to achieve a high level of visual transparency was a critical design consideration. Sasaki conducted an extensive community outreach program that gained consensus for the shelter design through an interactive design process with the community.

The third project for the San Francisco Waterfront is the Mid-Embarcadero Open Space and Roadway, the final portion of the redeveloped waterfront boulevard, connecting the North and South Embarcadero segments. Sasaki is part of a multidisciplinary team that is designing this central portion of the roadway. It involves multi-model transit issues, pedestrian access, and recreation open space programming—the development of a grand civic space. Significant components include the integration of the historic Ferry Building Plaza with Justin Herman Plaza and open space, and the successful linkage of Market Street to the waterfront and the Embarcadero.

Palm-lined boulevard

Mid-Embarcadero open space

The transit shelter design reflects the waves of the bay

Boston Waterfront

Location: Boston, Massachusetts
Client: Boston Redevelopment
               Authority
Project Dates: 1973-1976 (park),
               1988 (Rose Kennedy Garden)
Sasaki Staff: Stuart O. Dawson, Maurice Freedman,
               Dale Dennis, W. Gerald Venable,
               John R. Jennings, David Beede,
               Hideo Sasaki
Awards: Honor Award, The Waterfront Center,
               "Excellence on the Waterfront" Awards,
               1987; Merit Award, Boston Society
               of Landscape Architects, 3rd Professional
               Awards Program, 1986; Greater Boston
               Regional Award, Governor's Design
               Awards, 1986

Historic plan of Boston waterfront

Aerial view showing downtown Boston's relationship to the water

Late in 1973, Robert T. Kenney, then director of the Boston Redevelopment Authority (BRA), asked Stu Dawson whether Sasaki Associates might be interested in planning a new park in the downtown waterfront urban renewal area. Speed was critical, Kenney said: the goal was to open the park in the spring of 1976 during Bicentennial observances. At the same time, Atlantic Avenue, which ran through the park site, was being rerouted, and the BRA hoped to influence major utility relocations which would, in turn, have an impact on the park design.

Sasaki quickly developed several design options, ranging in size from one to eight acres, that were submitted to intensive BRA and community review. The 6-acre alternative which was finally agreed upon had 400 feet of frontage at the water's edge, swung the new Atlantic Avenue farther inland than originally planned, and designated 1.5 acres abutting the new roadway for mixed-use development.

The park was a key element in the "Walk to the Sea," a concept developed by I.M. Pei, Kevin Lynch, and Hideo Sasaki in the 1960s to connect City Hall Plaza through Quincy Market to Boston Harbor. To improve pedestrian access from the market area to the park, the BRA was able to arrange for removal of two ramps from the elevated highway that separated the waterfront and the North End from downtown Boston. The primary park entrance on the southern edge first related to the adjacent Long Wharf and the nearby New England Aquarium, and later to the hotel and park-side outdoor café developed at the landward end of Long Wharf. In response to the wishes of the adjacent North End neighborhood, Richmond Street was extended as a pedestrian path through the park to reestablish direct access from the residential district to the water.

Sasaki's design for the park—envisioned as a "window on the sea"—elevates the majority of the open space in order to offer better views, provide a better soil environment for plant material, and to stay well above the newly installed utilities. A gently sloped lawn, defined by continuous seat walls and a simple cobblestone plaza, faces out to Boston Harbor. Traditional marine bollards and heavy chain line the plaza at the water's edge. A granite-columned lamela wood trellis at the ridge of the park shades the benches and broad walk beneath and stands as an abstract representation of the wharf structures that once occupied the site.

Rose Kennedy Garden

Rose garden and fountain

Long Wharf redesigned for pedestrian access to the harbor

Tip of Long Wharf

View to Boston Harbor from trellis

Park from Commercial Wharf

Boston Waterfront

(continued)

1 Boston Harbor
2 Central Wharf
3 Atlantic Avenue
4 Rose Kennedy Garden
5 Locust grove fountain
6 Trellis
7 Sloped lawn
8 Cobble plaza
9 State Street
10 Marriott Hotel
11 Chart House
12 Old Customs House
13 Long Wharf
14 Central Wharf
15 New England Aquarium

Boston waterfront in 19th century

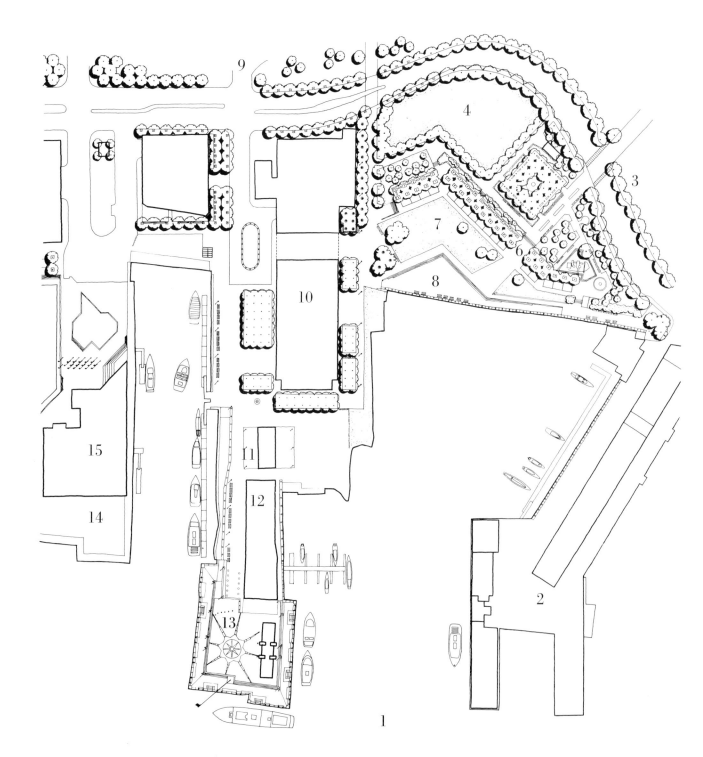

Site plan, Waterfront Park and Long Wharf

0   200 feet

West of the trellis are individual features relating to the smaller-scale spaces of the North End and waterfront. In response to extensive citizen input, these include a playground, a spray pool, a formal grove of locust trees for casual gathering and an occasional game of bocce, and numerous benches and low walls.

Several years later, the 1.5-acre parcel originally intended for mixed-use development was appended to the park and became the Rose Kennedy Garden, designed by the BRA with Sasaki. It is an intimate "park within a park" with rose parterres and a bubbling fountain.

Waterfront Park was opened in 1976, in time to welcome an international fleet of tall ships and to celebrate the nation's 200th birthday. The park was equally as important as a first step in opening Boston's waterfront to public access. It triggered major private investment in residential and commercial redevelopment and established the waterfront as the location for marinas, tour boats, and water taxis.

In 1979, the BRA commissioned Sasaki to develop a schematic master plan for the entire length of the downtown Boston waterfront from Commercial Wharf to the Fort Point Channel and into South Boston. The plan for this then-underutilized resource created a vision and a strategy for development of the harbor, with particular emphasis on public pedestrian access to and along the water's edge and alternative locations for commuter and excursion boat terminals. The concept plan that emerged from Sasaki's work helped shape the city's harbor development policy.

The firm subsequently undertook planning and design for the restoration of historic Long Wharf, the final piece in the Walk to the Sea. Phase I, completed in 1989, saw the wharf returned to its 1780-1820 configuration, with a broad upper wharf accented by a bronze and granite compass rose and a 100-foot marine flagpole, and a lower perimeter wharf designed to serve harbor cruise boats, commuter boats and water-shuttles, tall ships and private vessels.

Coping, bollards, benches, and trellis

Oak grove

Boat basin and park edge

Trellis walk

Wisteria-covered trellis

Locust grove and fountain near North End

Newburyport Downtown and Waterfront

Location: *Boardwalk and Inn Street*
                      Newburyport, Massachusetts
Client: *City of Newburyport and*
                      Newburyport Redevelopment Authority
Project Dates: *1974-1980*
Sasaki Staff: *Stuart O. Dawson, Maurice Freedman,*
                      John Jennings, Chuck Alden
In Association
With: *Anderson Notter Associates;*
                      Vorhees Associates
Awards: *Honor Award, Boston Society*
                      of Landscape Architects, 1994

Newburyport, Merrimac River, and Atlantic Ocean

Newburyport, which is located on the Merrimack River about 40 miles north of Boston, was a trading center in the 18th and 19th centuries. However, as is the case with many older waterfront communities where Sasaki Associates has worked, the economics of the 20th century have not been kind to this small city. However, starting in the early 1970s, the city administration worked with the redevelopment agency to articulate a vision for the future, which included the creation of a revitalized waterfront and the transformation of the historic commercial center into a pedestrian-oriented shopping district. Sasaki played an important role in the realization of that vision.

The first project was to reconfigure the traffic and create a handsome brick-paved Market Square from this recaptured space. An adjacent alley was closed to vehicles and became the Inn Street Mall, a lively shop-lined pedestrian space with a timber playground and a fountain of bronze tubes and salvaged granite blocks.

Sasaki then continued work on Newburyport's waterfront. Projects included an engineering feasibility study for construction of a new bulkhead—which would require a lengthy environmental permitting and approvals process—and the design of a 1,400-foot promenade and marina along the river's edge. The improvements create a destination for residents and tourists, with views of river activity, of the nearby marsh (which was cleaned to improve habitat), and of the shore and the sky. The water is deep enough for fishing from the boardwalk, and dock space is available for both fishing boats and pleasure boats, which are a continuing source of activity and interest. The design reinforces view corridors created by intersecting city streets, preserving vistas of the river from within the downtown and reestablishing the city's historic connection with the river. The wood-decked promenade includes benches and a planter/retaining wall built of salvaged granite and topped by a continuous planting of evergreens and roses to screen the adjacent municipal parking lots.

In the years since its completion, the boardwalk has enjoyed far greater popularity than was originally anticipated. A visit to Newburyport, now well established as a tourist destination, typically includes a walking circuit around the waterfront and Inn Street Mall, where visitors and residents alike enjoy the restored Federal architecture, and the shops and lively riverfront environment.

Inn Street Mall shortly after planting

Working waterfront

Boardwalk and embayment

Benches along boardwalk

Boardwalk and dock

Pedestrians only

Inn Street Mall

Timber play structure

Kuwait Waterfront

Location: *Kuwait City, Kuwait*
Client: *His Highness Shaikh Jaber Al Ahmed Al Sabah,*
the Amir of Kuwait; The Municipality of Kuwait,
Hamid Shuaib, Chief Architect
Project Dates: *1975-1985*
Sasaki Staff: *Paul Gardescu, Paul R. V. Pawlowski,*
Richard Foster, Daniel R. Kenney,
Clarissa Rowe, Richard H. Rogers,
David A. Mittelstadt, Frank D. James,
Michael F. Holland, Stephen E. Hamwey,
Varoujan Hagopian, David Miller,
David Berrarducci, Philip Sheldon
In Association
With: *Ghazi Sultan, Architect*
and Kuwaiti Engineers Office
Sub-consultants: *Research Planning Institute, Inc.;*
Geotechnical Engineers, Inc.;
Normancleau Associates, Inc.;
Keller Engineering;
John W. Bonnington Partnership

Shuwaikh Children's Water Park

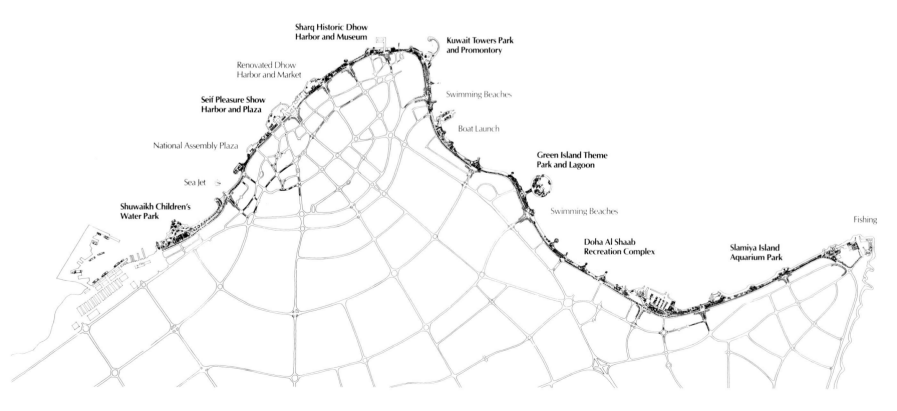

Sharq Historic Dhow
Harbor and Museum

Renovated Dhow
Harbor and Market

Kuwait Towers Park
and Promontory

Seif Pleasure Show
Harbor and Plaza

Swimming Beaches

National Assembly Plaza

Boat Launch

Sea Jet

Green Island Theme
Park and Lagoon

Shuwaikh Children's
Water Park

Swimming Beaches

Doha Al Shaab
Recreation Complex

Slamiya Island
Aquarium Park

Fishing

0   1 mile

Seeking to create a new urban edge along its 21-kilometer coastal road, an eroded and derelict area unsuitable to a rapidly urbanizing, oil-rich nation, the Municipality of Kuwait sponsored an invited competition among five international design firms. The successful Sasaki Associates scheme drew upon the designers' understanding of local cultural and environmental factors. The soft shoreline edge responded to the forces of wave and wind off the Arabian Gulf, and the restrained planting proposal respected the region's precious water resources. The scheme also integrated established neighborhoods and districts of Kuwait City with waterfront recreational and cultural resources, thereby improving access for residents and reestablishing Kuwait's historic links to the sea.

The team assembled to prepare the detailed master plan included consultants who provided the Sasaki planners with essential data on coastal processes, geomorphology, soil characteristics, and plant material suitability, none of which was available from published sources. The plan divided the waterfront into five zones that recognized the distinctive needs and character of the adjacent urban districts, which ranged from the commercial and governmental core at Sief Palace to the high-density residential blocks of Ras Al Ardh and the neighborhoods adjacent to the Shuwaikh port facilities. The master plan included marinas for recreational and commercial boating, a man-made, multi-use destination called Green Island, and playgrounds and boat launching ramps. Cultural features such as the Dhow Builders Yard and Museum, an aquarium, a traditional performance amphitheater, and *divaniyas* (coffee houses) were also woven into the waterfront fabric. To unify the area, the master plan advocated a vocabulary of design guidelines for planting, paving, lighting, signage, modular shade structures, and site furnishings.

The design team prepared for implementation of the $300 million construction effort in a series of stages: design brief, preliminary design, final design, and tender documents. In total, over 1,300 full-size drawings with accompanying technical specifications and estimates of quantity were produced over a four-year period. Sasaki obtained additional survey information, offshore bathymetry, borehole investigations, and geotechnical evaluation of sand sources for beach nourishment. To ensure that an ample supply of marine dolos (concrete tetrapod shore protection elements) were available in time for construction, Sasaki supervised their manufacture in Kuwait. Other shore protection elements consisted of beaches, rock revetments, groins, and breakwaters located in response to the varying wave energies encountered along the 21-kilometer shoreline.

The project's plant irrigation needs were met by creation of a separate water utility system, combining desalinated and well water via conduits, booster pumps, and in-ground storage tanks. Plant materials were grown-in and acclimatized to the seaside conditions prior to installation, in a municipal nursery adjacent to the site.

In the period between 1981 and 1985, the first two phases of the Kuwait Waterfront were constructed, at a total cost of US $120 million. At the time, the waterfront design contract and the companion contract for implementation of the construction were the two largest ever tendered by the Municipality of Kuwait. Construction of phases 3, 4, and 5 were delayed by budgetary priorities and ultimately by the occupation by Iraqi forces in 1990. The municipality is currently planning to co-sponsor development of the remaining waterfront phases with private for-profit interests, who will participate in the capital improvement financing and the operations and maintenance responsibilities through privatization agreements.

Palm grove and Kuwait Towers

Green Island from mainland

Green Island Lagoon

Children's modular bridge

Lighting grove

Common elements of precast concrete

Shore protection

Restaurant on Green Island Lagoon

Central Indianapolis Riverfront

Location: Indianapolis, Indiana
Client: US Army Corps of Engineers Louisville District;
                    White River State Park Commission;
                    City of Indianapolis
Project Dates: 1992-1997
Sasaki Staff: Stuart O. Dawson, Alistair T. McIntosh,
                    Varoujan Hagopian, Stephen E. Hamwey,
                    Takako Oji, Charles Coronis,
                    Michael Berry, Maurice Freedman,
                    Chandra Goldsmith, Xiao Wei Ma,
                    Jeremy Matosky, Catherine Oranchak,
                    Vince Rico, Bradford O. Saunders,
                    Norris Strawbridge, Maria Tucker,
                    Don Vitters

1   Celebration Plaza and Amphitheater
2   Canal extension
3   National Road
4   Flume Fountain and McCormick Terrace
5   Old Washington Street Bridge
6   Zoo entrance court garden
7   IMAX Theater
8   Baseball park
9   White River

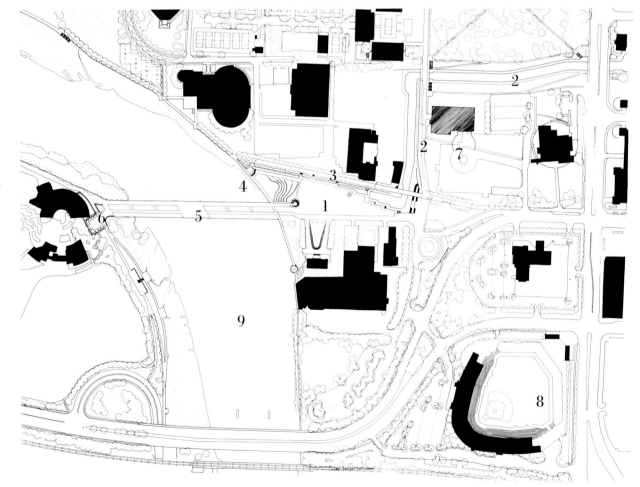

Master plan

0   500 feet

The Central Indianapolis Riverfront project transforms the urban reaches of the White River into a unified open space system. New links between the downtown and the river reconnect the citizens of Indianapolis with this long-neglected civic resource. Urban revitalization is a key theme in Indianapolis. The planning, design, and construction of new public space create and support development on individual riverfront sites, the buildings ranging from a new IMAX Theater and a state museum, to a baseball park and additions to the existing Indianapolis Zoo. The Indianapolis Riverfront exemplifies an equally important goal: to go beyond the practical provision of a recreational environment, creating landscape form and space that satisfy a community's deep desire for tangible, collective memory.

Sasaki Associates initially prepared a master plan for the nine-mile-long corridor formed by the White River as it flows through the city. The massive levees and flood walls constructed to protect the downtown from the river's periodic flooding form an effective barrier between the river and the city in all seasons. To minimize this separation, the master plan proposed continuous public access trails along both banks of the raised river. These riverfront promenades link the downtown with existing recreational corridors, taking their design cues from the varied urban conditions along the river. The plan also proposed the design of major public open spaces at key locations to connect the riverfront promenades with the adjacent urban fabric.

The first implementation phase of the project is Capital City Landing, the principal park link between the downtown civic and commercial core and the river. The site is layered with remnants of roads, bridges, industrial and commercial buildings, monuments, a power station, utility corridors, canals, flood walls, and levees that bear testimony to the city's growth over the past 175 years. Sasaki's designers translated these found conditions into the design forms of the park, not through an explicit historical restoration or imitation of the past, but by exploring and revealing meaning in the recreation and interpretation of the topographic inheritance of the place.

The principal organizing element is the extension of the historic Central Canal (renovated in the 1980s) to connect with the White River. The extension flows into a terminal basin that narrows into a mill flume—recalling the original flume that was on the site—then discharges over a fountain weir into the river.

The National Road Promenade, following the path of an early Indianapolis street, is the main pedestrian route to the river from downtown. The termination of the promenade is marked by McCormick Terrace, which commemorates the first bridge across the river and the site of the first settler's cabin.

The centerpiece of the park is Celebration Plaza, which lies to the south of the National Road Promenade. The plaza is oriented to the river via a grass and stone amphitheater that breaks through the existing flood wall between the flume fountain and the east approach to the Old Washington Street Bridge. The renovated Old Washington Street Bridge connects Celebration Plaza with a new entrance to the Indianapolis Zoo on the west bank of the river.

Capital City Landing

Upper promenade

Chevy dam with new elevated weir

Canal basin

Charleston Waterfront

Location: *Charleston, South Carolina*
Client: *City of Charleston*
Project Dates: *1979-1997*
Sasaki Staff:
Waterfront Park: *Stuart O. Dawson, Jay B. Faber,*
    Edward J. Fitzgerald, Maurice Freedman,
    Varoujan Hagopian, Kenneth M. Kreutziger,
    David French, David C. Clough,
    Jeanne Lukenda, Bert Ferris
VRTC Garage: *Larry R. Young, Varoujan Hagopian,*
    Stuart O. Dawson, Gary Anderson,
    Kevin MacNeill
Maritime Center: *Larry R. Young, Varoujan Hagopian,*
    Stuart O. Dawson, Kevin MacNeill
Sub-consultants: *Jacquelin Robertson; Ed Pinckney*
Awards: *Top Honor Award, The Waterfront*
    Center "Excellence on the Waterfront"
    Awards, 1992; Design Award,
    Boston Society of Landscape Architects,
    1991; Federal Design Achievement Award,
    Presidential Design Awards, 1991;
    Honor Award, The Waterfront Center
    "Excellence on the Waterfront" Awards, 1990

1 East Bay Street
2 Vendue Range
3 Parking garage
4 Development parcel
5 Vendue Plaza and fountain
6 Vendue Pier
7 Shade structures with swings
8 Fishing pier
9 Lawn
10 Four Oak Grove
11 Pineapple fountain
12 Restored marsh
13 Cooper River
14 Overlook
15 Community park
16 Restored Adger's Wharf

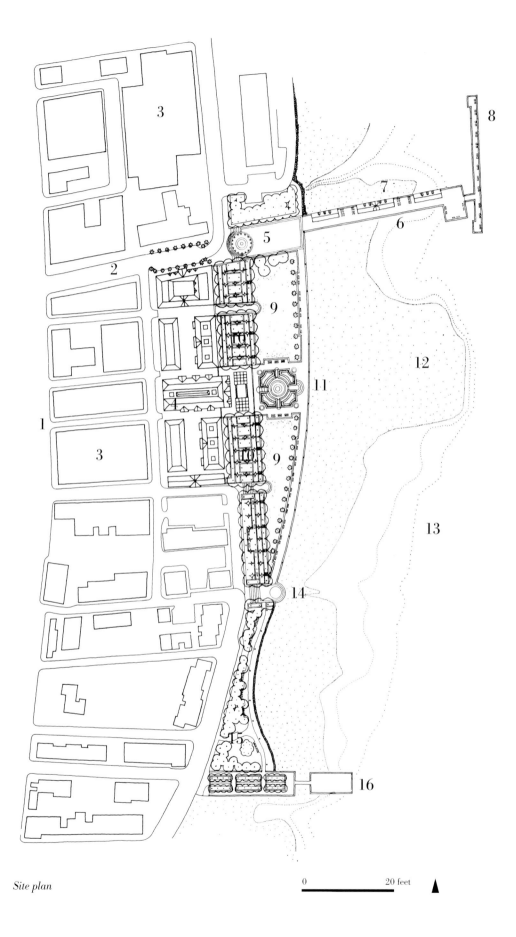

Site plan

0   20 feet

After completing an urban design master plan for Charleston's historic district, Sasaki Associates was retained to design the seven-acre park called for in the study, and to begin early-action restoration of historic Adger's Wharf at the southern edge of the park site. The derelict property, almost 1,300 feet in length, is defined by Adger's Wharf to the south, Vendue Range to the north, the Cooper River and marshes to the east, and little-used Concord Street to the west.

The client wanted to create a significant and memorable public open space that would be the first step in the redevelopment of the city's Cooper River waterfront, which had been reduced to rotting pilings, parking lots, and vacant commercial buildings. The park was envisioned as a place with civic stature that would become a landmark destination and would connect Charleston's historic residential and commercial districts with the river.

The first task was to replace the surface parking on the site with new garages nearby, which Sasaki's architects designed to be in keeping with the historic district. At the same time, four blocks of Concord Street, which run along the land side of the park site, were closed to traffic. The resulting pedestrian zone contiguous to the park will ultimately contain an inn, café, and shops. Its architectural style will be consistent with that of the historic district.

The park site required extensive modification before construction could begin. Except for the salt marsh, the entire site consisted of unstable fill, some of it put in place before the Civil War. Consequently, over a two-year period, the soil had to be compressed by surcharging the entire area with sand to a depth of eight feet while draining it by means of a network of wick drains. Despite these consolidation measures, the fountains, plazas, and other heavy park elements still needed to be supported on piles.

Another early issue was the South Carolina Coastal Council's requirement that the existing marsh grasses not be disturbed during construction. Salt marsh restoration and additional planting resulted in a total of five acres of marshland which complements the seven acres of the park itself.

To connect the new park with the adjacent historic districts, the grid of existing city streets and old wharves was extended as pedestrian ways through the park to the riverfront. At the terminus of Vendue Range, the bluestone-paved Vendue Plaza, with its fountain, is the principal park entry and connects all elements of the park. A 300-foot-long fishing pier parallel to deep water terminates the 400-foot-long Vendue Wharf, which aligns with the main park entrance. Shade structures with picnic tables and swings line the northern edge of the wharf.

A 1,300-foot-long gravel promenade parallels the river's edge to connect Vendue Plaza to the north with a residential community to the south. The promenade features traditional "Charleston" benches, a continuous row of palmettos, and decorative lighting which is integrated with the railing design. Adjacent to the promenade, raised seat walls define a simple, open, slightly crowned lawn that makes up the majority of the park's open space. A bronze and cast-stone pineapple fountain, symbolizing Charleston's well-known hospitality, occupies the center of the lawn.

Along the city edge, a more protected, intimate quality is created by four rows of live oaks which shade sidewalks, seating areas, and eight small gardens. These charming gardens, each with its own special character, provide intimate places to sit and have become settings for memorable events in the lives of Charlestonians, from marriage proposals to family gatherings to reunions with old friends.

Park and adjacent historic district

East Bay Street Garage

Palmettos and elevated seat wall

Restored salt marsh

View corridors, park, new garages, and development parcel

Vendue Plaza lawn and Four Oak Grove

Cooper River

Pineapple fountain

Charleston Waterfront
(continued)

When Mayor Riley dedicated the park in 1990, he described it as "a cathedral of the stars, a chapel of the wind, a temple of the sun, and a church of the sky." Charleston's waterfront park has indeed become a place where Charlestonians and visitors come together. Sasaki's most recent project in Charleston is the design for the Charleston Maritime Center. This city-owned marina serves both the local fishing industry and the City Parks and Recreation Departments. A two-story, 7,400-square-foot building is positioned broadside to the waterfront. The ground floor is devoted to fishing-related uses; the main space is a large workroom for fish packing and sorting. Overhead industrial doors open the entire space to allow full access to fishermen from the waterside, and to refrigerated trucks on the land-side. A retail space for selling fish is located at the north end of

the building. The second floor has a gift shop, a large multi-purpose community space with a kitchen, and offices for management of the marina.

The building's position on the site allows for both public use of open recreational space and the waterfront, and for private use by the fishing industry. The lawn area to the north of the building is intended for occasional public events, such as the start and finish of the British Overseas Challenge sailboat race, and for the ceremonies of sports fishing tournaments. Future use of the open space may include housing and retail development.

Executed in contemporary materials—steel frame and glass, with metal panels and roof—the building's design, nonetheless, takes inspiration from the traditional West Indian and Barbadian "single house," which appeared in Charleston as early as the 1730s, and has been built in

all eras and in all parts of the city. Like the typical "single house," the Charleston Maritime Center is a narrow, one-room-wide building with windows on both sides, high ceilings, and a broad, covered porch—all features which promote natural ventilation. In Charleston, covered porches, called "piazzas," provide shade along one long side of a building, as well as access to the interior spaces, and provide extra living space in the hot months of the year. In the case of the Charleston Maritime Center, the piazza also provides an exciting water view.

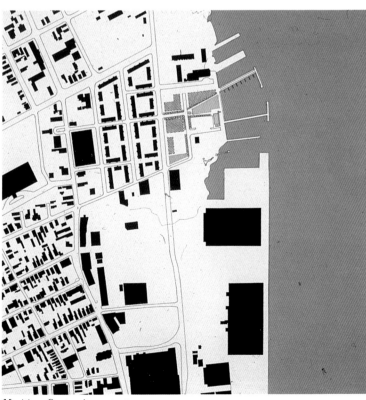

Maritime Center site context

Maritime Center entry road

Visitor Reception and Transportation Center Garage

View of Maritime Center from the water

Employees

1953-1996

1953
Hideo Sasaki

1954
Martin Gordon

1955
Steve Bochkor
Eddie Helfeld
Eric Hoyte
Paul Novak

1956
Robert Buchannan
George Connolly
Lee Lyman Dober
Robert Fenton
David Heldt
Bill Johnson
Peter Rolland
Peter E. Walker

1957
Stuart Dawson
Beatrice DeWinthuysen
Charles W. Harris
Dick Julin
Bill Potts
Julie Treide
John Wade
Larry Walquist

1958
Marvin Adelman
Richard Dober
John Frey
Frank Gehry
Allison Goodwin
Harold Goyette
Pierra Patri
Susan Patterson

1959
Katherine DeMay
Tony Guzzardo
Don Olson
Richard Rogers
Donald Sakuma
Jaquiline Wheeler

1960
Kenneth DeMay
Jean Furuichi
Richard Galehouse
Paul Gardescu
William Halsey
John Molloy
Jack E. Robinson
Carl Steinetz
Richard Strong
Minoru Takeyama
Chuck Wood

1961
John Adelberg
John Collins
Robert Fager
Gary Karner
Masao Kinoshita
Harry Porter
Samuel Stevens
Floyd Zimmerman

1962
Tom Blandy
Holly Carleton
John Emerson
Jean Falzone
Fred Furuichi
Eugene Futterman
Garol Galotti
Reginald Hall
James Hudson
Marlene Malek
Judith McBride

Beverly Meeker
Naomi Newell
John Newman
Steve Olds
Pauline Santorsola
Lindsay Shives
Roger Tinney
Kathryn Whetstone
Wayne Womack
George Yost

1963
Carlisle Becker
Dale Ikeda
Robert Page

1964
Kay Alexander
Richard Berridge
M. Perry Chapman
Muriel Fleming
Charles Fryling
Peter Gaffron
Peter Hornbeck
Philip Minervino
Stuart Solomon
Morgan Wheelock

1965
Konstancija Brazdys
Michael Buckley
Russell Burditt
Maurice Childs
Michaeleen Garabedian
David Longey
Samuel Otis
Peter Pollack
Jerry Spencer
Charles Tseckares

1966
Ken Arutinian
Ronald Basker
Mark Battaglia
Anthony Casendino
James Crissman
John Degenhart
Eric Doepke
Larry Gibson
Mary Grace
Richard Hardaway
James Haskell
Maureen Heffernan
Anne Jackson
Edward Jacobsen
Barbara Johnson
Thomas Johnson
Shirley Kirley
Andrejs Laivins
Paul Lu
Tsunekata Naito
Vincent Nauseda
Robert Ossman
Peter Page
John Perkins
Susan Ratta
Peter Thomas
Roger Trancik
Charles Turofsky
Chester Winter
Roy Viklund

1967
Shirley Ahern
Charles Alden
Arthur Barber
Mary Bernard
Douglas Burckett
Caren Cahoon
Jeanne Clancy
Timothy Coppola
James Coveney
James Crissman

John Gaffney
Chester Gasunas
Alton James
Diane Kelleher
George Kelso
Theodore Keosiyan
Michelle Khachadourian
Constance Lacashio
Elizabeth Lanier
Christian Larras
Kenneth Lupo
Richard Magnuson
P. McAce
Mary McGee
Robert McNary
Edmundo Medeiros
D. Mellen
Martina Mesmer
William Mitchell
Catharine Monaco
Takero Ogawa
Robert Oxman
Elias Rayna
William Reed
Keith Renner
Merle Rubin
Robert Scheele
Robert Seacat
Ruth Smiler
Susan Staub
Joseph Stichter
Andres Sammataro
Martin Van Valkenburg
Albert Veri
Victor Walker
Peter Wells
Bruce West
Ronald Williams
Shepard Williams
Thomas Wirth
Floyd Zimmerman

1968
Christine Albin
Maryanne Anderson
William Andlin
Kenneth Bassett
Vincent Bellafiore
Jeffrey Bentz
June Blanchard
Richard Carroll
Kathleen Carter
Donald Collins
Carolyn Cooney
Robert Copeland
Ellen Dawson
Larry Ervin
Matthew Falcone
Stanley Fink
Beverly Finn
Carol Fippin
Richard Forsyth
Cecily Freeman
S. Gallandet
David Gates
Stephen Gray
John Greene
Ann Hoffman
Roger Holtman
Kathleen Hunter
Jose Jiminez
Knox Johnson
Richard Joslin
Jerald Kamman
James Kiberd
Susan LaMontagne
Arthur LeCain
Joshua Lickerman
Karen Lidster
Robert Longfield
William Mann
Lee Miller
Wendy Mininberg
Ursala Mohr
R. Nald

Daniel Orwig
Pamela Playdon
Joseph Ryan
John Sanderson
Michael Smither
Dianne Stewart
Charles Studen
Walter Tryon
Wallace Gerald Venable
Elizabeth Wert
Franklin Wing

1969
Thomas Adams
Barbara Barney
John Barry
Patricia Basu
Allick Bhark
Ronald Boin
Dix Campbell
Carol Caputo
David Carter
Robert Chase
Constance Clark
Blanca Colannino
Judith Coleman
Ronald Crockford
Catherine Daniel
Hope Erwin
William Firth
Geoffrey Freeman
Michael Gebhart
Walter Grallert
David Hirzel
Rosemary Jones
Roger Kallstrom
Kenneth Kreutziger
Mary Jane Levy
Diane Maki
Anne McWalter
Keiji Miyagi
Christine Moreau
Karen Mortenson

*1957 Upjohn Corporation
Executive Offices
Kalamazoo, Michigan*

*1957 Foothill College
Los Altos, California*

*1958 Quincy and Leverett House
Harvard University
Cambridge, Massachusetts*

Michael Neculescu
Dennis Nolan
James Norton
Robert O'Nell
John Orcutt
Susan Otteson
Cruce Palmer
Paul Pawlowski
Ellen Pugliese
George Richards
John Ritter
Joanne Schnut
Geraldine Scotti
Helene Settle
J. David Smith
Linda Stern
Robert Straub
Ralph Sweinberger
Mary Beth Teas
Ronda Wacks
Douglas Way
Gisela Weis
Herman Weis
Ronald Wortman
Brenda York

1970

David Beede
Joanne Biscoe
Nancy Bogart
Merwin Brown
Alan Butler
Karen Cato
Carol DeDuc
Robert Dill
Resann Donahue
Paul Donavan
Joy Eaves
Gary Freebody
Maurice Freedman
Suzanne Gallaudet
Mary Gatto
Daniel Geary

Juliette Gelle
William Grundman
Robert Harris
Deborah Haviland
Maureen Henry
Arlyn Hertz
Barry Hughes
Abdel Ismail
Edward Johnson
Douglas Kelly
Theodore Krygier
James LaBarge
Lily Land
Ann Landreth
Carol Lee
Charles Leneten
James LeVine
Eugene Lewis
Maureen Little
Eleanor Lukes
Mary MacDonald
Leon Manoukian
Anthony Mantia
Charles March
Jane Merithew
John Molloy
Nubert Moloney
James Myers
Richard Orton
Ultich Raeber
Robert Ritter
Laurence Roeder
Gary Russell
Brian Sandy
Rin Sasaki
Robert Searson
Ingrid Skalicky
Frank Sparks
Peter Stone
Eda Todaro
John Turchan
Jonathan Unger
Walter Urbanek

Claire Viklund
John Welch
Ronald Wood

1971

Timothy Chubbuck
James Cunningham
Robert DiPace
Barbara Eldredge
Maria Epsimos
Jane Francisco
Ronald Getty
Frank James
Hiroo Kurano
Susan Laverty
Roger Loomis
John Massauro
Dale Moeller
Bruce Morimune
Mary O'Brien
Winifred Regan
Jeanne Silver
Donald Skop
Peter Swanson
Patricia Theophilos

1972

Ronda Andres
Edward Boiteau
Robert Cala
Victor Campominosi
Lawrence Carr
Donald Cato
Jeffrey Crane
Dale Dennis
James Edwards
Joy Hays
John Hillman
Duncan Hudson
Ronald Jarek
Otsuki Katsyoshi
Hartlie Kelley
Woo Kim

Robert Kochanowski
Delores LaDisa
Michael LaPlante
Arthur Laundon
Patricia Leighfield
Sandra Lessa
Jack Madanian
Gerald Marston
Leo Mayewski
Torru Miyakoda
Samuel Nuckols
Spiros Pantazi
Carl Peterson
Jerry Pulaski
Susan Skulley
Karen Smith
Jeffrey Sweeney
Samual Van Dam
Linda Volpe
Harold Wong
Larry Young

1973

Frank Armentano
Michael Azarian
Alex Barnes
Susan Beede
Debbie Bennett
Jeffrey Berg
Christine Berry
Richard Bertoni
Margaret Beyer
Richard Bond
Marcia Byrom
John Campbell
Rhonda Carey
Elizabeth Crimmins
Cynthia Cronin
Tamas Csabaffy
Neil Dean
Charles DeMarco
Marguerite Dunn
Jonathan Edwards

Diane Fainberg
Kathleen Fitzgerald
Jane Foster
Edward Fuller
Joseph Guerino
Efren Gutierrez
Paul Hemmerick
John Higgins
David Jones
Maura Kelley
Carl Kern
Nicky Kokoros
Sherri Kulkin
Younghoon Kwaak
Paul Lewis
Robert Livermore
Mary Helen Lorenz
Ann Lynch
Heather Lyttle
Michele McKay
Daniel Miller
Paul Morency
Nancy Moyer
Cherry Muse
Thomas Nelson
Barbara Nestler
William Patterson
Karen Rendini
Dana Rodman
Carol Rossi
Charles Sanders
Ann Sasaki
Robert Scarfo
Richard Shaw
Robert Shinbo
Michael Sico
Philip Siebert
Michael Smith
Tova Solo
Charlotte Suslavich
Yolande Tan
Helga Thompson
Kevin Thompson

Grant Thornbrough
Michael Timmons
Ann VerPlanck
Richard Watson
James Webster
Hideko Worcester
Juan Yerbes

1974

George Amendola
Beverly Bergonzi
Jack Bowersoz
Nancy Brigham
John Buckley
Rank Dembinski
John Fahy
Gayle Floyd
Richard Foulkes
Helen Garibotto
Agnes Gazelian
Dorothea Glynn
Virginia Kannenberg
Amy Kell
Daniel Kenney
Owen Lang
Brian Lunch
Francis McGuire
David Peterson
John Pollack
Donna Randles
Dennis Reinhardt
Patricia Ryuan
Donald Vahrenkamp

1975

Patricia Burroughs
Arline Westerman

1976

Kim Ahern
Betty Allen
Joyce Ashman
Eve Baltzell

Michael Bernard
Anthony Case
Thomas DeLucia
Pornpun Futrakul
Mark Gabriel
David Garofano
David Gerber
Kenneth Glidden
Leo Greene
Gary Gwon
Nancy Jaglowski
Alan Kaufman
Raymond Keegan
Mary Kelly
Lindsay Kirk
Angelica Lamas
Henry Law
Laura Llerena
Rebecca Moran
Gail Promboin
Cynthia Rice
Clarissa Rowe
Alexander Trakimas
Mary Wallace
Donna Watson

1977

Mary Arena
George Botner
George Burr, Jr.
James Capen
Peter Carnes
Frederick Clark
Jerome Corvan
Marcella Dickie
Rosemary Fahey
Robert Galehouse
Daniel Garbowit
Heidi German
Zachery Hagg
Lawrence Headley
John Henshaw
Michael Holland

1959 Constitution Plaza
Hartford, Connecticut

1960 University of Colorado
Boulder, Colorado

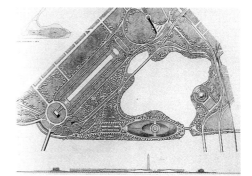

1960 FDR Memorial Competition
Washington, DC

Apryl Isaacs
Seddon Johnson
John Jurewicz
Anne Kendrick
Lisa Kinosian
Carol Krieger
Robert Kuckta
Christopher Lang
Walter Lewinski
William McClelland
Robert McIver
John Missell
Yoshiaki Morikawa
Christopher Munson
Brian Peterson
William Rabben
Leslie Reich
Henry Ricciuti
Alison Richardson
Christopher Rogers
Marcella Saunders
Elizabeth Shreeve
John Siff
Cynthia Smith
Hans Strauch
Judy Swanson
David Szlag
Bruce Von Alten
Helen Walker
James White
Sidney Zecher

1978

Michael Abend
Michael Allen
Joseph Barbato
Richard Burck
Edith Calzadilla
Lemuel Canady
Sho-ping Chin
Sukkuen Chin
John Coons
Judith Dempsey

Sylvia Dickey
Robert Dincecco
Karlson Greene
Michael Kaufman
Pamela Kennedy
Ruth Kessler
Sally Keys
Judith LaVacca
Joseph Leonard
Juan Lucero
Elizabeth Mahoney
Brad Meyer
David Mittlestadt
Michael Pape
Christine Prokop
Toby Reed
Amy Richardson
Lydia Richardson
Nina Rodriquez
Donald Rose
Charles Samiotes
Laura Serafin
Ann Sloan
Charles Sullivan
Alan Ward
Richard Westcott
Leslie Whalen
Carolyn Winkler
Ronald Zeytoonian
Michelle Zippel

1979

Wilbur Adams
Marcia Adkins
Guillermo Aguilar
Joseph Allen
Mark Anthony
Stephen Armington
Barbara Arsenault
Dwight Barefoot
Claire Beaudoin
Irma Boehm
Maureen Brannelly

Bobby Brown
Cornilia Brown
Ellen Chagnon
Antonia Clary
David Clough
Peter Coleman
Ann Collings
Mark Dawson
Francis Domurat
Ireneusz Domurat
Kathryn Drinkhouse
Heleodoro Feliciano
Jonathan Fitch
Joseph Frye
Arlene Ghiasik
Deborah Goldman
June Graves
Leah Greenwald
Varoujan Hagopian
John Hawes
Joseph Hibbard
Ken Hoffman
Mary Ann Hunt
Carsten Jacobs
John Jennings
Gail Keddy
Michael Kelly
Maria Knight
Mark Kopchell
Douglas Kornfeld
Maryellen Lanza
Virginia LaPusata
Ashan Lari
Lisa Leone
Jane Lueders
James Lyons
Stephen Mabee
Constance Maloney
James Martin
Leo Mayewski
Peggy McCarthy
Patricia McCobb
Mark McDonough

Agnes McManus
Leonard Melish
Stephen Messenger
David Miller
Donald Miller
Peter Miniutti
Christopher Moder
Meijean Moong
Matteo Moore
Varoujan Moubayed
Barry Mullen
Sharon Nixon
Geraldine Palma
Diane Pasiuk
Lauren Perry
Sandra Proctus
Edward Ransom
Richard Redmond
Nicholas Reed
Bruce Richardson
Jennifer Rogers
Susan Rogers
Carol Roscio
David Ross
John Rutherford
Cynthia Sarver
Cheryl Scott
Philip Sheldon
Heather Thompson-Ryan
Randy Thueme
Ingrid Tollefson
Judith Winters
Ronald Wong
Susan Ziegler

1980

Gary Abbott
Jose Aponte
Van Arend
James Ashbrook
Roberta Bates
Michael Beaver
Paul Beede

Kathleen Brannelly
Madeline Bunster
Bruce Buttner
Maria Caira
Louis Calzadilla
John Carthas
Thomas Caruso
Andy Chung
Thomas Coffman
Diane Costa
Ellen Costigan
Peter Davis
Ray Davison
Robert Donahue
Molly Feltham
Deborah Field
Peter Frayley
David French
John Gillon
Elizabeth Golden
Margaret Goodman
Diana Graves
Bozena Grocholski
Jean Gropp
Steve Hamwey
Richard Hayden
Elaine Hennebury
Wayne Hill
Anne Hogan
Barbara Humphries
Theresa Hynes
Karen Jordan
Ann Komara
Susan Lanigan
Ermina Larocca
Matt Leiner
Steve Levin
Paul Lindholm
Kathryn Madden
Cynthia Manos
Larry Marshall
William McDonough
Chris Meinhardt

James Mellows
Terry Meyer
Juan Morales
Doreen Munger
Suzanne Myra
Kathleen Nolen
Susan O'Connor-Welch
Janet Pearce
Frank Piscitelli
Armando Porto
Pam Robinson
Bradford Saunders
Alla Schmidt
Debra Singer
Ralph Sneed
Linda Stayton
Su-Fan Su
Octavio Suarez
John Supple
Lorraine Sweeney
Brian Swift
Barbara Waddington
Rosaline Wai
Mary Warriner
David Wilson
Jefferey Wyner

1981

Richard Backer
Robert Barbato
John Benson
David Berrarducci
Katherine Bleakney
John Brandolino
Brian Brickley
Richard Bridgeo
Heidi Butler
Joan Carmody
Anne Casey
Marann Cassell
Paul Cincotta
Allan Clark
Charles Crumpton

DeMontingny
Lucia Donahue
Arthur Duff
Ricardo Dumont
Jay Faber
Ellen Filppu
Edward Fitzgerald
Peter Frawly
Steven Gardescu
John Gaudette
Richard Gillis
Richard Heeley
David Hillier
Judith Katz
Laurence Keegan
Anne Kemble
Kim Kerdyk
Taryn Kontos
Rebecca Krinke
Nancy Leask
Matt Leiner
Joan Lodge
Rebecca Longley
Mary Lyons
Ernest Marsh
Richard McAllistar
Kelly McCauley
Edward Mullins
Margaret Mullins
Lori Murray
Leslie Nichols
Jesus Novoa
Joseph Nucciarone
Dennis O'Reilly
Robert Parente
Andrew Patton
Bary Pell
Laura Perez
Suzanne Peyser
Mona Rafferty
Laura Ricciardi
Miguel Rivera
Becky Roberts

1974 IBM, Thomas J. Watson Research Center Yorktown Heights, NY

1975 Ramapo College Mahwah, New Jersey

1975 Baxter-Travenol Laboratories Deerfield, Illinois

Charles Shepherd
Carol Silverman
Michael Smiley
Arthur Smith
James Smith
William Smith
Gregory Stevens
James Sukeforth
Joseph Tringale
Peter Ventola
Debbie Walsh
Barbara Welanetz
Sui Wong
Mark Yelland

1982
Paul Berkowitz
Stefan Bolliger
Kimberly Bondeson
Mary Burns
Elizabeth Chabot
Ilene Chaet
Mason DeMay
Barbara Drainoni
Phyllis Fogg
Yasmin Fozard
Beatriz Garcia
Jon Gardescu
Patricia Gardner
Olive Holmes
Todd Johnson
Craig Jones
Steven Kurz
Roy LaMotte
Sarah Lipson
Brian McCusker
Michael McNiece
Pamela Moreno
Cynthia Plank
George Pottie
Maureen Pratt
Sharon Price
Gwendolyn Richter

Lisa Rookard
Frances Rugo
Thomas Ryan
Mohammad Sadrolashrafi
Nelson Scott Smith
Robert Smith
Michael Sobczak
Christine Walkowicz

1983
Robert Augustine
Lori Barr
Joan Bartinelli
Charles Blackmore
Gregg Bleam
John Bociek
Robert Brown
Eric Carlson
Alicia Carrillo
Neil Cavanagh
John Cazzetta
Shawn Coady
Deborah Collins
Kimberly Corey
Daniel Crocco
Paul Crocco
Dwight DeMay
Paul DiBona
Maryjane Donohue
Daniel Douglas
Hussam El-alami
Richard Elliott
Richard Farrington
Lance Ferguson
Eileen Fitzgerald
Steve Freche
Alan Fujimori
Amy Galehouse
Margo Galloway
Rebecca Gardner
Elizabeth Gifford
Gail Goldberg
Eva Gurewitz

John Headerle
Suzanne Hopkins
John Leisinger
Allen Leland
Brenda Lonning
Elizabeth MacDonnell
Kathleen Matthews
Elaine McCabe
Edward McMahon
Frederick Merrill, Jr.
Deanne Munger
Scott Oglevee
Ida Perryman
Richard Potestia
Dorothy Redding
Vincent Rico
Rodrigo Rodriquez
Lori Rohr
Jill Sabota
Ellen Soroka
Leonard Staffa
Victoria Steiger
Anthony Stella
Leonard Stocker
Michael Strahm
Les Stucka
Ella Svirsky
Gary Tondorf-Dick
Victoria Union
Darlene Walsh
Margaret Weed
Frederick Winkler

1984
Gregory Ault
Lori Austen
Aristotle Bakalos
Naomi Baldwin
Donna Behrle
Martha Bennett
Patricia Birch
Wolfgang Bowhm
William Brownstein

Bethann Brush
Nancy Burns
Thomas Burns
David Burrill
Charlene Crouch
Aida Curtis
Scott Davis
Marianne DePamphilis
Thomas DiCicco
James Doolin
James Dunn
Mani Farhadi
Noah Fasten
Nancy Freedman
Jean Garbier
Diane Gavin
Darlene Gray
Peter Grover
Michael Hamilton
Kevin Hamrock
Michael Hatfield
Elizabeth Herman
David Holdorf
Bent Huld
Laura Jinishian
James Klien
Corinne Levesque
Anthony Mallows
Wendy Mandel
Michael Maxwell
Nancy Mayer
Mary McNichol
John Mele
Marie Morrissey
Christopher Nemethy
Ian Nestler
Pedro Ordenes
William Ormond
Diane Palmeri-Eller
Douglas Pew
Enrique Pezuela
Daniel Pierce
Mary Pitts

Maurice Ponti
Rayna Rambat
Robert Ravelli
Bruce Rein
Daria Riordan
Dorene Russo
David Samuelson
Camilo Santana
Jean Shanahan
Patricia Smith
Norris Strawbridge
Sidney Swidler
Caroline Taggart
Michael Tolajian
Carole Touzet
Peter Vasiliadis
Donald Vitters
Madgerie Woodbury
Robert Yacobian
John Yurewicz, Sr.

1985
Arthur Anderson
Gary Anderson
Nancy Armstrong
Jonathan Austin
Robert Ballou
Robert Berube
Carol Boerder-Snyder
Julie Boyce
Gary Brink
John Brittingham
Calvin Brook
Laura Burnett
Cynthia Burnham
Margaret Carney
Lucy Chamberlain
Deborah Champam-Harford
James Cogliano
Samual Coplon
Claudia Cox
Trudt Cronin

Oscar Cuello
Walter Daly
Diane Deblois
Bobby Deleveau
Ellen Deming
Gnanesh Desai
Linda Dole
Ray Dunetz
Manuel Echezarreta
Afsaneh Eghbalian
Elizabeth Emery
Hildy Feinstein
Mark Finneral
David Flaschenriem
Agostino Furtado
Lynn Gilligan
Kathleen Hansen
Philip Hart
Victoria Hibbard
Gary Hilderbrand
John Hollywood
Jeffrey Jacoby
Elizabeth Janofsky
Bradley Johnson
Michael Johnson
Spencer Johnson
Molly Jytyla
Nina Kim
Jutta Konopasek
Jeffrey Lakey
Martha Lampkin
Bruce Larkin
Maryann Laurinat
Carolyn Leaman
Richard Leisner
Larry Lewis
Eduardo Llano
Jose Lopez
Jeanne Lukenda
Stanton Lyman
William Lyons
Andrew Mann
Ellen Marhoney

Gerald Marston
Michael McGoldrick
David McIntyre
Frank Miller
Peter Miner
Rosellen Morey
Gaius Nelson
Doreve Nicholaeff
Robert Nichols
Lucinda O'Neill
Roxane Olson
Robert Osten
Robert Paladino
Kejoo Park
Joanne Pearson
Antonio Pereira
Minna Pyyhkala
Janis Reiters
Susan Renaccio
William Ridge
Cathy Ries
Terry Rookard
Frank Sabori
Stephanie Sawyer-Ames
Roberta Shaw
Sally Sheehan
Laura Sheffield
Michael Smith
Martin Sokoloff
Laura Solano
Patricia Sonnino
Andrew Sprague
Laura Stambaugh
Jeannette Szabo
James Taylor
Carole Twombly
Rosemarie Villegas
Timothy Von Aschwege
Kay Wagenknecht-Harte
Thomas Wang
Paul Weathers
Julie Weener
Mary Whatmore

1978 Waterfall Garden
Seattle, Washington

1978 National Arboretum
Washington, DC

1980 Winter Olympics
Lake Placid, New York

Timothy Whitney
Guy Winig
Suzanne Wissell
Ralph Wolfe
Sing-Charn Wong
Windy Wood
Robert Young

1986

Robin Aallen
Mahkameh Adnani
Jeanne Allen
Edward Alshut
Katherine Arbour
Eric Arthur
Roger Atwood
John D. Barry
Michel Beheshti
Darrell Bird
Sharon Bondiet
Marjorie Bortolotto
George Bregianos
Jonathan Buff
Donna Caracino
Charles Carlin
Walter Carlson
Alain Carroli
David Castagno
Jennifer Cave
Bradley Chaszer
Joyce Chestnut
Magda Christian
Kathy Christopher
Richard Ciardella
Bruce Clark
Douglas Cole
Chistopher Cooke-Yarborough
Patti Cristina
Doreen Curseaden
Ginette Dalberiste
Enrique DeLamar
Chris Delaney

Cathleen DiMarzio
Paul Donovan
Frederick Duplinsky
Vernon Eldringhoff
Brooke Emery
Lisa Esposito
Keith Everett
Carlotte Fanfan
Anne Fectau
Adolfo Fernandez
Carlos Ferre
Gary Fishbeck
Paula Fisher
Francis Ford
Thomas Fox
Paul Frazier
Clinton Fulton
Jorge Fuste
Glenn Garber
Arturo Garcia
Arpie Gennetian
Pamela Gorgone
Shiela Grady
Brian Greene
Dennis Hand
Kenneth Heath
Lori Hey
Delaine Hudson
Larry Hughes
Mark Kalin
Rai Karapetyan
Kathleen Kattredge
Pamela Kiley
Jess Kilgore
Andres Koenigsberg
Julian LaFerriere
Ellen Light
Veronica Lima
Julie Lindow
Francis Loughran
Deborah Maillett
Diana Miller
Wendy Morita

Clare Morris
Herbert Nolan
Susan O'Donnell
James Oglesby
Elaine Ognoto
Gary Olander
Stephen Oppenheimer
Sarah Orcutt
Louise Paiva
Marie Palleschi
Judy Paprin
Christopher Parrish
Janice Pender
Martha Porter
Roger Poulin
Robert Poulos
Joanne Powell
Marcia Reed
Camila Rincon
Pamela Rooney
Steven Rose
Audrey Salunier
Susan Sangiolo
Maria Sevely
Sheila Sheets
James Simmons
Kevin Sims
Michael Small
Edward Smith
Jennifer Smith
Karen Snow
Mark Stevens
Michael Stevens
Richard Streetman
Therese Sullivan
Dennis Swinford
Staci Tate
Tabitha Thomas
Jeannette Thomson
Jeffrey Townsend
Kimberly Trussell

Brenda Upson
Mario Viteri
Michael Wang
Jonathan Warner
Andrew Weaver
Wendy Welsh
Alan West
Michael William
Tyrone Williams
Randy Wood
Todd Worthley
Gabriel Yaari

1987

Kerry Adams
Duncan Alford
Daniel Beagna
Roger Behgam
Marie Benincase
Gail Bornstein
Michiko Bracket
Scott Cavaness
Diane Cavers
Joseph Chan
George Choueiry
Diana Clow
Loran Commins
Tammy Cook
Rita Coriani
Gina D'Andragora
Rebecca Davie
Suzanne DeMillar
Melissa Dhoku
Jaquiline Dickinson
Susan Didzinski
Brian Driscoll
Renee Dumas
Thomas Dunning
Elaine Dupre
Talitha Fabricius
Roberta Factor
Katrin Fox
Timothy Franke

David Fyffe
Lana Gokey
Mara Graman
Winston Hagen
Lisa Hall
Garry Harley
Nancy Harrod
Melissa Hellfrich
John Highes
John Highman
Jeffrey Horstmeier
Richard Johnson
Dale Jones
Sandra Shafer
Jeffrey Kagermeir
Penelope Karas
Lee Kreindel
Mary Lambert
David Lardon
Laurie Lebbon
Michele Lee
Denise Marini
Jay Marsh
Christine Martel
Nancy Matolak
Rachel Mello
Alexandra Mijares
Jean Milholland
Richard Mitchel
Marilyn Muldrow
Martha Murphy
Thomas Murphy
Marilys Nepomechie
Anne Nixon
Leo O'Brien
Sonja Olson
Anthony Orlando
Dennis Pieprz
Cynthia Potenze
Elizabeth Powers
Christopher Royer
Barbara Sansone
Jay Schulman

David Schuster
Kenneth Schwartz
Lawrence Schwirian
John Shields
Randi Simmons
Lydia Sowles
Beth Sykes
Peter Taschioglou
Annette Taylor
James Taylor
Robert Vigeant
Vincent Vignaly
Jennifer Viklund
Vitas Viskanta
Robert Von Elgg
Virginia Welter
Warren Wheeler
Heather Whitten
Deborah Williamson
Dennis Wilson
Ronald Wommack
Carole Youden
Helen Yung
John Yurewicz, Jr.

1988

John Amato
Paul Anderson
Kendall Bates
Kim Baur
Ruth Bednarzuk
Richard Boydack
Isabel Claudino
Linda Cooper
Dorothy Crowley
Michael Dechemin
Laurie Ewing
Leanne Fitzgerald
Joseph Flynn
Richard Ford
David Galehouse
Steve Garbier
Barbara Glinski

William Harris
Robert Holt
Susan Hoxie
Rachel Knighten
Rebecca Ko
Suzanne Lauriet
Harris Levitt
Joanne Lodi
Sheila Lynch-Benttinen
Jayne Mabie
Edward Malouf
Cynthia Maltenfort
Steven McHugh
Duncan Mellor
Donna Michitson
Sandra Mika
Christine Murphy
Jacqueline Patey
Eugene Peck
Martha Perkins
Juan Antonio Pineda
Angel Rivera
Steven Rooney
Bobette Rousseau
Ellen Rowan
Jennifer Rowan
Cynthia Russo
Deena Scaperotta
Pamela Schricker
Judith Sellers
Nancy Shapiro
Rachel Siegel
Rhonda Simard
Stephen Smith
Susan Spaulding
John Suarez
Lauren Tannen
David Wight
Jodi Williamson
Hope Woodcock
Judy Wynnemer

1984 St. Mark's School Dormitory
Southborough, Massachusetts

1987 Southwest Corridor
Boston, Massachusetts

1990 Vassar College
Poughkeepsie, New York

1989

Roy Ackerman
Harry Akiyama
Georganne Alpert
Sarah Ayres
Richard Ball
Denise Bannon
Andrew Bartolotta
Jan Becker
Todd Bennitt
Julie Berry
Bradley Black
Clive Booker
Robert Brooks
Robert Burt
Iris Carlo
Irene Carlson
Patricia Cavallaro
Anthony Chacon
Tun-sing Chen
Christina Chestre
Bruce Choen
Ya-tien Chuan
Marc Ciannavei
Ken Corey
Allison Crosbie
Laura Cunningham
Timothy Deacon
Rose Marie DeAngelis
Alain DeVergie
Paul Diaz
James Dietzmann
Karen Dove
Susan Duca
Charles Eggert
Thomas Ennis
Robert Evans
Anne Federick
James Ferdinand
Julie Fitzgerald
Sara Forbes
Kay Gan
Andrew Garvin

Vladimir Gavrilovic
Andrew Gil
Mark Gilbert
Glenn Gilbreath
Barbara Gould
Melissa Gramstad
Joseph Green
Phyllis Halpern
Kris Hansen
Sandra Hansen
Scott Henry
Romeo Hernandez
Eugene Hollingsworth
Ronald Izumita
Gary Joaquin
Ron Kagawa
Mark Killie
Betsy Klein
John Knickmeyer
Paul Kontoh
Karen Larsen
Eric Lassen
Marsha Lea
Marc Lindow
Anne Lyons
John Matthews
Jacqueline McDonald
Stephen McDonald
Roger McErlane
Jonathan McIntyre
Laurence McNulty
Sarah Medeiros
Vicki Meier
Gregory Miller
Brian Mitchell
Andrew Mooradian
Santiago Moreno
Anne Mullaney
Ernest Muniz
Charles Myers
Craig Myers
Pedro Nunex
David Partyka

Julia Pastor
Norman Pease
Raquel Penalosa
Mary Dixon-Presbey
Karen Preston
Daniel Reeder
Timothy Regan
Alan Resnick
Dominic Restagno
Cristal Rumber
Robert Sabbatini
Marija Sabic
Robert Salas
James Sandlin
Maria Santiago
Mustafa Sayer
Jim Schaefer
Stephen Schar
Claire Schiavi
Efren Sebastian
Dennis Selinger
Scott Simons
Parvinder Sodhi
Simin Soltani
Saeed Soltanik
Tracey Sonneborn
Timothy Stepeck
Paula Stone
Ivana Sturm
Eric Svahn
Su-sin Tang
Jane Tarlov
Andrea Thiringer
Graham Thomas
Peggy Thomas
Larry Van Vleet
Susan Vitters
Lisa Vokovan
Tzawe Wang
Robert Waslov
Deborah West
Peter Widmer

Robert Wiech
Jeffrey Wogan
Barbara Zewiey

1990

Suzanne Agcaoili
Ronita Alexander
Mitchell Alguadich
Robert Arthur
Thomas Berkeley
Marie Bernard
Corinne Capiaux
Dennis Carlberg
James Carver
Lorena Celis
Patrick Chang
Pauline Chin
Lewis Colten
Julia Conner
Lisa Connors
Patricia Coolberth
Martha Crowell
Regina Damico
Carmen Deffely
Enrico DiMaro
Barbara Dickey
Michael Dineen
Pat Doolin
Megan Doyle
Theresa Farrell
Liesel Fenner
Tracy Finlayson
Joanna Fong
Elizabeth Garcia
Jennifer Gilpatrick
Scott Gray
Andrew Guidry
Mary Harris
Gina Hawley
Wu-chang Ho
Mark Hoffheimer
Maureen Hosick
Susan Hoy

Siobhan Hundertmark
Jennifer Jackson
Anna Lacadie
Joseph Lafo
Nicholas Lennett
Jean-Christophe
Liermeier
Diahanne Lucas
Juan Machado
Barbara Manning
Patricia Moran
Kimberly Nelson
Ken Nguyen
Lan Nguyen
Takako Oji
David Oldman
Frank Oliva
Garth Paterson
James Podesky
Bradley Pontius
Nancy Prado
Lisa Rosen
Hector Ruiz
Catherine Runnals
Michael Schneider
Caroline Schwirian
Robert Sellers
Peter Silva
Gayle Sinopoli-Munoz
Harper Smith
Gregory Sparks
Thomas Takao
Betty Ty
Michael Wang
Wendy Wallace
Hans Warner
Jill Yuzwa
Joseph Yee

1991

Tomi Alvey
April Bauer
Robert Beerman

Robert Bell
Jo Bennitt
Hans Peter Bissegger
Laura Bobeczko
Cary Carpenter
Karen Charris
Timothy Crate
Paul Demosthenes
Kirstin Dewara
Gautam Dey
Ronald DiMauro
Kimberly Dodge
Mary Beth Ellis
Andrew Fairbairn
Cynthia Fordham
David Gallagher
Sumila Gulyani
Reaz Haque
Liesa Harwood
Gregory Havens
Vandee Jearkjirm
Eric Johnson
Jack Joseph
Dannette Kahn
James Keenan
Alex Kiritschenko
Michael Kissane
James Lyons
James Maloney
Esther Margulies
Marc Mazzarelli
Anna McErlane
Kevin McKowen
Nancy McLean
Elizabeth Meek
Sevak Meldonin
Carl Mills
Mary Beth Munson
Choy Ng
George Nichols
Lee Pearce
Vladimir Petkovich
Diane Plemenos

Christopher Porter
Dorran Prescott
Nora Quadros
Pam Rooney
Steven Shetler
Scott Silva
Susan Stainback
Eliza Sullivan
Maryellen Suziedelis
Sumio Suzuki
Dale Wall

1992

Robert Bell
Hilary Bidwell
Cristin Boots
David Brothers
Kim Brown
Robert Callaway
Jennifer Camero
Joseph Chambers
Romulo Co
Laurie Connell
Charles Coronis
Patrick Coyne
Antonio D'Agostino
Chantal Darling
Jody DeBye
Anne-Sophie Divenyi
Linda Dombrosky
Roberta A. Doocey
Michael Dumala
Rafael Fernandez
Kristin Fond
Kevin Gal
Gale Goldberg
Paul Harris
Cuyler Hennecy
Jennifer Jackson
Tina Jackson
Diahann Lucas
Frank Lucas
Kevin MacNeill

1990 Theater of the Performing Arts
Miami Beach, Florida

1991 Plymouth Library
Plymouth, Massachusetts

1992 Hana-Maui Hotel
Maui, Hawaii

Harold McCaleb
Bradley McCord
William McDonald
Alistair McIntosh
Nancy McLean
Suzanne Molloy
David Morgan
Kathleen Noonan
Brian O'Connell
Gerald Ohta
Ralph Ray
Pamela Robinson
Molly Simmons
Robert Titus
Glen Valentine
Susan Veronee
Midori Watanabe
Constance Weiting
Kathleen Winder

1993
Mohammed Alanni
Robert Benson
Samara Bercovitch
Daniel Boudreau, Jr.
Debra Caruso
Stacy Chambers
Jerry Chao
Colleen Creamer
Deborah Delorey
Laurie Ericsson
Diane Evans-Vorhis
Doreen Fantini
Miriam Fitzpatrick
Susan Foxlin
Richard Friedson
Eileen Glass
Janet Goyette
Jennifer Grimes
Stephen Hamwey, Jr.
Paul Heidrick
Stephanie Johnson
Koti Kalakota

James Keenan
Karl Leabo
Susan Lin
Xiao Wei Ma
Masaki Maruoka
Melissa A. McCann
Elizabeth McCoy
Rachel Miller
Emi Okawara
Stephen Pak
Taufik Prakasa
David Rust
Daryl Sequeira
George Sharpe
Michael Sherman
Timothy Stoaks
Emily Talcott
Mark Vinless
Susan Welch
William Winkler
Claudia Zander
Jian Zhao

1994
Diego Alessi
Barbara Apel
Diane Arone
Kim Azar
Neal Baker
Colleen Barry
Catherine Bell
Maria Bellalta
Henry Bobek
James Kyle Casper
William Colehower
Susan Dallas
Michael Earls
Eric Eldridge
Ann Elwell
Brian Erba
Ginger Fagundes

Julie Ferrari
Paul Furman
Chandra Goldsmith
Christina Grillo
Barbara Gugger
Suzanne Hafer
Ryan Hanson
Michael Harada
Michael Heath
Sarah Hirzel
I-Pai Hsu
Alexandra Hussey
Mark Kuskowski
James Lin
Patricia Madore
Jason McHugh
Boyd Morrison
Carol Moyles (Brower)
Tom Mullane
Nancy Peake
Brian Pearce
Lisa Picard
Roland Quirion, Jr.
Michael Regan
Steven Roscoe
Rita Ruskin
William Sasser
Maribeth Sawyer
Julia Smythe
Timothy Stevens
Nicholas Wagner
Constance Wieting
Craig Worley
Charlene Ying
Nella Young

1995
Sarah Adams
Matthew Allison
Chad Bennett
Paul Blanc
Chere Burdette
John Busby

Stephen Cast
Veronique Choa
Mary Crawford
Grace Cribbin
Richard Daniels
Caroline Darbyshire
Harriet Diamond
Michelle Djordjevich
Kelly Ehrgott
Yamileth Espinoza
Kenneth Fout
Leslie Goldberg
Teresa Gray-Pearce
Jessica Horwitz
Jie Hu
Gregory Johnson
Gregory Kaiser
Lisa Kent
Saeed Kheradmandnia
Janyce Knight
Debra Kully
Nani Kurniawan
Vladimir Lauture
Trung Le
Heather Little
Leo Ma
Jeremy Matosky
Andrew McClurg
Mary Miller
Jason Mirabito
Julia Monteith
Stephan Murphy
Kimberly Natale
Ruth Nugroho
Maureen O'Leary
James Olmsted
Daniel Richards
Tracy Rieckelman
Richard Smith, II
Renee Tiano
Kristine Waldman

1996
Elaine Abdul-Massih
Gillian Alexander
Lianne Ames
Arben Arapi
Lisa Aufman Gaffey
Grayson Baur
Susan Bellis
Brian Benko
Tom Berkley
Daniel Bernstein
Michael Berry
Jennifer Biller
Danielle Bruce
Robert Cahill
Robert Cahoon
Emily Chang
Ho-Ping Chueh
Richard Colavecchio
David Damon
Scott Delano
Rick Dumont
Linda Eastley
Mark Eclipse
Karen Ford
Jose Garcia
Vinicius Gorgati
Michele Hammer
Leekyung Han
Douglas Hartnett
Gwendolyn Horton
Teresa James
Leslie Jonas
Seonhee Jung
Christopher Kent
Alla Khlyap
Thomas Kinslow
Diana Kissil
Gregory Lyons
Mark Maniaci
Douglas Marshall
Nayana Mawilmada
Stephanie McGrath

Sheila Moe
Romeo Moreira
Julia O'Grady
Catherine Oranchak
J. Christoph Panfil
Maria Pierce
Jennifer Peters
Serge Plishevsky
Linda Poirier
Matilde Reyes
Brian Roessler
Jin Roh
Aya Sakai
Pablo Savid-Buteler
Jason Stabach
Kathryn Stearns
Alexander Stoltz
Michael Sukeforth
Maria Tucker
Kathleen Tackabury
Kenny Tsai
Christina Van Deusen
Melissa Wedig
Mark Yin
Richard York

1993 Dhahran Master Plan
Dhahran, Saudi Arabia

1994 Marquette Playing Fields
Milwaukee, Wisconsin

1995 Bethel College
Community Life Center
St. Paul, Minnesota

Notes

Photography Credits

Translations

Notes

Introduction

1. Pietro Belluschi to Richard F. Galehouse, April 2, 1988. Sasaki Associates Archives.

2. Ibid.

3. Hideo Sasaki, Memorandum to Dick Dober, February 21, 1959. Hideo Sasaki's files.

4. Richard P. Dober, "A Three and Five Year Plan for Sasaki, Walker and Associates, Inc.," January, 1959. Hideo Sasaki's files.

5. See Gary O. Robinette, *Landscape Architectural Education*, vol. 1 (Dubuque, Iowa: Kendall/Hunt Publishing Co., 1973), 76-89; and Peter Walker and Melanie Simo, *Invisible Gardens* (Cambridge, Mass.: MIT Press, 1994), 198-222.

6. Hideo Sasaki, taped conversations with the author, Lafayette, California, June 14, 1988; August 27, 1991; and May 18, 1996; and Hideo Sasaki, Memorandum to Reginald Isaacs, Chairman, Department of City Planning and Landscape Architecture, Harvard Graduate School of Design, December 9, 1954. Hideo Sasaki's files.

7. Hideo Sasaki, Memorandum to Reginald Isaacs, December 9, 1954.

8. Charles W. Harris, "The Once-Lonely Turf: New Directions for Landscape Architecture at Harvard from 1958 to 1970," in Margaret Henderson-Floyd, *Architectural Education and Boston: Centennial Publication of the Boston Architectural Center, 1889-1989* (Boston: Boston Architectural Center, 1989), 107. This article was an expansion of Harris's article, "The Once-Lonely Turf," *HGSDA News* (1970/3), 3-6. See also Melanie L. Simo, *The Landscape Reinvented 1953-1996* (forthcoming from Spacemaker Press, Washington, D.C., cat 1987).

9. Hideo Sasaki, taped conversation at Sasaki Associates, Watertown, Massachusetts, April, 1993. Author's transcription of audio tape, Sasaki Associates archives.

10. Hideo Sasaki, taped conversation with the author, Lafayette, California, June 14, 1988.

11. Hideo Sasaki, "Landscape Architecture and the Planning Effort," *Forsite '53*, student publication of the Department of City Planning and Landscape Architecture, University of Illinois, Champaign-Urbana; and Sasaki, "Urban Renewal and Landscape Architecture," *Landscape Architecture* (January, 1955), 100-101.

12. Hideo Sasaki, "Urban Renewal and Landscape Architecture" (1955); and Sasaki, "The City and the Landscape Architect," *Space 1956*, student publication of the Department of Landscape Architecture, University of California, Berkeley.

13. Josep Lluis Sert, in "Urban Design," condensed report of an invitation conference sponsored by the Faculty and Alumni Association of the Graduate School of Design, Harvard University, April 9-10, 1956, *Progressive Architecture* (August, 1956).

14. Hideo Sasaki, Ibid.

15. James A. Sukeforth, taped conversation with the author, Watertown, Massachusetts, April 11, 1996.

16. Kenneth Bassett, taped conversation with the author, Watertown, Massachusetts, April 11, 1996.

17. David Hirzel, taped conversation with the author, Watertown, Massachusetts, May 29, 1996.

18. Peter Walker, personal communication to the author, November 24, 1996.

19. Don Olson, Memorandum to Paul Gardescu, April 8, 1981. Sasaki Associates archives.

Campus Planning

1. M. Perry Chapman, taped conversation with the author, Watertown, Massachusetts, May 29, 1996.

2. M. Perry Chapman, "Social Change and American Campus Planning," *Planning for Higher Education*, vol. 22 (Spring, 1994), 1-12.

3. This summary of the early years has been derived from conversations with several principals at Sasaki Associates and their former colleagues, including Hideo Sasaki, Kenneth DeMay, M. Perry Chapman, Richard Galehouse, Alan Ward, Richard Dober, Charles W. Harris, and Peter Walker. Also useful were a series of articles by Chapman and some notes by Walker.

4. Allan Temko, "Foothill's Campus is a Community in Itself," *Architectural Forum* (February, 1962), 54-56.

5. Richard Galehouse, taped conversation with the author, Watertown, Massachusetts, June 3, 1996.

Urban Design

1. Stuart O. Dawson, "The Skyscraper's Base: Architecture, Landscape and Use," paper presented at "The Second Century of the Skyscraper," The Third International Conference on Tall Buildings, Chicago, Illinois, January 8, 1986. Author's files.

2. William H. Whyte, "The Blank Wall," speech delivered at the conference, "What Makes a City?" April 29, 1983, Dallas, Texas, sponsored by the Dallas Institute of Humanities and Culture.

3. *Government Center–Boston*. Prepared for the City Planning Board of Boston, Massachusetts, by Adams, Howard & Greeley, Consultants, in association with: Anderson, Beckwith & Haible; Sasaki, Walker & Associates; Kevin Lynch; John R. Myer; and Paul D. Spreiregen. Sasaki Associates archives.

4. Alan Ward, taped conversation with the author, Watertown, Massachusetts, May 8, 1996.

5. Hideo Sasaki to Edmund N. Bacon, April 29, 1963, with attached conceptual sketches and sketch plans. Sasaki Associates archives.

6. Alan Ward, taped conversation with the author, Watertown, Massachusetts, June 26, 1996.

New Communities

1. David M. Hirzel, "The Virginia Coast Reserve: Planning for Sustainable Development," paper presented at the AIA Conference on Sustainability, 1994. David Hirzel's files.

2. Richard Galehouse, taped conversation with the author, Watertown, Massachusetts, June 3, 1996.

3. Richard Galehouse, slide presentation, "Sasaki Associates, Inc., A Retrospective," with the Boston Society of Landscape Architects, Harvard University, Graduate School of Design, November 5, 1981. Transcript, Sasaki Associates archives.

4. John McPhee, *Encounters with the Archdruid* (New York: Farrar, Straus and Giroux, 1971), 92.

5. Philip Morris, "Charles Fraser," *Southern Living* (June, 1990), 58-59.

6. Richard F. Galehouse, "Kingsmill on the James River," *Landscape Architecture* (April, 1975), 212. See also Galehouse, "Land Planning for Large-Scale Residential Development," *Urban Land* (October, 1981).

7. Richard Galehouse, taped conversation with the author, Watertown, Massachusetts, June 3, 1996.

8. Richard Galehouse, Ibid. See "Designs on the Future" [Celebration, Florida], *Architectural Record* (January, 1996), 63-69.

9. Alan Ward, in "Designing New Towns," *Landscape Architecture Forum, Landscape Architecture* (December, 1988), 71.

10. Alan Ward, Ibid, 72.

11. David Hirzel, taped conversation with the author, Watertown, Massachusetts, May 29, 1996.

Design

1. Alan Resnick, taped conversation with the author, Watertown, Massachusetts, July 17, 1996.

2. Joseph Hibbard, taped conversation with the author, Watertown, Massachusetts, June 18, 1996.

3. Scott Smith, taped conversation with the author, South Sutton, New Hampshire, June 22, 1996.

4. Stuart Dawson, taped conversation with the author, Watertown, Massachusetts, December 13, 1988.

5. Stuart Dawson, taped conversations with the author, Watertown, Massachusetts, December 13, 1988, and April 11, 1996.

6. Kenneth DeMay, taped conversation with the author, Watertown, Massachusetts, June 12, 1996.

7. Richard Galehouse, taped conversation with the author, Watertown, Massachusetts, June 3, 1996; and David Hirzel, in a round-table discussion with Kenneth Bassett, James Sukeforth, Don Olson, Nancy Harrod, Alan Ward, and the author, Watertown, Massachusetts, June 26, 1996.

8. Richard Galehouse, in a round-table discussion with Perry Chapman, David Hirzel, and the author, Watertown, Massachusetts, June 27, 1996.

9. Nancy Harrod, taped conversation with the author, Watertown, Massachusetts, June 12, 1996.

10. Alan Ward, taped conversation with the author, Watertown, Massachusetts, June 16, 1996. For one discussion of emerging meeting places in cyberspace, see William J. Mitchell, *City of Bits: Space, Place, and the Infobahn* (Cambridge, Massachusetts: The MIT Press, 1995).

Photography Credits

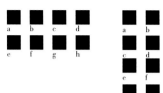

Sasaki Associates
Ambientes Integrados
Por Melanie Simo

En 1988, en ocasión del 35 Aniversario de Sasaki Associados, Pietro Belluschi envió sus felicitaciones junto con algunas memorias de la Firma; "Yo estaba en Cambridge para la época de su nacimiento", escribió al arquitecto urbanista Richard Galehouse, "y he seguido muy de cerca su crecimiento y éxitos, todo debido a una inusual combinación de talentos y sentido común en resolver los múltiples problemas que enfrenta nuestro medio ambiente".[1]

De la visión de un hombre, Hideo Sasaki, la Firma ha crecido a través de una sucesión de asociaciones y entidades corporativas: Sasaki & Novak, Sasaki & Associates, Sasaki, Walter & Associates, Sasaki, Dawson, DeMay Associates, asociados a Sasaki desde 1975, siendo hoy en día una firma planificadora, de diseño multidisciplinario, con oficinas en Boston (Watertown), Dallas, y San Francisco. Sasaki & Associates, es conocido por su trabajo de planificación de campo; diseño urbano; el desarrollo de nuevas comunidades; estudios ambientales y por el diseño de edificios individuales; jardínes; plazas y diseño paisajista, corporativo y comercial; así como por la planificación y diseño de interiores.

La Firma, es también conocida por algunos proyectos específicos que, con el tiempo han llegado a ser "clásicos" de su tipo o época: pequeños y discretos proyectos, tales como el jardín del techo de la Plaza Bonaventura, en Montreal, Quebec (1967) y el Parque Greenacre en Nueva York (1971); porciones significativas de contextos urbanos e institucionales, tales como la Plaza Constitución en Hartford, Conneticut (1959) y la Casa Quincy en la Universidad de Harvard, en Cambridge Massachussets (1959-60); y trabajos a gran escala en tierras sin desarrollo previo, tales como el College Foothill en Los Altos, California (1957-60); El Centro Administrativo de Deere & Company en Moline, Illinois (de 1963); riberas de agua en Boston y Charleston, South Carolina (1973 y 1979). Así como éstos, otros proyectos ejemplares han surgido y han contribuido a la acumulativa y siempre evolutiva identidad de la Firma multidisciplinaria Sasaki Associates.

Quizás menos evidente, es el papel histórico en el desarrollo de las áreas de Planes Maestros de Campus Universitarios y Diseño Urbano. Con su multidisciplinaria organización y sus lazos con el desarrollo de la teoría de post-guerra de Harvard y MIT, Sasaki Associates ha sido uno de los centros más importantes de experimentos para Planificación y Diseño en los Estados Unidos y en el extranjero. En adición se continúa la práctica y la enseñanza, lo que esbozamos más adelante. La Compañía ha ampliado la visión de dos generaciones de Arquitectos Paisajistas (colegas y estudiantes de Sasaki) quienes han trabajado con Arquitectos, Ingenieros y Planificadores en el mayor desarrollo de la postguerra, tanto de Instituciones, como del Gobierno y de la Industria.

En *Planificación de Campus* (1963) y *Diseño Ambiental* (1969), Richard Dober documentó su trabajo (por la Firma Sasaki y otras Firmas) con planos, fotografías y descripciones. Dober, fue alumno de Kevin Lynch en MIT y un colega en la firma Sasaki, y en estos trabajos él también pone de manifiesto algo del idealismo (así como el pragmatismo) que fortalecen estos esfuerzos de la postguerra, en el Planeamiento de Campus y Diseño Urbano. La apertura del Centro Conjunto para Estudios Regionales y Urbanos en MIT y Harvard, en 1957, fue uno de esos signos de esperanza. En esta época, Belluschi era el Decano de la Escuela de Arquitectura y Planificación en MIT; Josep Lluis Sert era el Decano de la Escuela Post-Grado de Diseño de Harvard. Sasaki, (quien en breve sería nombrado Director de la Escuela de Arquitectura Paisajista en Harvard) trabajó armoniosamente con ambos, en esos años seguros, cuando todo parecía que no había problema que no pudiera ser resuelto por medios racionales y con un verdadero espíritu de colaboración.

Esos eran los años de "heroísmo" o la fase individualista del modernismo, caracterizados por los trabajos de Eero Saarinen, Paul Rudolph, I. M. Pei, Minoru Yamasaki, Gordon Bunshaft y otros, que fueron llamados; los grandes creadores de la forma. Sasaki trabajó con estos hombres y se ganó su respeto, sin aspirar al mismo título de creador de formas. Esto fue aún mas evidente en la planificación de campus, en donde Sasaki trabajó frecuentemente con Belluschi en el diseño de amplios marcos de trabajo en nuevos desarrollos, tal como la expansión de la Universidad de Colorado en Boulder (en 1960). Más acusiosos que la mayoría de diseñadores de la época, tanto Belluschi como Sasaki conceptualizaban, más allá del edificio individual o el espacio claramente definido, al contexto total del proyecto. Ellos buscaban establecer enlaces dentro y fuera de la propiedad del campus. En la locación de las nuevas estructuras, heterogéneas y a veces monumentales y aisladas, se esforzaban por obtener un grado de armonía y unidad en el ambiente.

Por muchos años, este fue el legado de la asociación entre Belluschi, Sasaki y sus colegas, esta huella se puede identificar en trabajos mas recientes de Sasaki Associates, que incluyen la expansión del Western Wyoming College, en Rock Springs; el Interlochen Center for the Arts, en Michigan; y otros proyectos, en donde se sigue esta característica. En todos estos proyectos en colaboración, el diseño de la arquitectura y el lugar, ha evolucionado partiendo de una apreciación general, al gran ambiente natural y cultural.

Con el tiempo, Belluschi hizo una evaluación de los trabajos de Sasaki, centrándose en el ambiente para la construcción: "Todos tienen cualidades convincentes infinitas, las cuales, en mi opinión, prueban que la arquitectura es como un gran Arte de nuestro tiempo, más allá de modas y tendencias."[2] Sasaki se mostró favorable a este punto de vista, y lo paso a sus socios y asociados, conjuntamente con otros valores que él compartía con Belluschi: Respeto por el contexto total; apreciación por lo simple, reserva, proporción, permanencia; y una convicción en el proceso de colaboración. En muchos aspectos, Belluschi se volvió su modelo; Sasaki, también sirvió como "jefe crítico de diseño" dentro de su propia firma, sutilmente dando forma y estructura al ambiente en donde se construye. Sasaki era acusioso en cuanto a la tierra en sí. Su entrenamiento, a pesar de ser variado, estaba centrado en la arquitectura paisajista.

Las personas en su Firma estarían listos a contestar "Oh, Sí, pero él nunca se consideró un Arquitecto Paisajista." De alguna forma esto es cierto, pero la evidencia histórica, archivada en viejos memorandums, en ensayos olvidados y entrevistas transcritas durante muchos años, sugiere lo contrario. El planeamiento y diseño de la tierra, no como una comodidad, pero si como un recurso natural, como asentamiento para la acción humana, y como depósito de la memoria personal y cultural, era fundamental para la visión del fundador, su profesión y su Firma. En la prática, por supuesto, el lado pragmático era enfatizado más a menudo. Tal como Sasaki recordaba al planificador Richard Dober en 1959 (cuando Dober todavía no era Director Ejecutivo de la Firma), "Todos los edificios, ciudades, instituciones, casas, etc., van sobre la tierra. Si nosotros pudiéramos proveer servicios competentes y necesarios, no habría límite en nuestro crecimiento."[3] Un mes antes, Dober había señalado, "nuestra función principal como consultores de diseño, es y debería ser, relacionada con el paisaje y planeamiento de lugares. Una segunda área en la que nos deberíamos involucrar es la de diseño urbano, esto quiere decir; un continuo proceso de evolución de ricos ambientes físicos, ligando lo individual y privado, así como también lo comunal y público.[4]

Como sucedió, Dober y Sasaki no siempre estaban de acuerdo. Sin embargo Sasaki tomaba diversos puntos de vista, civilizadamente, abierto a otras visiones.

Entonces parecía adecuado el introducir la diversidad de puntos de vista, tipos de proyectos y ambiciones de la Firma Sasaki Associates de ese entonces, considerando en primer término la visión de su fundador, un extraordinario y ambicioso joven, quien mas bien era modesto, antes que tímido. El estaba determinado a transformar una profesión que muchas veces parece limitante y algunas hasta letárgica. Pero él, también estaba consciente de sus limitaciones: él no podía hacerlo por sí solo.

En 1953, cuando Sasaki abrió la empresa que luego sería reconocida como Sasaki Associates, él había recorrido un largo camino desde el Valle Central de California, su lugar de nacimiento. En su adolescencia, durante los últimos años de la "gran depresión," su curiosidad intelectual lo había dirigido de sus estudios generales universitarios, a cursos universitarios de negocios y de bellas artes. El también se sentía intrigado acerca del campo de la "Planificación," que lo llevó del sur de California a la Universidad de Berkeley. Allí fue introducido a la Arquitectura y Arquitectura Paisajista, lo mismo que a la Planificación. Una inclinación natural a trabajar con ideas relacionadas con elementos naturales, lo llevó a acercarse más al área de la Arquitectura Paisajista.

Estos estudios, fueron abruptamente interrumpidos en diciembre de 1941, cuando los Estados Unidos entraron a la segunda guerra mundial. Sasaki, pasó un período de tiempo en el campo de reclusión para Japoneses-Americanos en Poston, Arizona. Después de esto, realizó una serie de trabajos en y alrededor de Denver y Chicago, los que lo condujeron a completar sus estudios en Arquitectura Paisajista en la Universidad de Illinois en Champaign-Urbana, después de la guerra en 1946. En este entonces, las fábricas estaban en una rápida transición de tiempos de guerra a tiempos de paz, y los recursos y la voluntad de planificar y construir eran evidentes. Después de recibir su licenciatura en Bellas Artes, "suma cum laude," Sasaki recibió una beca para un trabajo de post-grado en Harvard. Hasta este punto, parecía que él estaba conduciéndose por los canales apropiados para asumir una responsable posición en una buena profesión... Sin embargo, él tenía ciertas reservas.

En la Universidad de Illinois, Sasaki estudió con profesores maduros y altamente competentes, incluyendo al arquitecto paisajista y planificador; Karl B. Lohmann, y Harland Bartholomew, (quién tomo un año de su práctica en planificación para enseñar). El profesor de Arquitectura Paisajista, Stanley White había trabajado para "Olmsted Brothers" en Bookline, y después brevemente en proyectos de planificación en el nuevo pueblo de Greendale, Wisconsin bajo patrocinio del Gobierno Federal. A través de sus estudios y trabajos a medio tiempo para Lobman, Sasaki observó como la continuidad en planificación y diseño podrían operarse relativamente a gran escala, entre profesionales que hubiesen consolidado sus propias carreras sobre una base de estudios en Arquitectura Paisajista. Sasaki estudió cuidadosamente por su cuenta los escritos de Frederick Law Olmsted, encontrando en ellos precedentes para planificación y diseño de "sistemas de parques extensos en las ciudades," en Boston, Buffalo, Chicago y en otros lugares. En conjunto, con la percepción del valor socio-cultural y psicológico del área diseñada en cualquier escala, ya fuera pública o privada.[5]

Pero si los profesores de Olmsted e Illinois se encontraban lo suficientemente confiados, los miembros de la Sociedad Americana de Arquitectos Paisajistas, no lo estaban. En ellos, Sasaki percibió un cierto sentido de inferioridad de los Arquitectos Paisajistas, ante los Arquitectos e Ingenieros. Este hecho lo condujo a escribir el ensayo: "El complejo de inferioridad y los Arquitectos Paisajistas". Nunca fué publicado, pero su determinación a cambiar este estado de cosas permaneció con él, aún en Harvard. De hecho, esta determinación se intensificó más.

En Illinois, Sasaki había conocido educadores y practicantes que habían hecho la transición de los métodos de Bellas Artes de Planificación y Diseño, a intentos frescos para tratar con problemas urgentes del ambiente contemporáneo, sin temores acerca de la teoría modernista de la expresión formal. White, un hombre educado liberalmente, versado en artes y ciencias, con énfasis en diseño a gran escala y diseño a la medida exacta, sin ataduras a teorías ni ideas preconcebidas. Sin embargo en Harvard, el Modernismo era un punto de discusión. En la Escuela de Graduados de Diseño, Walter Gropius y sus antiguos estudiantes representaban una fuerza revolucionaria, basada en ideas estéticas y sociales definidas previamente en Bauhaus. Esto le dió energía a los estudiantes de la post-guerra, presentando una postura de amenaza para la vieja generación de educadores en la Arquitectura Paisajista. En ésta época, la Arquitectura Paisajista todavía estaba siendo impartida en una "cierta forma clásica", recordaba Sasaki. Planeamiento de ciudades era un departamento separado (había surgido de unos pocos cursos de Planificación, impartidos inicialmente en el Departamento de Arquitectura Paisajista). Mientras tanto, en Arquitectura, por lo menos desde el final de los años treinta, los estudiantes habían venido luchando con problemas de renovación urbana, vivienda, nuevas comunidades, etc. En ese ambiente, Sasaki se sentía atraído hacia los estudiantes, en la facultad de Arquitectura y Planificación. El escuchaba atentamente las conferencias de Gropius, y aprendió mucho de sus compañeros estudiantes de Arquitectura, quienes más adelante le traerían comisiones para Planificación y Diseño de espacios.[6]

Después de recibir su título de Master en Arquitectura Paisajista, de Harvard, en 1948, Sasaki pasó otros cinco años ganando experiencia en la práctica y la enseñanza antes de montar su propia oficina en las cercanías de Harvard, en 1953. El trabajó en las dos oficinas de Skidmore Owings & Merrill (SOM) en Chicago y en Nueva York, y enseñó en las Universidades de Harvard e Illinois. Paralelamente, él trabajó con el Planificador Reginald Isaacs en proyectos de renovación urbana y esfuerzos de investigación dentro y alrededor de Chicago. Fue Isaacs quien como el nuevo Director de Planificación de Ciudades y Arquitectura Paisajista de Harvard, hizo volver a Sasaki a enseñar ahí en 1953. Y fué a Isaacs a quién Sasaki hizo su primera proposición de transformar la profesión de Arquitectura Paisajista, empezando con Educación Profesional en Harvard, en donde muchas de las próximas generaciones de Educadores y Profesionales podrían ganar sus grados académicos avanzados. Entre otras cosas, Sasaki recomendó un nuevo balance entre personalidades, habilidades y conocimientos académicos, la clase de balance que él también buscaría dentro de su Firma. Idealmente debería haber por lo menos cuatro Instructores, (a tiempo parcial y a tiempo completo): "Un hombre de genio creativo; una persona productiva y llena de energía; uno altamente técnico y uno más moderado." El hombre de genio creativo, sería alguien del calibre de Roberto Burle-Marx. El moderado, sería Sasaki.[7]

Los detalles de los esfuerzos de Sasaki de transformar la Educación Profesional y la práctica, en Arquitectura Paisajista, se dan en cualquier lugar. En resumen, un colega cercano, Charles W. Harris, escribió: "bajo el liderazgo de Hideo Sasaki, la década de cambio evolucionario (1958-1968) casi tuvo un impacto revolucionario sobre los máximos programas educacionales y oficinas profesionales,"[8] estas transformaciones dependieron de una sola y simbiótica relación. Mientras era Director del Departamento de Arquitectura Paisajista de 1958 a 1968, Sasaki apoyó el Departamento con Instructores a medio tiempo y recursos financieros de su Firma. El, enriqueció ambas cosas; la enseñanza y el proceso de aprendizaje, induciendo a Profesionales activos y a Especialistas en nuevos campos, (tales como la interpretación de fotos aéreas y aplicaciones en computadoras), a enseñar por períodos cortos. A los estudiantes más prometedores, se les ofrecía trabajos a medio tiempo en su oficina y empleos después de su graduación. Durante este tiempo, se les solicitaba enseñar a medio tiempo, (por poca o ninguna paga), dando de esta forma alguna retribución a la institución que los había formado.

En este proceso, las barreras tradicionales entre la práctica y la enseñanza se volvieron permeables, aún con las diferencias tradicionales entre Arquitectos Paisajistas, Arquitectos, Planificadores, Ingenieros, y otros, estas barreras se volvieron menos agudas, en algunos momentos, hasta irrelevantes. Como Sasaki destacó recientemente en una visita reciente a Sasaki Associates, "en esa época, cuando había un espíritu investigador y excitante, ya fuera con Arquitectos o Arquitectos Paisajistas, no importaba con quien se estaba trabajando, algunos eran generosos en conceder el mérito por alguna obra, nosotros trabajábamos juntos para alcanzar la solución que creíamos era la más apropiada o creativa para una situación particular."[9]

Con su característica modestia, Sasaki ha descrito la evolución de su Firma multidisciplinaria como algo natural, llevándose a cabo sin un plan definido, pero con un sentido de las posibilidades abiertas para equipos de diferentes adiestramientos, profesionales de altas destrezas, unidos en su creencia de que un mejor ambiente podía, (y debía), ser creado. Gropius, por mucho tiempo había apoyado el ideal colaboracionista de Bauhaus y desde las postrimerías de 1945 se había comprometido con sus antiguos estudiantes en la nueva Firma. Los Arquitectos Colaboracionistas (TAC). Poco tiempo después, TAC había atraído gente de diferentes disciplinas, así como SOM lo había hecho en el pasado. La característica más notable de este precedente, sin embargo, era que la Firma Sasaki habia sido fundada sobre las bases de la Arquitectura Paisajista. Esta base, según creía Sasaki, permitió a la multidisciplinaria Firma avanzar más allá de la tradición que creció directamente de la Revolución Industrial y la mecanicanización. Para muchos modernistas inspirados por libros como "La Mecanización toma mando" (1948) de Siegfried Giedon, "la naturaleza era algo para tocar superficialmente" según recuerda Sasaki, "Pero nuestra concepción era que la naturaleza es para trabajar en conjunto con nuestra economía."[10]

En poco tiempo Sasaki contrató Planificadores, Diseñadores Gráficos y Diseñadores de espacio, pero eventualmente, conforme a la demanda de clientes permanentes, también se comenzó a diseñar edificios. Con el tiempo, los Ingenieros se encontraron con complejos problemas técnicos, tales como los muros de contención de riberas urbanas y el impacto, a largo plazo en el estado del medio ambiente, de 1970 en adelante. En esta década, otro cambio de rumbo de la práctica común en Firmas multidisciplinarias fué evidente; el acuerdo principal de promover, cuando menos a un Profesional en cada una de las disciplinas de las Firmas, a un nivel de Director, Accionista y partícipe en la toma de decisiones.

Para 1970 Sasaki ya no escribía para publicaciones. En sus pocos artículos publicados, virtualmente todos de 1950, Sasaki, esbozó la gama de oportunidades específicas para Arquitectos Paisajistas, desde el Planeamiento Ambiental hasta el Diseño Urbano. "Se necesita que haya un estudio ecológico, basado en las fuerzas naturales operando desde el lugar o área a ser planificada," escribió en 1953."Ese estudio, deberá determinar cómo las formas culturales deberán ser ajustadas favorablemente a las fuerzas naturales, de tal modo que las variadas tensiones ecológicas operantes, deberán ser tomadas de manera que estimulen la creación de una mejor forma-diseño, de la que podemos evidenciar en nuestro escenario actual." En 1955, él subrayó la dimensión cultural: "El Arquitecto Paisajista puede contribuir con sus destrezas y, junto con otros, puede crear un buen medio ambiente, no solamente en términos de funcionamiento económico, sino como una expresión visual satisfactoria, la cual en algunos aspectos es la medida del logro cultural de una civilización."[11]

En los años cincuenta, mientras él y su Firma trabajaban en proyectos en Boston, Filadelfia y Chicago, Sasaki señaló algunos de los problemas urbanos más fundamentales. La ciudad se encontraba amenazada en su función y expresión cultural, escribió él en 1955. En 1956, él específicamente se pronunció acerca del nuevo campo de Diseño Urbano. "El Arquitecto Paisajista, debido a su conocimiento especializado, deberá contribuir significativamente al campo del Diseño Urbano...El deberá, conjuntamente con el Planificador, determinar los aspectos relacionados con el uso de la tierra y deberá, más adelante, determinar el diseño estructural y la forma del proyecto en general."[12]

En abril de 1956, una conferencia sobre Diseño Urbano en la Escuela de Graduados de Diseño de Harvard, reunió a Richard Neutra, Garrett Eckbo, Jane Jacobs, Lewis Mumford, Charles Abrams, Edmund Bacon, Charles Eliot y otros, en la búsqueda de una base común para un trabajo conjunto de Arquitectos, Arquitectos paisajistas y Planificadores. El anfitrión, Dean Sert, estaba en ese entonces colaborando con la Firma Sasaki en unos proyectos en Harvard, involucrando estos; Diseño Urbano y Planificación y Diseño de Campus Universitarios, tales como el Centro Holyoke, el edificio de vivienda para estudiantes casados, el Centro para el Estudio de Religiones del Mundo, y otros. En esta conferencia, Sert enfatizó la necesidad de equipos má grandes de especialistas para resolver problemas de Diseño Urbano. " Después de muchos años de trabajo individual y aislado, estamos llegando lógicamente a una era de síntesis", señaló él. El Diseño Urbano es el "más creativo", aún siendo el menos explorado en las fases del planeamiento de la ciudad, debería efectuarse por su medio, una recentralización de la ciudad, hacia lo cuál, Sert estaba comprometido. Desde su punto de vista, la ciudad era un contribuyente a la grandeza de América, no solamente como un lugar de negocios, sino también como un centro de cultura y aprendizaje.[13]

Sasaki aprovechó esta ocasión para enfatizar ciertos desarrollos desordenados de los tiempos modernos. El lamentó la falta de significado en el conformismo del estilo arquitectónico (de conformar el presente, lo mismo que en eras pasadas), a lo cual llamó "eclecticismo sin significado." También era inquietante la "monumentalidad sin significado," o falta de escala. Sasaki observó que edificios de una escala tecnológica, podrían expresar una dimensión nunca observada anteriormente; pero eran los seres humanos quienes tendrían que habitarlos y comprender estas estructuras. Un tercer desarrollo desordenado, era la falta de relación con los alrededores. Una vez tomando conciencia de estos contornos, se podría escoger el actuar humildemente o por el contrario, con audacia y osadía. Sin embargo, el buscar lo espectacular por pura novedad era, para él, un concepto detestable.[14] Estos puntos (muchos de ellos extractados de las páginas de "Progressive Arquitecture"), ofrecen una penetración al razonamiento, al pensamiento analítico y la sensibilidad humana del fundador de Sasaki y Asociados.

Verdaderamente, los aspectos humanos de su práctica en Planificación y Diseño fueron determinantes para Sasaki. La armonía y totalidad que él buscaba sacar del gran medio ambiente, también fueron cualidades que él trató de mantener en su Firma. Esto era muy difícil y un asunto muy delicado, (como él libremente admitía), porque los talentosos individuos que él reunía a su alrededor eran a menudo hombres de personalidad fuerte y temperamento volátil. Siempre, muy cautelosos por sus propias limitaciones y compromisos, Sasaki escogió como segundo en mando al Arquitecto Paisajista Paul Gardescu, una persona calmada e imparcial de reconocida integridad. Por más de veinte años como Director Ejecutivo, luego como Presidente, Gardescu atendió relaciones humanas, contratos, y otros aspectos poco notorios del negocio del diseño, con ecuanimidad y una actitud de apertura hacia otras culturas, que todavía son recordados con cariño por sus colegas, en Sasaki Associates.

Sasaki se retiró en 1980 aunque permanece como consultor de la Firma. Gardescu se retiró en 1984, después de lo cual, James A. Sukeforth, C.P.A. y M.B.A., fue elegido Presidente, cargo en el cual sirvió por nueve años. Por razones de su propia admisión, Sukeforth no podía dirigir la Firma por sí solo; él, más bien tenía que crear un balance entre su propio liderazgo financiero, con el liderazgo profesional en las cuatro direcciones de las disciplinas: Richard Galehouse, en Planificación; Kenneth Basset, en Arquitectura Paisajista; John Orcutt, en Arquitectura y Maurice Freedman, en Ingeniería. "Nosotros cinco, esencialmente dirigimos la organización." Expresaba Sukerforth.[15] Después de que él salió de la Presidencia, al finales de 1992, una nueva fórmula de balance fue aplicada; Kenneth Basset, asumió la Presidencia, pero continuó reuniéndose frecuentemente con su predecesor. Bassett y Sukeforth ocupan ahora oficinas contiguas.

Bassett, actualmente Presidente de Sasaki, se desplaza fácilmente de un tipo de proyecto a otro dentro de la Firma. El se siente orgulloso de su habilidad para escuchar, así como también el de su habilidad para comprender el amplio marco estructural de una situación específica, y así poder llevar hacia adelante la herencia de Sasaki, bajo sus propios términos: "Nuestra cultura ha nacido del balance de dos disciplinas", es una cultura en la cual debe de haber un poco de *mano libre*, lo mejor surgirá de un lugar como éste, cuando le das un sitio de descanso, a personas que están muy embebidas por la disciplina en que se encuentran. Pero al mismo tiempo tienes que hacerlos volver gentilmente a su lugar y decirles: También hay un todo aquí adentro. Tú tienes que templar tu comportamiento, tu actitud y tu forma de trabajar para reconocer que si todos estamos juntos, somos un equipo y tendrás que seguir las reglas del juego, no puedes dirigir este lugar en una forma rígida, se debe hacer prestando atención a un indeterminado número de intereses distintos. Me gusta eso," dice él.[16]

En las páginas siguientes, conocerán más acerca de los directores actuales de Sasaki Associates, y por sus propias palabras, interpretaremos el trabajo y la visión de la Firma. A continuación tres perspectivas del legado de Sasaki, que podrían servir como resumen: Una mezcla de filosofía, ambición y relaciones humanas. El Arquitecto Planificador David Hirzel, recuerda conversaciones con Arquitectos que amaban trabajar con Hideo en sus primeros años. "Ellos afirmaban cuán refrescante era trabajar con alguien que creía en la colaboración, la participación y el apoyo, como algo opuesto a la competencia. Los grandes egos de los Arquitectos, estaban muy contentos de tener ésto. Estos rasgos de Hideo reflejaban quién se quedaba y quién no. Aquellos que querían hacer lo correcto y poder tener su propio nombre, en la puerta que atraviesa este lugar."[17]

Peter Walker, un Arquitecto Paisajista que se retiró de la Firma, recuerda con orgullo: "Como Thomas Church, en su taller de San Francisco, introdujo el modernismo en el campo de la Arquitectura

Paisajista en los años treintas y cuarentas, la óptica Neo-Olmstediana de Hideo, ha definido el propósito, la forma y la naturaleza de la práctica del paisajismo para todos desde 1955, aceptando el reto de la gran expansión de la post-guerra. El ideal Bauhausiano de que la colaboración en el Diseño iguala, es pocas veces alcanzado en una base únicamente de Arquitectura. Ha sido tratado de alcanzar por cuatro generaciones de Arquitectos Paisajistas, Arquitectos, Planificadores e Ingenieros, y persiste hasta ahora en Sasaki Associates. Es un sueño sustentado en un mundo bellamente construido, visto como un todo.[18]

Don Olson un Arquitecto Paisajista que se quedó en la Firma, en 1981 observó: "No muchas compañías han seguido nuestras huellas, tampoco nosotros las de ellos. Las oficinas que ya existían antes que nosotros, presumiblemente estaban en una mejor posición para responder a las mismas oportunidades de crecimiento. Sin embargo, parece que las cualidades especiales de el ser humano son esenciales para poder lograr ésto." [19]

Planificación de Campus Universitarios

"La Planificación de una Universidad se basa en que, en ella se preserva la conexión entre el saber y el gusto por la vida, a través de unificar lo antiguo y lo moderno, considerando la parte creativa del aprendizaje. La Universidad provee la información, en una forma imaginativa... Un hecho no se considera concreto, sin involucrar todas sus posibilidades. Ya no es solamente una carga en la memoria; es revitalizante como el Poeta de nuestro sueños, y como el Arquitecto de nuestros propósitos."
—Alfred North Whitehead

Esta cita, fue usada como el épigrafe del Plan Maestro de la Universidad Estatal de Cleveland, el 28 de junio de 1968. Sasaki, Dawson, DeMay Associates (SDDA), trabajaron en éste plan con los Arquitectos Don. M. Hisaka & Associates. Del Plan Maestro, la firma de Sasaki pasó a proporcionar servicios Arquitectónicos Paisajistas para un nuevo edificio de Educación Física y a diseñar una nueva plaza para un nuevo Centro Universitario. Esta fue una obra grande en aquel entonces. Vale la pena agregar esta experiencia a la impresionante historia de Sasaki Associates en Planificación y Diseño de Campus Universitarios, en donde se aplicaron las ideas trascendentales de la función universitaria, según fueron articuladas por Whitehead, y posteriormente redescubiertas, como una expresión de los valores, en la Firma Sasaki.

M. Perry Chapman, era entonces un joven Arquitecto Planificador, que había sido contratado por la Firma Sasaki en 1964, para trabajar inicialmente en el Plan Maestro de la Universidad de Rochester. En poco tiempo, él se encontró inmerso en las complejidades del Planeamiento y Diseño de Campus Universitarios, siendo esta área, la de más rápido crecimiento en la práctica de la Firma, en los años sesentas. Treinta años más tarde, cuando Chapman decidió escribir un ensayo acerca de la Planificación de Campus Universitarios, en los Estados Unidos durante la post-guerra, entrevistó a Sasaki y escribió un bosquejo que comenzaba con la época prolífica de los sesentas. Un editor lo indujo a comenzar el escrito abarcando períodos anteriores. " Cuando comencé a profundizar en los años cincuentas, me di cuenta que hechos muy significativos e interesantes habían ocurrido en Diseño de Campus en esa época," recuerda Chapman.[1]

El ensayo de Chapman, *"El cambio social y el Diseño de Campus Universitario Americano"* (1994), eventualmente lo llevó hacia a un estudio completo del tamaño de un libro.[2] En éste se podía notar las contribuciones de la Firma Sasaki. Poco tiempo después de que Hideo Sasaki comenzó su enseñanza en Harvard en 1953-54, invitó al nuevo Decano en MIT, Pietro Belluschi, para observar qué era lo que él y sus estudiantes estaban haciendo en Harvard. Belluschi aceptó la invitación y encontró en Sasaki un espíritu semejante al suyo, empezó a buscar la asistencia de Sasaki en proyectos que le llegaban, primordialmente para Campus Universitarios. Las universidades estaban en ese entonces experimentando un crecimiento fenomenal, debido en parte, a la presencia de veteranos que estaban estudiando amparados bajo la declaración de los Derechos del Soldado. Belluschi se había reinstalado en Cambridge, sin tener una oficina propia, después de haber ejercido una significativa práctica en Portland, Oregon. A finales de los años cincuentas y principios de los sesentas, él trabajó con oficinas asociadas de Arquitectos, tales como: Robinson, Green & Beretta, en el proyecto del nuevo desarrollo de edificios para residencias estudiantiles en la Escuela de Diseño de Rhode Island (RISD), y en la oficina de Carl Koch, en la nueva biblioteca de Bennington College. En cada uno de estos casos, Belluschi involucró a su amigo Hideo Sasaki como Arquitecto Paisajista.

Los Presidentes de éstas y otras Instituciones, pronto solicitaron asesoramiento sobre los grandes problemas del crecimiento y planificación de los Campus Universitarios. Belluschi contactó a Sasaki en su pequeña oficina de entonces, contrataron personal y formalizaron estas investigaciones, organizando el equipo multidisciplinario requerido para afrontar problemas tales como infraestructura, estacionamiento, área peatonal, y locación de edificaciones.

Algunos estudios conjuntos entre las Escuelas de Diseño y las de Educación, en Harvard, habían comenzado a explorar la relación entre programación educacional y planeamiento físico tri-dimensional. El trabajo de la Firma Sasaki surgió en el resultado de estas exploraciones: Para Sasaki y algunos de sus colegas en esto: Richard Dober, Jack Robinson, Kenneth DeMay, y Don Olson, quienes también eran estudiantes o instructores parciales en la Escuela de Diseño, Sasaki aportó destrezas en organización y práctica en la edificación a estos estudios. El también visualizó su empresa, en cierto modo, como una escuela, en donde el marco exploratorio de la mente y el interés pragmático en la búsqueda, eran algo crítico para manejar los problemas repentinos en el Planeamiento de Campus Universitarios: crecimiento rápido, continuidad histórica, infraestructura y equipamiento de edificaciones y el control de la calidad visual en la Arquitectura en el paisaje. Se usaron varios modelos en la contratación de personal por Consultores y Autoridades Universitarias. Se desarrolló un proceso en la determinación del programa de construcción. Se formaron Comités Consultores dentro de la Universidad, para revisar las diferentes etapas del trabajo. El punto focal ya no eran únicamente los edificios, sino los conjuntos, las secuencias, la circulación y los espacios abiertos. Un nuevo marco para el desarrollo había surgido.

Los resultados de estas investigaciones se acumularon, formando un conjunto de teoría y datos, que fue usado por Dober para escribir *Campus Planning* (1963). Cuando Chapman leyó este libro, poco tiempo después de su publicación, quedó intrigado. El libro tuvo un impacto tal, que fue comparado con el que causaron el de Jane Jacob: *The Life and Death of Great American Cities* (1961)y el de Gordon Cullens: *Townscape* (1961).

Estos trabajos ampliarion el horizonte de la persona, mientras la regresaban a los pequeños e importantes detalles de la vida diaria. Ellos ofrecieron el gran cuadro y la pequeña viñeta, los ideales sustentados y los hechos. Estos conceptos permearon rápidamente las Profesiones del Diseño.

La magnitud y frescura del nuevo trabajo en Planificación de Campus y Diseño hizo que de inmediato Sasaki ganara rápidamente reputación a nivel nacional, su planificación física y diseño comprensivos y al mismo tiempo humanos, se volvieron de mucha demanda. La Firma creció ganando la atracción de graduados de Harvard, MIT, y otras Escuelas. Después de algunos años, en la oficina de Watertown, algunos de estos Planificadores y Diseñadores jóvenes se mudaron a empleos en sus regiones nativas. Unos dejaron la Firma para dedicarse a la enseñanza. Otros aceptaron trabajos dentro de Instituciones y después regresaron a Sasaki Associates, para ayudarles a cumplir con las nuevas responsabilidades de planificación.[3]

Los Planificadores y Diseñadores jóvenes, que se quedaron en la oficina de Sasaki, trabajaron en algunos proyectos excepcionales de Campus Universitarios nuevos y en otros ya existentes, en varias regiones de los Estados Unidos lo mismo que en Canadá. Por ejemplo FootHill College, en Los Altos, California, se volvió prototipo para algo más que una colección de edificios académicos. Empezando en 1957, Sasaki y sus colegas trabajaron de cerca con los Arquitectos Ernest J, Kump & Associates, y Masten and Hurd, para integrar los espacios abiertos y los edificios de Foothill, a las renovadas cumbres de dos colinas. El Teatro, la Biblioteca, el Gimnasio (en donde ocasionalmente ejecuta la Sinfónica de San Francisco), y las plazas y patios; grandes y ceremoniales o pequeñas e íntimas, todas se volvieron sitios de congregación para estudiantes y demás miembros de las comunidades circundantes. Foothill fue conocido en poco tiempo como una verdadera Acrópolis, era según la visión de Allan Temko, un "lugar de altura, consagrado a los altos valores de su joven comunidad. " De esta manera, Foothill sentó las bases para el desarrollo de un nuevo tipo de Institución: los dos primeros años de Universidad que como un "recurso cultural de multiusos" sirviendo a la comunidad y la región.[4]

Después de Foothill College, llegó una larga serie de grandes y complejos proyectos de etapas múltiples en Planificación de campus y el diseño, que comprometerían la Firma Sasaki por muchas décadas. En los tempranos años sesentas, en Sasaki Asociates, se encontraban algunos profesionales jóvenes, cuyos talentos e inclinaciones naturales se adaptaban bien en ese trabajo. Entre éstos, estaban Richard Galehouse y Jack Robinson, quienes habían sido entrenados en ambas disciplinas: Arquitectura y Planificación. Estos hombres, junto con Chapman y Kenneth DeMay, jugaron papeles de liderazgo en el desarrollo de la práctica de la Firma en el planeamiento de campus y su diseño. La Universidad de Colorado, en Boulder, comenzó como un Proyecto Maestro de planificación para la expansión de post-guerra del Campus. Esto condujo a una serie de proyectos arquitectónicos, en colaboración con algunos Arquitectos prominentes, incluyendo a Pietro Belluschi, Harry Weese & Associates, y DeMars and Reay. Junto a éstos, en Colorado surgen las Firmas de William C. Muchow Associates, Hobart D. Wagener & Associates, y otros. Quizás, en retrospectiva, ningún trabajo de campus ganó mayor reconocimiento y número de premios en los primeros años, que Foothill y la Universidad de Colorado. Otros proyectos significativos, llegaron a la Oficina en los años sesentas y setentas, incluyendo la expansión de la Universidad de Massachusetts, en Amherst, nuevos edificios en la Universidad de Rhode Island, en Kingston y la Universidad de Virginia en Charlottesville, así como planes maestros y diseño de edificaciones en el Campus de Amherst de la Universidad Estatal de Nueva York en Buffalo.

Galehouse sirvió de Planificador para algunos de estos proyectos, incluyendo la Universidad de Massachusetts en Amherst, él gustaba de coleccionar historias que narraban las formas como se solucionaban los problemas en el proceso de colaboración entre las personalidades fuertes de estos eminentes profesionales, con diferentes antecedentes. Galehouse ha expresado mucho menos acerca del papel de su permanencia en esos tempranos días, sin embargo, describe a sus famosos colegas, Sasaki y Belluschi como: Dos hombres que compartían un profundo compromiso con la colaboración y parecían enriquecerse con este tipo de ambiente de trabajo. "Belluschi era un caballero, como los de los viejos tiempos," según expresaba Galehouse. Su estilo y destrezas eran asombrosos. Yo creo que realmente disfrutó su relación con Hideo. "Los dos eran unos caballeros."[5]

En varios artículos, Chapman hace notar los mayores logros de la Firma en Planificación de Campus, década por década. En los años cincuentas y a principios de los sesentas, se hicieron Planes Maestros con nuevas estructuras para abrir mas espacios, los cuales a menudo atrajeron comisiones para Diseño de Paisajes lo mismo que para diseño Arquitectónico. A finales de los sesentas, se les encomendaron algunos edificios académicos, independientes de los trabajos de Planes Maestros; y las disciplinas Arquitectónicas, auxiliadas por una gran fortaleza en Ingeniería Civil, pronto surgirían como una gran fuerza con todos sus derechos. En los años setenta, con la acumulación de inquietudes acerca de la guerra en el sur de Asia, la recesión económica, la inflación, la crisis energética y la disminución en las carteras de dotaciones, la Planificación de Campus se apaciguó por un tiempo. A finales de los años setentas algunas Universidades solicitaron asistencia a Sasaki Associates para desarrollar sus tierras circundantes, a fín de acomodar espacios de uso múltiple, (comerciales, corporativos, investigación y desarrollo, etc.), y de esta forma, generar empleo en sus comunidades y así también nuevas fuentes de ingreso.

Los años ochentas y noventas, han traído un retorno al Planeamiento de Campus, a menudo con presupuestos más estrictos y con nuevos intereses: para readaptaciones en su uso, más que nuevas edificaciones; para instalaciones que ayuden los Campus a ser competitivos para estudiante en una época de bajas inscripciones; para una expansión selectiva, más que para los grandes esquemas edificados en áreas verdes; para el uso de materiales mas tradicionales y formas que encajarían en un contexto ya existentes; para un planteamiento de poco mantenimiento y para una mayor seguridad. Sobre todo, se necesitaba una estrategia para integrar las computadoras y otros equipos tecnológicos en los espacios existentes, mientras se alienta a más personal en intercambios de persona a persona, los cuales han estado, tradicionalmente, en el corazón de la vida académica.

Muchos Directores de Sasaki Associates, consideran que en la creación de espacios para reuniones, se disfruten por un simple contacto humano, en cualquier escala, dentro del Campus o fuera de él, es algo que está en el corazón de su práctica multidisciplinaria. A Chapman le gusta citar un Planificador de Ciudades quien recientemente preguntaba: "¿ Por qué no nos podemos concentrar en la necesidad del espacio público, con la misma energía que nos estamos concentrando en la de un espacio cibernético?", Chapman admite que esto es únicamente una anécdota, "Pero yo, creo que ahí hay algo."

Diseño Urbano

Cuando Stuart Dawson presentó una disertación en la Tercera Conferencia Internacional sobre Edificios Altos, en 1986, invitó al público a que se olvidaran por un momento de ésos edificios. Ya hay demasiada atención a la silueta proyectada en el horizonte ¡Demasiada atención al crecimiento individual y de grupo; demasiada atención a un ventanaje único...; a la seguridad...; a los materiales. Demasiado afecto por los automóviles y muy poco interés para la gente en las calles! [1]

El tema de Dawson en esa ocasión, fue la creación de grandes avenidas, específicamente el diseño urbano maestro para el nuevo Distrito de Arte de Dallas, para el cual, él era el Director a cargo. Este proyecto vinculó la transformación de una fría vía pavimentada, recorriendo el centro del Distrito, en el noreste del centro de Dallas, a un gran boulevard con tres carriles, amigable para los peatones. Se le dejó el antiguo nombre de Calle Flora , mientras algunas nuevas estructuras de baja altura, ayudaron a definir y ennoblecer la calle. Se incluyó una sala de conciertos por I.M.Pei, el nuevo Museo de Artes de Dallas, por Edward L. Barnes y lugares para ser usados por pequeños comercios, tales como sitios de entretenimiento y algunos restaurantes, los que fueron intercalados con torres de oficinas, escuelas, la histórica mansión Belo y otras edificaciones. Para explicar la creación de esta gran vía, Dawson proporcionó amplios detalles legales, financieros, horticulturales y arquitectónicos que, cuando fueron adecuadamente coordinados, produjeron un gran espacio para la coexistencia de peatones y automóviles, rascacielos y pequeñas joyas arquitectónicas. La imagen final de Dawson, sin embargo, fue inspirada por el mundo natural. Citando las palabras de William H. Whyte, quien dijo: La calle es el río de vida de la ciudad. Los mejores lugares públicos son aquellos en los cuales usted no sabe en dónde termina la calle y en dónde empieza el lugar. [2]

De hecho, el río es una imagen recurrente en alrededor de cuarenta años de Diseño Urbano en Sasaki Associates. Movimiento sugestivo, continuidad, vitalidad y un marcado paso por las inclinaciones y el ritmo propios de la naturaleza, el río era un elemento natural, literal y metafórico, que llegó a nuestras mentes en los años cincuentas y sesentas, cuando Dawson, Kenneth DeMay, Richard Galehouse, Don Olson, y otros antiguos Directores de entonces en Sasaki Associates, colaboraron en proyectos de Diseño Urbano con los nuevos líderes en ese campo. Por ejemplo, en 1959, la Firma estaba trabajando con Adams, Howard & Greeley; Anderson; Beckwith & Haible y los Consultores Independientes; Kevin Lynch, John R. Myer, y Paul D. Spreiregen, para diseñar el gran marco para varias estructuras a ser construídas en el nuevo Centro de Gobierno de Boston. Conscientes de la tendencia, poco afortunada, para esquemas de renovación urbana que permanecieran aislados de el tejido de la ciudad existente, este grupo de Consultores, enfatizó la integración de lo antiguo y lo moderno, y la secuencia de espacios que podrían ser vistos y experimentados por la gente en movimiento. Los Consultores también hicieron la propuesta de que una cadena de espacios públicos abiertos, que corriera como un río hacia el Valle, entre edificios bajos, y eventualmente ésta se dirigiese al puerto. Más adelante, en un momento de inspiración, alguien se refirió a esta secuencia como: Una caminata hacia el mar. El concepto era interesante, y la frase sobrevivió. [3]

Al paso de los años, la firma Sasaki ha tomado retos aún mas complejos, particularmente durante las décadas en las que miles de regulaciones se aplicaron, en referencia a la protección del medio ambiente y se tomó en cuenta la opinión del publico en general, dentro del proceso de planificación. Pronto surgieron más voces que escuchar y más factores a considerarse. A menudo, tal como en las delicadas negociaciones sobre el reciente proyecto de La Puerta de Entrada a Cleveland (Cleveland Gateway), la Firma fue designada para supervisar la conciliación de los intereses de distintos grupos públicos y privados, antes de que el proceso tradicionalmente conocido como Planificación Urbana, pudiera comenzar. Alan Ward, Diseñador Director para el proyecto de La Puerta de Entrada a Cleveland explicó: Dos Firmas Arquitectónicas fueron seleccionadas al mismo tiempo que nosotros: HOK Sport, para el Estadio de Béisbol y Ellerbe Becket, para la Arena Deportiva. Nosotros eramos la parte coordinadora de las edificaciones en el lugar, de el tráfico y de el estacionamiento, asi como también eramos los representantes del interés público y debíamos actuar como una parte neutral, entre la ciudad, las autoridades responsables del desarrollo y la población. [4]

Problemas de Diseño Urbano, como aquellos de Planeamiento de Campus, tienden a sacar de Sasaki Associates su clásico esfuerzo colaboracional a largo plazo, el cual ellos encuentran muy satisfactorio, y no es sorprendente, que en estos proyectos, tiendan a ser más competitivos. Los problemas tienden a ser grandes, complejos y únicos, demandando destrezas y comprensión que ningún profesional podría ofrecer individualmente. Más bien, el Arquitecto, el Arquitecto Paisajista, el Ingeniero y el Planificador; cada uno, brindaría una solución para superar el problema, para lo cual, no existe ningún precedente.

Sin embargo, sí hay un precedente histórico, por el puro hecho del interés de la Firma y su capacidad para este tipo de proyectos. El precedente no es un proyecto particular, tampoco un momento único en el tiempo; es un acercamiento evolutivo para resolver problemas complejos, en donde no existe ningún profesional, ningún maestro en construcción, ni héroe alguno, en quién se podría confiar para el logro de una gran solución formal. En vez de ésto, un grupo de personas especializadas en diferentes disciplinas, profesionales con respeto mutuo, tienen el deseo común de trabajar unidos, reprimiento su ego, para mejorar el ambiente urbano en su medio

Por supuesto, ningún indivíduo, Firma o país, podría adjudicarse el monopolio en este enfoque. Sin embargo parece que este enfoque ha sido desarrollado en unos pocos lugares, en donde la ambición y los ideales del Diseñador eficiente de un grupo o de una Escuela, podrían ser controlados por los ideales y valores de otro. Un lugar en donde ésto ocurrió, fué en Harvard en los años cincuentas.

Cuando Josep Lluis Ser fue nombrado Decano de la Escuela de Graduados de la Facultad de Diseño en 1953, se efectuó un cambio importante en el estudio para Maestría, que Walter Gropius ofrecía a estudiantes avanzados en Arquitectura; éste se volvió multidisciplinario. Algunos de los mejores estudiantes de Arquitectura Paisajista de Hideo Sasaki y los mejores estudiantes en Planificación de Ciudades, de Reginald Isaacs se unieron después a estudiantes avanzados de Arquitectura en la investigación de los problemas más complejos de Arquitectura, esencialmente, aquellos de Diseño Urbano. Este estudio de Maestría, más tarde se volvió el modelo para el nuevo Programa de Diseño Urbano de la Escuela, establecido en el período comprendido entre 1960 y 1961, como un área de especialización para estudiantes avanzados en Arquitectura y Arquitectura Paisajista. El Programa reclutó estudiantes de todos los Estados Unidos y del extranjero, y sus graduados encontraron empleos en oficinas de Diseño en las cercanías de Harvard y en el área de Boston, en la oficina de Sasaki especialmente.

Debido a la naturaleza multidisciplinaria de la oficina y su creciente reputación en la Planificación de Campus, Renovación Urbana y Diseño Físico, algunos de los estudiantes de Diseño Urbano de Harvard trabajaban en la oficina, a tiempo parcial y unos pocos, eran invitados a unirse a la Firma. En ésta época, los Planificadores en la oficina, incluyendo a Richard Dober, John Adelberg y Richard Galehouse, tenían todos experiencia, primordialmente en Arquitectura. Estos Planificadores trabajaban con graduados del Programa de Diseño Urbano, tales como Masao Kinoshita. En el proceso, los elementos físicos y programáticos del nuevo campo del Diseño Urbano estaban integrados o fusionados. En adición a ésto, con la Escuela como una base teórica y la oficina Sasaki como un centro de práctica, el campo del Diseño Urbano se encontraba redefiniéndose continuamente, según surgían nuevos problemas.

Ahora, cuando vemos hacia atrás, después de varias décadas de Diseño Urbano de Sasaki Associates, en numerosas ciudades desde Boston hasta Dallas y desde Postdam hasta Taipei, podríamos trazar una creciente complejidad de factores integrados, y aún así, reconocer alguna continuidad en la visión amplia y en la visión cercana. La ciudad todavía es vista como un lugar que necesita estructuras, patrones, contrastes y una poderosa imagen memorable. La ciudad todavía es un lugar en donde uno trata de crear secuencias de espacios y panoramas, para ser experimentados en una escala humana; a pie, igual que en la carretera, y lo mismo que desde el aire. En 1963 cuando Hideo Sasaki le envió a Edmund Bacon (un Planificador de Ciudades de Filadelfia) una serie de sugerencias para el mejoramiento de las riberas de zonas acuáticas de esa ciudad, éstos iban acompañados de unos fluídos bosquejos, preparados por la oficina. El enfatizó en la trayectoria y la continua calidad del río Schuylkill. La gente podría sentarse o pasear a lo largo de un sendero especialmente diseñado para este fín, con pasos peatonales para atravesar la línea férrea y con sitios de reposo en áreas y campos tranquilos. En el fondo habría densas hileras de árboles, las cuales definirían ambas; las orillas del río y el tejido urbano. [5]

Recientemente, algunas teorías de Diseño Urbano han fijado su atención en desarrollos habitacionales tradicionales; el Urbanismo Nuevo . Estos son esfuerzos concienzudos, a menudo impulsados por fuertes propósitos sociológicos y ambientalistas, para mencionar sólo algunas de las tendencias que eran nuevas hace sesenta o setenta años. Estos son enfoques modernos al Diseño Urbano. Para Alan Ward, un Arquitecto que estudió en Harvard Arquitectura Paisajista y Diseño Urbano, a fines de los setentas, antes de unirse a la firma Sasaki Associates, parecían existir más precedentes para estos nuevos prototipos de Diseño Urbano, que los que las actuales teorías podrían sugerir. Cada época quiere hacer su propia revolución y así poder decir, estamos comenzándola. Pero actualmente, hay mucha continuidad en la materia, observó Ward.

Al recordar el trabajo de Frederick Law Olmsted con Calvert Vaux, en Riverside, Illinois (1869), y el trabajo de Sir Raymon Unwin con Barry Parker, en Letchworth, Hertfordshire, en Inglaterra (1904), Ward detectó una evolución del pensamiento de la Planificación y el Diseño Urbano. El cree que existe una amenaza que nace desde el trabajo de Olmsted, Unwin y los Arquitectos Paisajistas Planificadores de principios de siglo: John Nolen, Elbert Peets y otros, llegando hasta las postrimerías de este siglo con los trabajos de Sasaki Associates y sus contemporáneos, con los diseños de nuevas comunidades. El rompimiento dramático, con este desarrollo evolutivo, ocurre dentro del movimiento moderno, en los prototipos más revolucionarios de Le Corbusier y otros. Este movimiento, nunca fué tan homogéneo como algunos lo visualizan, en una percepción tardía, sus soluciones a los problemas de Diseño Urbano eran variadas. Aún ahora, los éxitos y fracasos del Diseño Urbano Moderno, todavía continúan siendo evaluados.

Mientras tanto, Ward se muestra interesado en problemas más a la mano, no los ideológicos, pero si los concretos, poniendo más urgencia en aquellos de la ciudad existente en América o en cualquier otro lugar del planeta. El verdadero problema, cree él es cómo reparar básicamente la ciudad actual. Si usted observa el Urbanismo Americano como un experimento, parecería que han transcurrido varios cientos de años, empezando con el asentamiento en el Oeste. A través de los años, nos hemos, simplemente mudado a las afueras y agrandado la ciudad, tratando de mejorar el pasado, en lugar de situar la ciudad en él, tal como han hecho en Europa, desde hace mucho tiempo. Yo creo que ha llegado la hora de establecer algunos límites y decir: Corrijamos los primeros y fallidos experimentos y tratemos de hacer lo correcto. En esta forma, se puede tratar de reconstruir la ciudad existente, procurando reforzar un sentido de comunidad en los ambientes públicos. Si tu puedes hacer ese ambiente más denso y urbanizado, el espacio público se volvería más importante. Esto, es parte de nuestro trabajo por hacer.

Ward vacila a medida que más problemas y más oportunidades se le vienen a la mente; ecológicas, sociológicas y artísticas. Siento, que el problema fundamental por venir, es el cómo nuestra cultura se relaciona con la naturaleza. Yo, todavía pienso que en ésto radica el reto que enfrentamos. [6]

Comunidades Nuevas

"Viajando a través de la Costa Atlántica de Maine a Florida no se encuentra otro lugar como éste. Playas arenosas se extienden ininterrumpidamente por kilómetros y kilómetros y atrás de las dunas de arena, se hallan extensiones incontables de pantanos de agua salada, adornados por ensenadas serpenteantes y bahías de poca profundidad... Explorar la costa Este de Virginia es como regresar en el tiempo y visitar una generación en donde la vida estaba unida a la tierra y las familias eran mantenidas por las dádivas del suelo y el mar" –Curtis Badger para, *The Nature Conservancy*

Hace alrededor de cinco años, Sasaki Associates comenzó a contribuir a una serie continua de esfuerzos de planificación, que dio inicio "The Nature Conservancy" con el fín de mantener los ámbitos naturales tradicionales (habitats) tanto del hombre como de la abundante vida silvestre de la Costa Este de Virginia. Estos esfuerzos de planificación abarcan alrededor de 45,000 acres conformadas por una barrera de islas; pantanos de agua salada y tierras altas a lo largo de la Costa Atlántica de la Península de Delmarva. Esta área se encuentra ahora bajo un programa de estudio excepcional el cual no proviene únicamente de grupos de ciudadanos locales, sino también de Comisiones de Planificación; Grupos de Negocios; Consejos de Turismo; Fideicomisos Habitacionales y el Capítulo Local de la NAACP. En 1979 Las Naciones Unidas declararon la Costa Este de Virginia una "Reserva Biósfera Internacional"; en esencia, un modelo de cómo los seres humanos pueden vivir en armonía con la naturaleza. La organización "The Nature Conservancy" ha definido este ecosistema excepcional como "Un último y grandioso lugar." Una frase con insinuaciones de maravilla, deleite y quizás también de presentimiento y urgencia.

Las contribuciones de Sasaki Associates a los esfuerzos de "The Nature Conservancy" en la Reserva Natural de la Costa de Virginia se describen en términos de estrategias, prototipos, pautas de diseño, etc. Aún inéditas se encuentran las convicciones personales del Director Principal involucrado: David Hirzel quien ha desempeñado diferentes cargos administrativos y profesionales desde que se unió a la firma en 1969. Entonces era un joven Arquitecto graduado de Harvard con una Maestría en Bellas Artes. Ahora es uno de los socios Directores de Sasaki más elocuentes en la materia de la defensa del medio ambiente. Como ponente en la conferencia del AIA sobre Defensa del Medio Ambiente en 1994, Hirzel enfatizó el vasto número de iniciativas dentro de los programas de "The Nature Conservancy" a lo largo de la Costa Este de Virginia con el fin de proteger desde los lugares más frágiles, hasta alcanzar el mejoramiento de la economía familiar a través de la pesca, la agricultura, el arte, las artesanías y las pequeñas industrias. "Nosotros hemos aprendido que ningún proyecto por sí sólo, puede cumplir con todo," les recordaba a sus compañeros arquitectos. Cada proyecto ofrece la oportunidad de dar un paso hacia adelante, para alcanzar la meta. "Como profesionales enfocados en el planeamiento y el diseño del ambiente para la contrucción, debemos asumir el liderazgo en uno de los problemas más críticos de nuestro tiempo," concluía él. [1]

Richard Galehouse, un Arquitecto Planificador asociado a Sasaki, estaría en un principio de acuerdo, pero expresaría sus convicciones de una manera diferente. "Nosotros estamos siempre buscando la solución ambiental, la solución bella, pero también la solución que tenga sentido económico. Siempre ha habido una preocupación por la calidad de la tierra, su carácter inherente y sus propiedades y la forma en que éstas afectarían a los economistas, para hacer algo al respecto."[2] Galehouse quien se unió a la Firma en 1960 tiene grandes perspectivas en cuanto al involucramiento de la Firma en el planeamiento y diseño de nuevas comunidades. Galehouse ha sido por muchos años Director de planificación en Sasaki Associates, y como tal, frecuentemente ha abordado los aspectos ambientales, al planificar éstas comunidades, mientras ha dictado conferencias, en escritos en publicaciones profesionales o involucrando a un cliente en el sub-arrendamiento de un proyecto nuevo. Típicamente, su punto de partida es "Sea Plants Plantation." un proyecto que llegó a la Firma tres o cuatro años antes de que él llegara. Galehouse sirvió como Planificador en la segunda fase del desarrollo de este proyecto comunitario, localizado en Hilton Head Island, en la costa de Carolina del Sur.

Galehouse ha observado que "la industria del desarrollo considera a Sea Pines como el primer punto recreacional y comunidad de retiro contemporáneo, después de la Segunda Guerra Mundial. Los niveles de desarrollo que estableció este proyecto marcaron los de toda la industria."[3] El crédito por este éxito se debe no sólo a Hideo Sasaki y sus Asociados, planificadores, diseñadores del lugar y arquitectos para esta nueva comunidad que se comenzó en las postrimerías de los años cincuentas, sino también al cliente, Charles Fraser quien era entonces un joven graduado de la Escuela de Leyes de Yale, con alguna experiencia a los aspectos legales del planeamiento del uso de la tierra, incluyendo restricciones de escrituras y convenios.

Fraser ha tenido un interés permanente y especial afecto por el paisaje natural de la isla, incluyendo su flora y fauna. John McPhee señaló que los lagartos y los venados del lugar fueron protegidos por la fuerza policial privada de Fraser.[4] Casi cuarenta años después del comienzo del proyecto, en alrededor de 4,500 acres, la visión de Fraser de "armonía y cohesión" ha sido ampliamente realizada. "Hay playas intactas, extensos paisajes acuáticos. En lo alto, se extiende un dosel continuo de bosques y un sinnúmero de paisajes bordeando el horizonte. A pesar del intenso desarrollo de las últimas tres décadas éste sereno paisaje todavía domina el carácter de Hilton Head." escribió un periodista en 1990.[5]

Galehouse ha servido, a menudo, como planificador de paisajes llenos de agradables sorpresas naturales, tales como islas costeras, altos riscos en donde se divisan paisajes de ríos y relativas tierras bajas con abundantes corrientes de agua. En un artículo escrito por él sobre "Kingsmill on the James," una comunidad nueva cerca de Williamsburg, Virginia, Galehouse enfatiza las consideraciones ecológicas que fueron los precedentes sobre otros factores en el proceso de desarrollo. "El análisis ecológico de Kingsmill demostró que los pantanos de las mareas y el sistema de canales con suelos frágiles que se erosionan fácilmente eran los elementos ambientales naturales más sensibles." Esto fue expresado por Galehouse antes de definir las consideraciones más importantes en el Plan Maestro que se completó en 1972. Los detalles técnicos, tales como movimientos de tierra, tala de árboles y la red de servicios de alcantarillas se trataron de manera que su impacto ambiental fuera el mínimo, guardando los costos económicos en forma "competitiva". Aún sin resolver, se encontraba el complejo problema de los restos de edificaciones de las antiguas plantaciones de la zona, situados en el lugar de futuras construcciones. La compañía cervecera Aheuser-Bush, que pertenecía al padre del dueño, acordó patrocinar un programa arqueológico intensivo para preservar estos sitios históricos. Las sesiones de trabajo fueron largas y algunas veces tediosas, según admitió Galehouse. Pero al final, las preocupaciones de todos; el Dueño del Desarrollo; Ambientalistas; el Servicio de Parques Nacionales, Williamsburg Colonial, la Comisión de Sitios Históricos de Virginia y de otras partes interesadas fueron resueltas dentro del plan mestro.[6]

La supervisión de Galehouse en la planificación y diseño de nuevas comunidades se caracteriza por el uso de un tono moderado y equilibrado. No hay un sólo problema, ni un objeto de uso universal, como las vallas de contensión de las carreteras o una escala de desarrollo particular, que dominara su visión de la práctica de la Firma, o sus sentido de que era lo que quería lograrse, respecto a estructuras y las formas de una nueva comunidad, Galehouse permanecía atento a las circunstancias y al lugar elegido. "Nosotros dejamos que la tierra tome una buena parte en la decisión" según él lo explica. "En Kingsmil se encuentra un paisaje policromado, lleno de pequeños salientes y hondonadas; no se puede forzar una valla en ese paisaje." En "Las Hamacas", una comunidad nueva de 1,100 acres en Dade County, Florida, catorce millas al sur de Miami, la Firma introdujo formas curvilíneas en la red de carreteras del condado. Se creó un lago interior y sistema de parques. Parcelas pequeñas de desarrollo a escala de vecindarios fueron creadas, cada una con 25 acres, se orientaron hacia los lagos. Instalaciones comunales, tales como, escuelas, iglesias, una casa comunal y servicios comerciales agrupados en tres aldeas y un centro de la ciudad. Galehouse recuerda: "En los años setentas la planificación de Las Hamacas fue aprobada únicamente por sus características de planificación de ciudad."[7]

Recientemente Galehouse ha participado en algunos diseños y planificación de mesas de discusión en Celebration, Florida, la nueva comunidad que está siendo construida por la Corporación de Desarrollo Disney. En una de esas reuniones él se encontró con Charles Fraser, Jacqueline Robertson, Robert A. M. Stern y algunos ejecutivos de Disney para discutir los problemas de diseño y mercadeo del área de vivienda. "Cada vez que Disney quiso negociar con los grupos de enfoque al proyecto; las personas que iban a habitar en él, éstos no querían tener nada que ver con el problema de las vallas. Esa era la constante," recuerda Galehouse. El lugar a cualquier costo era difícil de construir. De un total de 10,000 acres, únicamente en la mitad es factible construir, el resto son áreas húmedas protegidas.[8]

En contraste, el paisaje de Brambleton, que se discute más adelante, promete ser más compacto, pero en alguna forma, de carácter más urbano. Está concentrado en 375 acres de terreno. El Director de Diseño para este proyecto rural en el condado Loudoun, Virginia, es Alan Ward y él considera el potencial socioeconómico del plan básico de vallas de contensión, el que él y sus colegas, adaptaron a las calles existentes y la topografía de esta relativamente tierra plana. "Creo que es más fácil y más atractivo el introducir un espectro habitacional más amplio dentro de un patrón de red vial, que es lo que se usa cuando se diseñan áreas residenciales exclusivas o residencias individuales en las que todas las casas tienen un valor unitario. Dijo Ward en un forum de Arquitectura Paisajista con George J. Pillorge, Robert C. Kettler, Sam Bass Warner Jr. y Lewis D. Hopkins. "No se trata solamente de vivienda a diferentes escalas de precios, es también viviendas para los ancianos." continuó Ward. "El Plan Brambleton comprende casas para ancianos cerca de la calle principal dentro de corta distancia del centro de la ciudad... Ahora nosotros podemos introducir (continuando con las comunidades con cuidados especiales) una escala de cuadra a cuadra, siendo mucho más aceptable que teniendo estas comunidades a la orilla de asentamientos residenciales exclusivos."[9]

Finalmente Ward y sus colegas se distrajeron charlando acerca de sus sitios favoritos. "Lo que nosotros amamos de Annapolis, Maryland, es la escala de sus calles, la densidad de su actividad, la expresión cívica en donde ciertas calles terminan en maravillosos edificios y áreas públicas en una escala apropiada," dice Ward, con el conocimiento que la necesidad de diseñar áreas para la circulación de automóviles, complica actualmente el trabajo del diseñador. " Esa escala peatonal estrecha y compacta, que hace Annapolis tan vibrante y llena de vitalidad, está a una escala diferente a la de las autopistas regionales, se requiere de una transición de la autopista a los boulevares y calles principales. De forma tal que nosotros subordinemos el vehículo, lo introduzcamos en este tejido urbano y hagamos que se comporte apropiadamente."[10]

Existen ocasiones en Sasaki Associates en donde los Directores deben decidir unánimemente. Sin embargo, en conversaciones individuales o de grupo, lo que generalmente se tiende a oír es una diversidad de opiniones, algunas de una oposición aguda, otras difieren sutilmente, según las posiciones son refinadas o corregidas. Hirzel encuentra esto muy normal dentro del espíritu de colaboración y comprensión que trata de mantenerse dentro de la Firma. "Yo encuentro que, con un proceso de involucrameinto en la atención, respuesta y múltiple incorporación de todos los puntos de vista conflictivos, se obtienen mejores decisiones," dice él. "Y cuando veo alrededor de esta oficina, veo a Ken Bassett, Allan Ward, Dick Galehouse y Don Olson, veo a personas que por su disposición tienen un espíritu incorporado al enfrentamiento de las cosas. Y esto es fundalmentalmente diferente a casi todas o muchas otras firmas en este negocio," [11] afirma Hirzel

Diseño

Alan Resnick, Director en Sasaki Associates y Jefe de Disciplina Arquitectónica de la Firma, en Watertown, está muy complacido con los jóvenes talentosos y llenos de energía que recientemente se les han unido. "Vienen con ideas frescas y un intenso entusiasmo, pueden no estar al tanto de la historia de la Firma, pero tienen el sentimiento que Sasaki Associates es un lugar especial, todo lo que quieren hacer es un buen trabajo con buenas personas," [1] observa él.

Comentarios similares se escuchan de diseñadores en las otras disciplinas de la Firma, el énfasis se hace en el trabajo, su complejidad, su diversidad y sus muchos desafíos y en la gente que se desarrolla dentro de esos retos y oportunidades. Con el tiempo, estas personas aprenden algo de la Firma y su ilustre pasado, así como de la cultura que ha evolucionado dentro del proceso de colaboración e interacción multidisciplinaria. La historia permanece como una propiedad remota, más lejana, probablemente por el estribillo escuchado, no sólo dentro de la Firma, sino en todo el entorno, durante los primeros años de la post-guerra. "No es el mismo lugar. No es el mismo mundo, debe haber un cabo suelto en algún sitio..."

De hecho, hay algunos hilos que unen al trabajo y a la gente de Sasaki Associates, desde los tempranos años cincuentas, al presente. La voluntad de trabajar en equipo, de reprimir (al menos temporalmente), el ego de cada uno, de escudriñar a través de las diferentes escalas de factores, prioridades y posibilidades, en la búsqueda de la mejor solución a un problema. Dicho en pocas palabras, trabajar a través de un proceso de colaboración es un proceso en conjunto... El interés y aún el placer por integrar las habilidades y los pensamientos propios con los de los demás, quienes tienen diferentes experiencias y escalas en las disciplinas de planificación y diseño. Hay una consistencia dentro de los tipos de proyectos en los que ha trabajado la Firma durante cerca de 45 años, especialmente en Planificación de Campus Universitarios, Diseño, Diseño de Comunidades Nuevas y a gran escala: Paisajes corporativos y comerciales, rurales y urbanos. Stuart Dawson, Don Olson, Richard Galehouse y sus colegas, han disfrutado relaciones con clientes que han permanecido largo tiempo fieles a la Firma, quienes han continuado utilizando los servicios de ésta en series de proyectos, durante largos períodos. Esta continuidad representa un hilvanado, así como un delicado equilibrio de los intereses funcionales y pragmáticos, cualidades expresivas y significado cultural. Aparte de éste y otros entretejidos, está el cuestionamiento del tejido que ellos crean, cuando juntos entrelazan con gran habilidad, la destreza conocida en síntesis, como "diseño."

También en este tema se oyen muchas voces en armonía y no necesariamente al unísono. Joseph Hibbard, Director y Jefe de la disciplina de Arquitectura Paisajista, ha adaptado un enfoque al diseño, que absorbió de sus mentores: Hideo Sasaki (quién se retiró poco tiempo después de que Hibbard fuera contratado) y Don Olson. Este enfoque es: Resolver los problemas funcionales primero; hay que preocuparse de la composición y expresión después. No hay que olvidarlas, pero no hay que tratar de resolverlas desde el primer día." Hibbard también ha reconocido las diferencias sutiles en la forma en que él y Olson enfocan un problema de diseño. Hibbard observa: Olson comenzaría con una clase de "objetividad científica," sin abandonar su intuición; él posee una fuerte intuición acerca de la composición y acerca de qué es lo que funciona. A Olsen le gusta examinar un problema en todo su contexto, se abre al análisis y a las posibilidades antes de determinar la dirección de un diseño en particular. Hibbard en cambio, actúa de forma parecida pero en alguna forma con menos investigación y análisis. "Yo tengo un método de deducción, pero disfruto haciéndolo de la forma más rápida," explica. Al final, como muchos de sus colegas, él determina cuál de entre las variables, es crítica, después, se traslada a la concepción de un fundamento estructural, para resolver los particulares problemas del diseño. En este enfoque del diseño, se pueden acomodar las contribuciones de muchos colegas y colaboradores. La solución es enriquecedora y en general satisfactoria, es así como criterios de distintas disciplinas, se suman para apoyar la solución del problema. Aún así, el proceso de resolver un verdadero diseño sintetizado en forma física, permanece como un misterio, un proceso mental único para cada Diseñador o Director a cargo. Para Hibbard, es una cuestión de varias actividades ocurriendo simultáneamente. "La Arquitectura Paisajista trata de estilo, forma, calidad sensorial y estética, al mismo tiempo trata con la funcionalidad y la utilidad. Se tienen que obtener las dos cosas, funcionando al mismo tiempo, a la misma alltura, en pro de resolver satisfactoriamente el problema. [2]

Scott Smith, Arquitecto y Director de la oficina de Sasaki en San Francisco, recuerda que él fue atraído a la Firma, primordialmente por su práctica en trabajos de colaboración, "Pero realmente no sabía que tan fuerte me iba a sentir al respecto, hasta que pasé un tiempo en la Firma," observa. A principios de los ochentas, en uno de sus primeros proyectos en la Firma, la expansión del Western Wyoming college, trabajó con Galehouse, Hibbard, John Orcutt (quien fue Jefe de la disciplina arquitectónica de la Firma) Sasaki (quien estaba como consultor) y otros, al igual que con otras Firmas arquitectónicas asociadas. Particularmente por algunas percepciones que tuvieron marcado efecto en la locación o forma de expansión en la construcción, Smith le acreditó estas palabras a Hibbard: "Si un Arquitecto se aventura sólo por su propia elección, no creo que las edificaciones hubieran evolucionado hasta donde se encuentran ahora." El reafirma que; "Una de las cosas a las que le doy mayor valor en nuestra práctica, es la colaboración."

En el proceso del diseño en sí, Smith prefiere dirigirse primero al contexto completo; él afirma: "La Arquitectura es un arte social, está conformada por las culturas en las que vivimos y por las personas. Por supuesto el proceso toma tiempo, cuando el profesional debe entregar su arte a la inspiración, las edificaciones no son diseñadas por una democracia. Existe un líder que diseñó la edificación. El éxito de ésta, depende en que tan bien este líder absorbe un buen número de cosas; visitas al lugar elegido, las reuniones públicas, el proceso interno y así sucesivamente. Nosotros gastamos mucho tiempo y energía con el grupo de enfoque, les hacemos preguntas. El reto mayor del proceso creativo es, escuchar con atención." [3]

La disposición para escuchar es uno de los hilos más fuertes dentro de la firma Sasaki a través de sus casi 45 años de práctica. Pero la naturaleza de cómo escuchar, ha variado en alguna forma a través de los años. La perspectiva de Stuart Dawson acerca de este tema, se remonta a las postrimerías de los cincuentas, cuando como un joven graduado en Arquitectura Paisajista se unió a la entonces pequeña firma de Arquitectos Paisajistas, Planificadores y Arquitectos. Ahora, como Director y antiguo socio de la Firma, ha enfatizado la escala de voces que deben ser escuchadas cada vez más, especialmente en proyectos urbanos; las Agencias de Nuevos Desarrollos; los Consejos y Comisiones de planeamiento, las Organizaciones comunitarias y otros grupos de interés como los Mercadólogos y algunas veces los Administradores y los colaboradores artísticos, lo mismo que los propios colegas tanto de la oficina, como de otras firmas asociadas. Dawson es especialmente receptivo a la voz del cliente. El observó: "Hay suficiente espacio para escuchar con creatividad, requiere mayor madurez profesional el poder guiar el sueño del cliente, un poco hacia la visión propia, pero creo que es exitante. Hemos realizado obras que, en la primera charla con el cliente, creímos imposible de hacer, pero gradualmente, todos los involucrados se convencieron de que existía una mejor alternativa." [4]

Durante los años cincuentas y sesentas, si el cliente era un Arquitecto, Dawson algunas veces se encontraba prestando mayor atención a sus colegas en la oficina, que a ese Arquitecto. Por ejemplo, recuerda Dawson, Eero Saarinen mostró considerable interés por el paisaje en donde iba a edificar. "Era muy interesante, a él le importó mucho sólo la etapa del modelo, pero después que nosotros le dimos nuestra visión, cómo sería, qué colores tendría, el bosquejo de las texturas, algunos detalles (no muchos), entonces nos dejó solos y así esperaba que hiciéramos un buen trabajo. Esto también sucedía con Kevin Roche, quien se involucraba sólo en la primera etapa del proyecto, la visión." Cuando trabajaba en las oficinas principales de Deere en Moline, Illinois, entonces Dawson escuchaba la crítica de Sasaki a su trabajo y las recomendaciones para alguna forma específica de plantar; (colocar elementos juntos en una sola masa). Por ejemplo, agrupando los árboles de maple y los robles de la misma forma, como grandes corrientes, moviéndose con el ondulado paisaje. Al terminar este proceso de diseño, se le proporcionó un ambiente noble y sutil al edificio de Sarinen, almismo tiempo que Dawson obervó todo el proceso, desde su diseño conceptual, hasta los ensayos y los éxitos logrados, con dificultades en la instalación del paisaje completo. Satisfechos Saarinen y Deere & Company, continuaron utilizando los servicios de Sasaki por muchos años.

Para Dawson, el proceso de diseño ha evolucionado de acuerdo a los cambios en las condiciones. Como él refleja en sus comentarios: "Creo que los problemas eran simples en los años cincuentas, el cliente al que escuchábamos, generalmente traía consigo una agenda simple, dejaba mucho espacio para la innovación. La gente de ahora es mucho más sofisticada, pide mucho más de tí y dice mucho más si se le escucha." Mirando hacia atrás en los primeros años, es inevitable acordarse de anécdotas y de las condiciones de la práctica que eran simplemente circunstanciales, de una capacidad del tamaño de la oficina y de la juventud del personal. "Creo que eramos mucho más informales en esos días, podíamos trabajar toda la noche, después salíamos a jugar, si sentíamos que teníamos demasiado trabajo," afirma Dawson, toma una pausa, como para dejar fluir los recuerdos, "pasamos una excelente época. Hicimos modelos a escala y todo tipo de cosas. Hicimos un diseño de instalación de luces completamente a escala. Hicimos todo en una forma exploratoria." [5]

Dentro de los espíritus jóvenes, llenos de optimismo, de los tempranos años de la post-guerra, existía también un penetrante sentido de expansión, derivado, en parte de una floreciente economía nacional y de la necesidad de reconstruir y construir, no sólo dentro de los Estados Unidos, sino también en el extranjero. Existía también una base expansiva en donde, todo tipo de comprensión y conocimiento se creía esencial, o por lo menos relevante para el diseño y la planificación. Estudios en Sociología, Urbanismo, Antropología, Estética y Psicología del Diseño y los problemas tecnológicos del aire acondicionado, iluminación, ventilación, orientación solar y otros controles ambientales, eran cada vez más integrados dentro del curriculum profesional.

Como lo expresamos anteriormente, la oficina Sasaki ha mantenido fuertes lazos con instituciones educativas, especialmente con las Escuelas de Diseño en Harvard y MIT, dirigidas por Josep Lluis Sert y por Pietro Beluschi, respectivamente. Estos lazos no sólo atrajeron proyectos hacia la oficina de Sasaki, sino también para Sert y Belluschi, que permanecieron como colaboradores cercanos con la oficina por muchos años. Además esta relación aseguró que las nuevas formas de conocimiento y entendimiento mantuvieran actualizada la oficina. Algunos de los primeros Asociados, eran Profesores a medio tiempo, a la vez que ejercían su profesión. Para estos diseñadores y sus colegas en la Escuela y en la Oficina, el aprendizaje continuaba. Un seminario, un libro en proceso o un problema en estudio, podría producir una nueva teoría o una simple hipótesis, que después podría ser probada en la práctica en un proyecto. Algunos proyectos eran pequeños, aislados en el tiempo y el espacio. Otros, en un Campus Universitario o dentro de una ciudad, podían estar inter-relacionados dentro de un gran contexto, eran factores a ser considerados durante largos períodos de tiempo. Algunas veces, series de comisiones podrían ser llevadas a la Firma por el mismo contexto o por contextos similares. En este caso, una secuencia de soluciones en el diseño, podrían ser probadas y los diseñadores, podrían desarrollar una intensa comprensión de un problema grande.

De estos problemas grandes y complejos, surgió una visión más amplia que la suma de las partes. Allí evolucionó un sentido de unidad difícil de articular en palabras, sin embargo, identificable cuando se lograba. Con el tiempo, se volvió palpable para algunos diseñadores, el que esta unidad no se comprobaba por simple geometría o personalidades dominantes, tampoco por la consistencia del material, estilo o escala. Más sutil y evasiva, esta cualidad de unidad permanecía intangible, casi inexpresiva y extraña. Uno podría simplemente sentirla en ciertos ambientes en donde la gente, la elaboración de formas y espacios, y los elementos naturales parecían haber alcanzado el equilibrio.

Para Kenneth DeMay, uno de los primeros arquitectos contratados por Sasaki, el sentido de unidad en la construcción llegó en parte, por la forma natural en que la práctica de la arquitectura evolucionó en Sasaki Associates. Al principio, la pequeña oficina fue absorvida por proyectos de planeamiento y diseño de lugares. Los encargos llegaron de Arquitectos tales como: Sert, Belluschi, Skidmore, Owingsand Merrill, I. M. Rei, Ernest Kump y William Wurster, todos, personas a quienes les gustaba trabajar con Sasaki y su Firma. "Trabajábamos muchas y largas jornadas, trabajábamos tanto y tan diligentemente, que se volvió algo profundamente arraigado en nosotros," recuerda DeMay. Empezaban ayudando en diferentes formas, DeMay pronto enfocó sus esfuerzos en el Desarrollo de Planes Maestros Institucionales, los que a menudo los conducían a trabajos en construcción, él y sus colegas les daban forma, observabando el Campus desde un punto de vista general. Después, trabajando en menor escala, se encaminaban hasta llegar a diseñar la construcción.[6]

Si se puede decir que la práctica arquitectónica de Sasaki Associates se expandió partiendo de la planificación, esto también es cierto en otras áreas. Galehouse ha explicado que la práctica del diseño urbano creció, partiendo de las disciplinas de la planificación, así como de los servicios ambientalistas y de las capacidades gráficas. Estos desarrollos ocurren naturalmente, en una forma evolutiva y su rastro puede ser seguido hasta el hecho de que, "Planificación, " en Sasaki Associates, ha sido siempre comprendido como planeamiento físico. El producto final de los planificadores de la Firma, muchos de los cuales también tienen título de arquitecto, es usualmente un trabajo de construcción, o de espacios y estructuras. "Los planificadores tienen éxito (dentro de esta Firma) únicamente si poseen la habilidad de sentir realmente la dimensión física," observó Hirzel recientemente. Destrezas dentro de las políticas, por ejemplo, a pesar de ser útiles, no son suficientes. Hirzel ha hecho notar, similarmente que; "los Arquitectos que sobreviven aquí, son aquellos que pueden vivir en un mundo contextualizado."[7]

Smith está de acuerdo, destacando que "contexto" involucra más que el ambiente arquitectónico y natural de un proyecto. El enfatiza que el programa, la región, el clima, aún la Arquitectura Tecnológica usada en particular, todo contribuye a lo que se entiende como "contexto". El puede señalar una larga lista de edificaciones y paisajes diseñados por Sasaki Associates, que permanecen eminentemente en la medida del contexto, en el amplio sentido de la palabra. Sin embargo, él está al tanto de ciertas limitaciones que dicho trabajo conlleva. "Sasaki Associates no tiene sello Arquitectónico. Si usted observa nuestras edificaciones, usted no tiene por qué que saber cómo surgieron o quién las hizo." según él observa. Por el contrario, el diseño de una edificación es orientado por varios factores, que a menudo son paisajes naturales distintivos o asentamientos urbanos o instituciones que han sido edificadas y reafirmadas durante un largo período de tiempo.

Esta falta de "sello," es una forma de anonimato que los arquitectos paisajistas conocen y contra la que han luchado por muchos años, y también tiene otras implicaciones. En la tradición continua de colaboración con otras firmas arquitectónicas, lo mismo que con sus propios colegas, la contribución de la Firma en un edificio en particular, a menudo pasa desapercibida. En muchos Estados, la construcción es reconocida generalmente en ambas formas, formal e informalmente, como la obra de un Arquitecto dentro del Estado o de una Firma, "los registros de Arquitecto." Ahora, como en los años cincuentas y sesentas, mucho del trabajo arquitectónico es un esfuerzo de colaboración con otros arquitectos, para quienes Sasaki provee servicios de diseño. Aunque la Firma reciba reconocimiento público por este trabajo, el diseñador puede ser dejado del lado por algunos factores, fuera del control de la Firma. Sin embargo, a Smith le nace una gran satisfacción personal derivada de las relaciones de trabajo que surgen durante el proceso, dentro y fuera de la Firma. Un cliente o un colega, llega a ser un buen amigo. Algunas veces una edificación emerge como cierto tipo de "sello," no necesariamente para el diseñador o para la Firma, pero siempre dentro de su propio contexto. Smith dice con orgullo: "Las edificaciones son el sello dentro del campus."

Hablar acerca de "sellos" es crear cuestionamiento de identidades, individuales y colectivas. Algunos diseñadores en Sasaki Associates, maduran y confían en sus propias habilidades, han pasado toda su vida profesional en el ambiente multidisciplinario de colaboración de la Firma, no conocen otra forma de práctica. Algunos, han trabajado en otras oficinas, pero encuentran que prefieren la forma de colaboración, a otros modelos de práctica, en parte por la amplia y fascinante gama de tipos de problemas para resolver y el éxito de resolverlos. Después de muchos años, algunos permanecen fascinados con la idea de la colaboración, un ideal poderoso por el que uno se esfuerza diariamente en armonía con los otros. Irónicamente, en el mundo exterior, tanto los profesionalescomo el público en general, tienden a pensar en Sasaki Associates como una firma de planificación, una firma de diseño, una firma de arquitectura paisajista, una firma de arquitectura o una firma de ingeniería. Galehouse afirma: "Nosotros somos conocidos por nuestras partes, el mensaje central de la idea colaboracional, simplemente no parece llegar."[8]

Hirzel señala: "Bueno, nosotros sabemos que es lo que hacemos por nuestros clientes." Explicarlo en detalle involucraría una revisión más completa e histórica, en imágenes y palabras como es posible en estas páginas. Aquí a cualquier costo, las miradas retrospectivas, junto al trabajo reciente y al pensamiento de los profesionales en Sasaki Associates, ofrecemos el sentido de la identidad colectiva de la Firma.

Observaciones hechas por los recién llegados a la Firma, son también ilustrativas. Para Nancy Harrod, Directora y Jefe de la disciplina de Interiores (que se desarrolló a través de la disciplina arquitectónica), el tiempo en el que un proyecto se debe discutir en las reuniones iniciales, ha sido reducido dramáticamente desde que ella llegó a Sasaki Associates en 1987. Las fechas límite son más apretadas, los recursos son más limitados y la demanda es mayor. Ella admite que "requiere más y más energía cada año," reconociendo que a medida que se trabaja más de prisa, puede ser más exitante. Equipos trabajando de manera más rápida y eficiente, pueden ver el resultado de su trabajo (y aprender de ello) más pronto.[9] Otra parte del desarrollo es la fase programática en donde, como en otras disciplinas, yacen las mayores oportunidades para la creatividad. Los clientes observan a Harrod y su equipo, así como observan a Smith, Hibbard, Bassett, Galehouse y otros, buscando ayuda en variadas disciplinas, para resolver un problema, satisfaciendo de esta forma una compleja variedad de necesidades, expectativas y obligaciones.

Un desarrollo que puede encontrar implicaciones profundas en el proceso de diseño, es es la introducción de tecnologías, particularmente computadoras y otros equipos electrónicos. En Sasaki Associates, el entusiasmo por el diseño por computadoras o el sistema auto-CAD y tecnologías asociadas, varía de un profesional a otro. La mayoría de diseñadores visualizan éstos, como unos instrumentos más para el diseño, talvéz hasta indispensables, ultimamente las nuevas tecnologías también representan un número de problemas causados por la vasta escala de computadoras y otros medios electrónicos que son introducidos en los Campus Universitarios, oficinas Corporativas, Instituciones Financieras y otras más. Como mencionamos anteriormente, Perry Chapman ha encontrado que los administradores están haciendo cada vez más énfasis en la necesidad de integrar estos instrumentos en espacios existentes, lo mismo que crear o rediseñar espacios en donde los estudiantes puedan mezclarse y socializar cercanamente, después de pasar muchas horas frente a un monitor.

Mientras algunos escritores elaboran teorías acerca de la decreciente necesidad de espacios físicos públicos, con mira a los lugares electrónicos de reunión que definitivamente se van a crear dentro del espacio virtual. Alan Ward es más cauteloso: "Yo estoy de acuerdo que el medio electrónico afecta fundamentalmente cómo trabajamos y cómo visualizamos el mundo. Esto cambia los hechos. El medio nos ha alejado de los lugares en donde vivimos, de nuestro sentido comunitario. Yo no creo que el mundo físico va a volverse un mundo virtual. Yo preferiría mirar en otra dirección, en vez de pensar que este mundo físico a nuestro alrededor se está disolviendo, mejor traslademonos a algo más, yo mejor trataría de reclamar lo que es fundamentalmente humano."[10]

Esto también es lo que Sasaki Associate ha hecho por sus clientes. El reinvindicar, rediseñar y construir nuevos espacios físicos, fundamentalmente humanos, y que su consecusión ha sido de mucha importancia en el pasado y continúan siendo de las metas primordiales de esta práctica colaboracional. Con el tiempo, estos lugares también formarán parte de la identidad colectiva de la Firma.

Diálogos

Hunter Morrison, Director de Planificación, Cleveland, Ohio
Joseph Riley, Alcalde, Charleston, Carolina del Sur
Por David Dillon

Sasaki Associates ha trabajado en Cleveland y Charleston por 30 años, habiéndose puesto varios sombreros; como Planificador, Arquitecto Paisajista, Diseñador Urbano, Ingeniero, Abogado Público y proporcionando la amplia visión para planificar y la guía específica, para ejecutar los proyectos.

Hace treinta años, las firmas multidisciplinarias eran escasas, aún hoy en día, cuando la mayoría de firmas grandes emplean ingenieros y arquitectos paisajistas y cada quien se llama a sí mismo planificador, pocos conservan la trayectoria de colaboración tan constantemente, como en Sasaki. Asociaciones duraderas, así como los matrimonios largos, tienen sus altibajos. Algunos proyectos tienen éxito, otros no. Algunos Alcaldes promueven el buen diseño, a otros no les importa. No obstante la expectativa es que una historia compartida, condimentada con buena voluntad y con el estar siempre alerta a las limitaciones y fortalezas de cada uno, siempre producirá mejores trabajos, que oportunas alianzas transitorias de extraños. Este ha sido el caso para Sasaki en Charleston y Cleveland.

El involucramiento en el Centro de Cleveland comenzó a finales de los años setentas con el rediseño de la Plaza Pública, un espacio cívico formal que data desde la fundación de la ciudad y continuó con la planificación del Centro de la Puerta de Entrada y el Puerto de la Costa Norte, entre los años ochentas y noventas. Haciendo una conexión de estos puntos, se obtiene un mapa del renacimiento actual de Cleveland.

Los años setentas fueron una década obscura para Cleveland, cuando su política estaba en caos, una coalición de grupos privados dirigidos por el Club de Jardinería de Cleveland y la Corporación del Centro de Cleveland, seleccionó a Sasaki para renovar la Plaza Pública. Cleveland es una ciudad conservadora con rasgos del pragmatismo Yankee. Cleveland desdeña las tendencias en el diseño. Se requería simplicidad y reserva, y eso es lo que Sasaki produce. La Firma efectuó unos cuantos cambios modestos en cada uno de los cuadrantes de la Plaza, agregando fuentes, árboles ornamentales con flores y lugares en donde sentarse, dejando más césped en un área y más pavimento en otra. Por último, el proyecto era menos acerca de detalles de Diseño Urbano y más acerca de tomar un espacio público de los tecnócratas y devolverlo a la gente de la comunidad. Con la ayuda del Departamento de Ingeniería y la Agencia Regional de Tránsito, Sasaki hizo las calles más angostas, acortó los cruces peatonales, eliminó las paradas de autobuses innecesarias y, en general, le dió a los peatones un lugar determinante en el corazón histórico de Cleveland. "La renovación de la Plaza Pública demostró que Sasaki había comprendido la tónica de la ciudad." Ellos entregaron un proyecto crítico en un momento en que no era fácil hacerlo y lo hicieron sin perder la compostura," es la opinión del Director de Planificación de Cleveland, Hunter Morrison.

Este precedente constituyó una prueba invaluable una década más tarde, cuando Sasaki fué nombrado el Planificador Maestro en el Centro para la Puerta de Entrada a Cleveland, un desarollo de $400 millones de dólares, en un área desarrollada anteriormente, situada en el borde sur del Centro de la Ciudad. Anclada por nuevos hogares para los Indios de Cleveland (Cleveland Indians) y los Caballeros de Cleveland (Cleveland Cavaliers), la Puerta de Entrada representó la gran jugada de una ciudad luchando contra el bloqueo al centro de la ciudad, el alcalde Michael White, dijo directamente que a menos que la Puerta de Entrada albergara a más personas que en un Estadio y una Arena, no iban a recibir un centavo público. Tendría que llenar de energía todo el centro de la ciudad y generar beneficios económicos que todos pudieran compartir.

La asignación de Sasaki era plegar el Parque de Pelota y Arena, para que encajaran sutilmente en el Centro de la Ciudad. Sus otros cargos, mas bien sociales que arquitectónicos, eran el ser el intermediario, comisionado de desagravio y policía para varios de los participantes. La Firma debía articular la agenda pública tan fuertemente como los Indios y los Caballeros estaban articulando la privada. Mr. Morrison expresa: "Sasaki tenía un sentido de la escala del reto, lo que otras firmas no tenían. Ellos enmarcaban la cuestión en general en vez de pensar únicamente como arquitectos interesados en diseñar las edificaciones. Ellos comprendieron que nosotros necesitábamos un marco dentro del cual colocar la arquitectura, tanto como necesitábamos la arquitectura por sí sola." Este marco de trabajo consistía en un Plan Maestro para el lugar de 28 acres, y con lineamientos que permitieran a la ciudad poder decirle a los equipos y a los inversionistas en perspectiva, "Esto está bien," y "Esto no está bien."

El movimiento inicial de Sasaki fue rotar el parque de pelota hacia el norte, en dirección al Centro de la Ciudad y hacia la red histórica. La familia Jacobs, dueños de los Indios y comerciantes astutos, conocían el valor de mostrar el producto, que en este caso eran los Indios y la nueva proyección del Centro de la Ciudad, que ellos mismos habían ayudado a desarrollar. Usando el Centro de la Ciudad como fondo del béisbol, proyectaba una imagen de sofisticación urbana, para una ciudad que era famosa por sus ríos, los que una vez tomaron fuego por su estado de contaminación y alcaldes controversiales. Al mismo tiempo, Sasaki persuadió a los arquitectos del parque de pelota: HOK Sports Facilities Group, a bajar la parte de butacas, para lograr hacer de la explanada principal una extensión de la acera. Esto eliminó las rampas en caracol, y las escaleras en torre, que desfiguran muchos estadios. Esto presentaba un agudo margen a lo largo de la calle Ontario. En el Plan Maestro, lo mismo que en la historia de la Firma, los bordes y el acoplamiento son tan importantes como los edificios.

Dentro del llugar, Sasaki delineó una serie de plazas, más sociales que ceremoniales y boulevares diseñados con arquitectura paisajista, para orientar el flujo deseado de visitantes de una parte a otra, entre la Puerta de Entrada y el Centro de la Ciudad, forma en que los centros de compras, hacen a los compradores ir y venir entre sus tiendas estratégicas. Las esquinas del parque de pelota se dejaron abiertas para que los transeúntes pudieran ver hacia adentro, asi como también para que los aficionados pudieran admirar la ciudad.

Las intenciones de Sasaki eran tanto poéticas como pragmáticas, tal como explicó el Director Diseñador Alan Ward: "Nosotros queríamos crear un conjunto de espacios memorables según te ibas acercando al parque, puedes ver la pantalla, puedes oír el ruido del bate de béisbol pegándole a la pelota y quizás, hasta un jonrón pudiera caer a tus pies. Nosotros queríamos que la gente mirara, oyera y sintiera el parque, aunque no hubiera asistido al juego."

Las grandes ideas del diseño urbano de la Puerta de Entrada, dependen de cientos de pequeñas ideas acerca de vistas, materiales, dimensiones, entradas y salidas. Jugar con la idea sensible y romántica, pero al mismo tiempo conceptual de "un campo verde, un campo de sueños", el legado de lineamientos de Sasaki abarcaba todo; desde vallas de árboles, hasta áreas de estacionamiento. Algunos eran sutiles, como la colocación apropiada de las barricadas policiales después de un juego; mientras otras cambiaron el Centro de la Ciudad en forma significativa. El plan de estacionamiento de Sasaki, limitaba el érea a 3200 sitios en 2 espacios, acomodando a todos los demás automóviles en lotes de estacionamientos ya existentes, unos abiertos y otros techados. Los Indios y los Caballeros querían más, pero ya que la meta del plan era fortalecer el Centro de la Ciudad, no pavimentarlo, la ciudad y Sasaki no iban a cambiar su posición. Usando lotes abiertos y techados ya existentes obligaban a los aficionados a caminar, a ver las vitrinas de las tiendas, y a participar en el proceso de redescubrir el Centro de la Ciudad. Hunter Morrison explica: "Nosotros no creemos que el Parque de Pelota y la Arena sean arreglos rápidos, ellos son sólo parte de una estrategia a largo plazo para reestablecer el Centro de la Ciudad. Atando el Parque al tejido de la ciudad, nosotros creemos que la gente se va a inclinar más a circular a través de ésta, vaciando sus billeteras en el proceso, en vez de apresurarse hacia sus vehículos."

Cerca de dos docenas de restaurantes y clubes nuevos, han abierto alrededor del Parque y sus áreas adyacentes. Un distrito histórico de bodegas a lo largo del río Cuyahoga, está ahora conectado a la Puerta de Entrada y al Puerto de la Costa Norte (en donde se encuentran el Salón de la Fama y el Museo del Rock), por medio de una ligera baranda, planificada y diseñada por Sasaki. Diversidad de hoteles se encuentran en contrucción, y al menos media docena de edificios de oficina, están siendo transformados en lugares de vivienda. La mayoría no habían sido tocados por 50 años. Sin la Puerta de Entrada, habrían seguido desintegrándose por otros 50 años. El Proyecto ha cambiado el concepto del público respecto al Centro de la Ciudad. Repentinamente, es el lugar en dónde estar. "El mayor impacto en el proyecto de la Puerta de Entrada, fue el área de estacionamiento y la planficación del tráfico." dice la Asistente al Director de Planificación, Linda Hendrickson. "Si esto hubiera fallado, todo lo demás también hubiera fallado. Poner a dos equipos deportivos, a dos propietarios y a todos esos egos de acuerdo, fue fenomenal." La Presentación de Sasaki a Charleston fue en 1957, con el Plan Maestro para la plantación " Sea Pines" en la isla "Hilton Head", el cual incluía el lugar para Harbourtown. Charleston fue el modelo para Harbourtown, y el inversionista Charles Fraser insitía en que cualquiera que hubiera trabajado en este proyecto tendría que comprender el original. Fue así como Ken DeMay, Don Olson y otros, se volvieron intrusos esporádicos en Charleston, haciendo estudios de su historia y terreno, fotografiando sus edificaciones y en general, almacenando todas sus impresiones para ser usadas en proyectos futuros. Más adelante, el Director Stu Dawson señalaba irónicamente: La Firma "ha establecido raíces en Carolina del Sur, antes de que tuviera raíces en Nueva Inglaterra."

El "proyecto futuro" llegó en 1979, cuando Sasaki ganó un concurso para diseñar el área de 7 acres de terreno en la ribera del mar, lo que sería el "Waterfront Park". Para entonces, la orilla de la ciudad había sido reducida a una hilera de rompeolas en mal estado, bodegas abandonadas, estacionamientos sin pavimentar, intercalados con edificios de aprtamentos, lo que provocaba un sombrío comentario acerca de la decadencia del vecindario.

El Alcalde Joseph Riley prometió cambiar todo esto, creando un parque que renovaría la ribera y áreas adyacentes. No un parque elegante para dueños de botes y vacacionistas CEO (directores ejecutivos corporativos) sino un espacio público, con un muelle de pesca, jardínes y fuentes que alentaría a los habitantes de Charleston, a reestablecer una íntima relación con el mar. El Alcalde conocía el trabajo de Sasaki en Newburyport y Boston, dos puertos históricos con riberas decadentes. El Alcalde consideraba de mucho valor el concepto de Sasaki de no construir grandes estructuras a costa del cliente. "Ellos son una gran Firma, con buena reputación, sin embargo mostraron una verdadera sensibilidad hacia lo que nosotros teníamos aquí, sin ningún ego en absoluto," dijo el Alcalde. Pero al igual que en Cleveland, Sasaki fue contratado finalmente por su capacidad de comprensión del problema urbano de Charleston. "Ellos comprendieron que nosotros no íbamos a solamente crear un parque, nosotros íbamos a desarollar nuevamente todo el margen de la ciudad," dijo el alcalde Riley. El "Waterfront Park", se extiende 1300 pies a lo largo del río Cooper, tomó 11 años el completarlo, y mucho de este tiempo se invirtió en la preparación del lugar. Los arquitectos de Sasaki tomaron el liderazgo, ellos diseñaron 2 espacios techados para estacionamiento a fin de acomodar los carros que serían desplazados por la construcción del nuevo parque. Esto tardó 3 años. Después, hubo que compactar el suelo lleno de deshechos ("mayonesa negra" para los habitantes de Charleston) del lugar. Recubriéndolo con 9 pies de arena. Lo que duró otros dos años, durante los cuales, la pila de arena fue bautizada con el nombre de "La Montaña de Riley" y pasó a ser el blanco de las burlas de sus oponentes políticos. Aún después de compactado el suelo no podía sostener las fuentes, plazas y puertos sin una estructura subterránea elaborada con pilotes y plataformas. Cincuenta por ciento del costo del parque está bajo tierra, invisible al público. Al construir los nuevos muros de contensión, se perturbaron los pantanos, los que Sasaki tuvo que restaurar, junto con el histórico muelle Adger, hacia el sur. Unicamente una Firma fuertemente integrada y acostumbrada a trabajar a través de disciplinas podría haber resuelto estos problemas técnicos y todavía producir un diseño atractivo y coherente.

El Alcalde Riley probó sorpresivamente ser un político paciente y un colaborador entusiasta. Participó en numerosas reuniones de trabajo, trazando líneas y escogiendo colores. El verde en los estacionamientos del Centro de la Ciudad es de él. Siempre estaba recordando a los administradores, su gran responsabilidad social: "Muchas ciudades encargan este trabajo a personas más jóvenes y nunca se vuelve a ver al Alcalde otra vez, es la regla,"la excepción era Joe Riley, el estuvo presente en todas las reuniones públicas. El nos presentaba, servía de anfitrión, observaba cuando hablábamos con las personas adecuadas. "El dirigió el proyecto entero como un Director de Orquesta, "recordaba Stu Dawson.

El parque completo, combina formalidades clásicas con la soltura vernácula, típica de Charleston. Las decisiones acerca de las atracciones principales; la explanada, los puentes, los engramados, el bosquecillo de robles, la transición del duro pavimento en el extremo norte, a un paisaje suave en el extremo sur, se aceptaron rápidamente. Los detalles se tardaron toda una vida. El Alcalde y los arquitectos recolectaron 50 tipos de grava, antes de seleccionar la mezcla para las aceras. La altura de la pared en donde se sentarían alrededor del pasto y la colocación de las palmeras, fueron temas debatidos con intensidad jesuítica. Los caminos de ladrillo, en la orilla este, tuvieron que ser reconstuídos debido a que el patrón del ladrillo corría en dirección opuesta. Si tan sólo buenos ingenieros pudieron construir la estructura subterránea del parque, tan sólo Arquitectos Paisajistas, que habían estudiado el subsuelo, pudieron resolver correctamente los cientos de pequeños detalles a tomar en cuenta. Los pasos de ladrillo conectan 8 pequeños jardínes, que representan una reminiscencia de los jardines privados que se encuentran en Charleston, como antecámara del gran espacio público. El Alcalde Riley requería que hubiese uniformidad en el exterior, con la diferencia suficiente para que si "Un caballero le propone matrimonio a su enamorada en uno de éstos, lo pueda recordar para el resto de su vida." Un programa entero, en una oración.

Vease notas en la pagina 190.

ササキ・アソシエーツ：統合された諸環境

メラニー・スィーモ
訳／金 一

1988年のササキ・アソシエーツ設立35周年の際に、ピエトロ・ベルスキは事務所にまつわる二、三の思い出を添えて祝辞を送った。彼は建築家兼プランナーであるリチャード・ゲールハウス宛てに「事務所が設立されたとき、私はケンブリッジにいて、その成長と成功を非常に間近に見守ってきた。全ては、環境が直面する多くの問題を解決する際に彼らが発揮する、才能と社会常識の並々ならぬコンビネーションのおかげであった」[1] と書いた。

ヒデオ・ササキという一人の人間のヴィジョンから、事務所は一連のパートナーシップや共同体（ササキ・アンド・ノヴァック、ササキ・アンド・アソシエーツ、ササキ・ウォーカー・アンド・アソシエーツ、ササキ・ドーソン・デュメイ・アソシエーツ）を経て成長し、1975年以降現在のササキ・アソシエーツになった。今日、大都市ボストン（ウォータータウン）、ダラス、サンフランシスコにオフィスを構える総合的設計デザイン事務所として、キャンパス・プランニング、アーバンデザイン、新しいコミュニティの開発、環境アセスメント、個々の建築、庭園、広場、そして企業体のコマーシャル・ランドスケープのみならず、インテリアの設計デザインでもその名を知られている。

ササキ・アソシエーツは、時を経るうちにその時代を代表する「クラシック」となった、特色のあるプロジェクトによっても著名である。小さいが思慮に富むプロジェクトとしては、ケベック州モントリオールにあるボナヴェントゥーラ広場のルーフガーデン（1967）、ニューヨーク市のグリーナカー公園（1971）が、都市または公共の広大なコンテクストを扱ったものとしては、コネティカット州ハートフォードの憲法広場（1959）とマサチューセッツ州ケンブリッジのハーヴァード大学クインシーハウス（1959-60）が、そして土地開発を含む大きなスケールの作品としては、カリフォルニア州ロサンジェルスにあるフットヒル・カレッジ（1957-60）、イリノイ州モリンのディーア・アンド・カンパニー社管理センター（1963-）そして、ボストンと南カリフォルニアのチャールストンにおけるウォーターフロント（1973-、1979-）がある。こうした代表的プロジェクトが完成後社会の中で成熟し、ササキ・アソシエーツの独自性がいっそう明らかとなった。

この事務所が果たしたキャンパス・プランニングと都市デザインの発展への歴史的役割については、たぶんあまり知られていないであろう。その多分野にまたがる総合的組織化と、ハーヴァードとMITで発展した戦後理論との早い時期からの結びつきによって、ササキ・アソシエーツは米国内外における実験的設計デザインの、最も重要な活動拠点の一つとなった。更に、以下に述べる指導と実践の連続によって、二世代にわたるランドスケープ・アーキテクトたち（つまりササキの同僚や学生たち）の視野が広がった。彼らは、公共団体、政府、そして産業における、戦後の代表的発展に携わる建築家、エンジニア、プランナーたちと常に仕事を共にしてきたのである。

その著書「キャンパス・プランニング」（1963）と「環境デザイン」（1969）の中で、リチャード・ドーバーはササキ事務所とその他の歴史的役割を、平面図、写真、そして解説文によって記録した。以前、MITでケヴィン・リンチの学生であり、ササキ事務所の同僚でもあるドーバーは、戦後のこうしたキャンパス・プランニングと都市デザインにおける努力に潜む、理想主義とプラグマティズムをも明らかにした。1957年にMITとハーヴァードにおいて領域と都市の研究を目的とする共同研究機関が設立されたことは、多くの将来性のある兆候のひとつにすぎない。当時は、ベルスキはMITのスクール・オブ・アーキテクチャー・アンド・プランニングの学部長であり、ジョセップ・ルイス・サートはハーヴァードのグラデュエート・スクール・オブ・デザインの学部長であった。すぐにハーヴァードのランドスケープ・アーキテクチャーの主任教授になることとなるササキは、この自信に溢れる年代にある二人の両方に協力した。当時は、合理的方法や、真の協力の精神によって解決できないものはなにもないように思われた。

また、偉大なフォルムを生み出すエーロ・サーリネンやポール・ルドルフ、I.M.ペイ、ミノル・ヤマサキ、ゴードン・バンシャフトらの仕事によって特徴づけられる、「英雄的」もしくはかなり個人主義的な段階のモダニズムの年代だった。ササキはこうした人々と共に働き、フォルムを創出するといった彼らと同様の役割を目指すことはせずとも、彼らの尊敬を得た。このことは、ブルダーのコロラド大学拡張計画（1960-）に代表されるような、ササキがベルスキとよく共に行った、新しい開発の大幅な枠組みをデザインするキャンパス・プランニングの分野で最も明らかである。当時のデザイナーたちの誰よりも徹底的に、ベルスキとササキは個々の建物に左右されることなく、プロジェクトのより広いコンテクストにのっとってスペースを定義した。彼らはキャンパスにおける所有境界線の中での連続や、それを越えた関係性を確立しようとした。そして異質の、多くの場合モニュメンタルで独立した新しい建物を配置することによって、彼らは大きな環境の中での調和の程度や全体性を追求するのである。

これが、ベルスキとササキ、そして彼の同僚たちの幾年にもわたる伝統である。その軌跡は、ロックスプリングスにあるウェスタンワイオミング大学の拡張計画、ミシガンのインターロッケン美術センター、そしてこの作品集で特集された他のプロジェクト等の、ササキ・アソシエーツのより最近の作品に見ることができる。これらの全ての共同のプロジェクトでは、建築や敷地のデザインは、より大きな自然環境と文化的環境の入念な理解から展開する。

構築された環境に焦点を絞って、ベルスキとササキのプロジェクトを幾年にもわたり調査してきた。彼曰く、「それらは全て説得力があり、時を経ても色あせない質の高さを持つ。そのことこそが、流行や時代の傾向を越えた、我々の時代の偉大なる一芸術としての建築の試金石なのだ。」[2] この考え方に共鳴して、ササキはそれをベルスキと共有する他の価値観と共に、パートナーや所員たちに伝えていった。その価値観とは、より大きなコンテクスト、簡潔性、慎み、プロポーション、そして永遠性の尊重である。様々な点において、ベルスキは彼の手本となった。そしてササキもまた彼の事務所で、構築された環境に微妙な構造と形態を施しながら、自らの事務所のデザインを先頭に立って批判した。しかしながら、実際のところ、ササキは土地そのものについて意識していたのだった。彼の受けた教育は様々だが、中心はランドスケープ・アーキテクチャーにあった。

「ああ、確かに」と彼の事務所の人々は即座に返答する。「けれど、彼は決して自分自身をランドスケープ・アーキテクトだと思ったことはない。」あるレベルでは、それは本当かもしれない。しかし、古いメモや、長い間忘れられてきたエッセイ、そして何年にもわたるインタビュー記事といった史料は、そうは言っていない。「商品としてではなく、資源、人間活動の場、そして個人的文化的な宝庫としての土地」のプランニングとデザインは、彼の職業の創設者と彼の事務所にとって根本的である。当然ながら実践においてはプラグマティックな側面が強調されるのである。まだリチャード・ドーバーが事務所の取締役になる以前の1959年に、ササキは設計者ドーバーに以下のように注意を与えている。「全ての建物、都市、公共施設、住宅等は土地の上に立つ。もし我々が、適格で 必要とさ

れるサーヴィスを提供できるなら、我々の成長がある領域にとどまる必要はない。」[3] それよりひと月前、ドーバーは「デザイン・コンサルタントとしての我々の第一の機能は、ランドスケープとサイトプランニングに関連しており、またそうでなければならない。我々が関わりを持つべき第二の領域は、都市デザイン、つまり『個人と公共を結びつける、より豊かな物理的環境を発展させる一連のプロセス』である。」[4] と記していた。

このように、ドーバーとササキは常に同意するわけではない。しかし、他の考え方に敬意を表し寛容であるような多様な意見を、ササキは歓迎した。ここで、最初に事務所の創設者（控えめで、どちらかというと内気でもあった極めて野心的な青年）の展望について考察しながら、現在のササキ・アソシエーツの多様な見解、野望、そしてプロジェクト・タイプについて紹介するのがよいだろう。ササキは、往々にしてあまりに限られた、時には不活発にさえ見えるこの職能を変貌させる決意をした。しかし、また彼は自分の限界をも知っていた。自分一人でそれを行うことは無理だったからである。

1953年に、後にササキ・アソシエーツとして知られるようになる事務所を開設したとき、彼は自分の生まれ故郷であるカリフォルニアのセントラル・バレーから遥々やってきた。大恐慌の最後の数年と重なる十代の時に、彼の知的興味は短期大学での一般教養から、大学のビジネスと芸術のコースに移行した。彼はまた、いわゆるプランニングの新しい分野にも興味をそそられ、南カリフォルニアからカリフォルニア大学バークレー校にやってきた。そこで彼は建築とランドスケープ・アーキテクチャー、そしてプランニングに出会い、アイデアや自然の要素を対象に設定する彼の個人的傾向のため、ランドスケープ・アーキテクチャーの分野に一層近づいていった。

彼の勉学は合衆国が第二次世界大戦に参戦した1941年十二月に、突然中断された。ササキはある時期をアリゾナ州ポストンの日系アメリカ人収容キャンプで過ごした。そして、デンバーの辺りとシカゴでの一連の仕事に啓発された彼は、シャンパン・アーバーナにあるイリノイ大学でランドスケープ・アーキテクチャーの勉強を修了した。戦争直後の1946年であった。当時、産業施設は戦時下から平時への激急な変化を経験しており、新しい計画と建設のための財源と意志が揃っていた。美術の学士号を主席で取得したササキは、ハーヴァード大学大学院で学ぶための奨学金を手に入れた。この時点まで、彼は将来すばらしい職業で責任のある地位を得るための、的確な経路を辿っているように見えた。しかし、そこには但し書きが付くのである。

ササキは、イリノイ大学において幾人かの円熟した、きわめて有能な教授たちに学んだ。その中には、ランドスケープ・アーキテクトでありプランナーでもあるカール・B・ローマンと、一年にひと月プランニングの実践から離れて教えていたハーランド・バーソロミューがいた。ランドスケープ・アーキテクチャーの教授、スタンレー・ホワイトは、それまでにブルックリンのオルムステッド兄弟のもとで働いていたし、後にはジェイコブ・クレーン、エルバート・ピーツ、そしてバーソロミューといったプランナーたちと、プランニングのプロジェクトや、連邦政府が資金援助をしていたウィスコンシン州のグリーンデールという新しい町についての仕事を短期間だが共に行った。大学で学んだことや、ローマンの下でアルバイトをした経験から、ササキは、かなりのキャリアを積んでいた専門家たちの中でも際だって、ランドスケープ・アーキテクチャーの研究に基づいて、いかにプランニングとデザインの連続を比較的うまく作動させるか、ということに注目していた。そしてササキは独力でフレデリック・ロウ・オルムステッドの著作を熟読し、そこに、パブリックなものからプライヴェートなものまで、あらゆるスケールの計画においてデザインされたランドスケープの持つ、社会的、文化的、心理的価値への見識のみならず、ボストンやバッファロー、シカゴ等における都市規模で公園を体系化するためのプランニングとデザインの先例をも見いだした。[5]

しかし、たとえオルムステッドとイリノイ大学の教授たちが彼を元気づけたとしても、アメリカ・ランドスケープ・アーキテクト協会の古い体制は、そうはしなかった。そこでは、建築家やエンジニアと対峙するランドスケープ・アーキテクトたちが、かなりの劣等意識を持っていることをササキは発見した。この経験から、ササキはエッセイ「ランドスケープ・アーキテクトの劣等感」を書いた。このエッセイは決して出版されることはなかったが、この状況を修正しようという決心はハーヴァードにいた頃の彼の心の内に留まっていた。いや、それどころかこの決意は強化された。

イリノイでササキが出会ったのは、モダニストたちのいう理論や形態表現に煩わされることなく、ボザール式のプランニングとデザインからも離れて、現代の環境が抱える噴出する難問に取り組むための新しい試みへと向かった教育者たちや実践者たちであった。幅広い教育を受けて美術と科学に精通していたホワイトは、大きなスケールのデザインと、先入観や理論に縛られない、敷地に適合したデザインを強調した。しかしながら、ハーヴァードではモダニズムは一つの主流であった。グラデュエートスクール・オブ・デザインにおいては、ウォルター・グロピウスと彼の元学生たちが、それまでにバウハウスで定義された審美的社会的理想に影響されて、革命的な力を振るっていた。このことは、ランドスケープ・アーキテクチャーの分野の古い世代の教育者たちを脅かすと同時に、戦後世代の学生たちを活気づけた。当時は、ランドスケープ・アーキテクチャーは依然として「古典的手法で」教えられていたとササキは記憶している。アーバンプランニングは別の学科であった。（それは、初めはランドスケープ・アーキテクチャー学科で開講された若干のプランニングのコースから発展したのだった。）他方、建築においては、少なくとも1930年代の終わりから、学生たちは都市の再開発、住宅供給、新しいコミュニティーのあり方といった問題と格闘していた。こうした状況の中で、都市とプランニングに携わる学生たちと教授陣の方に、ササキは引き寄せられていった。彼はグロピウスの講義を熱心に聴講し、後年になってサイト・プランニングとデザインの仕事をもたらすことになる同僚の建築の学生たちから、多くを学んだ。[6]

1948年にハーヴァードからランドスケープ・アーキテクチャーで修士号を得てから1953年にハーヴァードの近くで自身の事務所を開設するまでの五年間を、ササキは実践の場で経験を積むことと教えることで過ごした。彼はニューヨークとシカゴのスキッドモア・オーイング・アンド・メリル（SOM）の事務所で働き、イリノイ大学とハーヴァードで教えた。その傍ら、プランナーであるレジナルド・アイザックスと、シカゴとその近辺の都市の刷新計画と調査の仕事を共に行った。1953年に、ハーヴァードのアーバンプランニングとランドスケープ・アーキテクチャーの新しい学科長となったアイザックスは、そこで教えさせるためにササキを呼び寄せた。そしてササキは他でもないアイザックスに、先ず、次世代の多くの教育者や実践者たちが高い学位を得るであろうハーヴァードの専門教育から、ランドスケープ・アーキテクチャーの職能を変え始めるべきだという意見書を書いた。特にササキは、彼の事務所の中でも求めていたのだが、学校においても建築の個性と技術の新しいバランスが保たれることを提唱した。理想的には専任と非常勤をあわせて少なくとも四人の教師がいるべきである。つまり、創造に長けた天才、活発で生産的な人、高い技術を持った者、そして一人の穏健な人物。創造に長けた天才とは、ロベルト・バール＝マルクスのような手腕を持った者を意味し、穏健な人物とはササキのような人のことである。[7]

ランドスケープ・アーキテクチャーの専門教育と実践においてササキが行った努力の子細については、他の箇所で述べられている。親しい同僚であるチャールズ・W・ハリスは、「ヒデオ・ササキのリーダーシップの下での１９５８年から１９６８年の十年間の進展的変化は、ほとんど革命的衝撃をアメリカの主要な教育プログラムと設計事務所にもたらした」[8] と、まとめている。こうした変革は、独特な共生的関係に頼るところが大きかった。ランドスケープ・アーキテクチャーの学科長であった１９５８年から１９６８年の間に、ササキは自分の事務所から非常勤講師と資金を提供することによって学科を支えていたのである。また彼は、航空写真の解釈やコンピューターの応用といった新しい分野に従事している人やその専門家たちが、短期間学生を指導する制度を導入することによって、教えることと学ぶプロセスとの両方を豊かにした。最も将来性のある学生たちは、彼の事務所でのアルバイトや卒業後の仕事の機会を与えられた。同時に彼らはパート・タイムで（少額かもしくは無償で）教えることを求められ、このようにして彼らを養成した教育機関に何らかのお返しをするのであった。

このプロセスによって、実践と教育との間の伝統的障壁が透過的になり、それはまさにランドスケープ・アーキテクト、建築家、プランナー、エンジニア等の間の伝統的区別が明白でなくなり、時には無意味にさえなってきたのと時を同じくしていた。最近ササキ・アソシエーツの各事務所をを巡視した際にササキが述べたように、「当時は建築家と一緒であろうがランドスケプ・アーキテクトと一緒であろうが、探求と品揚の精神があった。誰と働くかは問題ではなかった。躊躇することなく、おおらかに何事かを信じる人々もいた。特別な状況のための、最も適切もしくは最も創造的だと思われる解決策を達成するために、我々は共に働いたのだった。」[9]

彼らしく謙虚に、ササキは、自分の多領域で活動する事務所の進展をあたかもきわめて自然なことのように、いかなる綿密な計画もなく、しかしどちらかというと「よりよい環境は創造できるし、そうでなければならないという信念の下に集う、異なる訓練と高い技術を持った専門家たちの集団にこそ可能性は開かれているのだ」という意識と共に達成された進展として語ってきた。グロピウスはバウハウスの協力の理想をずっと掲げてきたし、１９４５年の末以来、ザ・アーキテクツ・コラボラティブ（ＴＡＣ）という新しい事務所を組織した彼の元学生たちと関わってきた。間もなく、ＴＡＣはＳＯＭがそうした様に組織に専門の訓練を受けた人材を組織に導入した。しかしながら、ササキの事務所が（建築ではなく）ランドスケープ・アーキテクチャーを出発点として創設されたことは、こうした先例からの大きな飛躍である。この多分野で活動する事務所が産業革命や機械化から直接成長した伝統を飛び越えることが出来たのは、この出発点のおかげであるとササキは信じている。ジークフリード・ギーディオンの「機械化が権利を握る」（１９４８）といったような本に鼓舞された多くのモダニストたちにとっては、「自然とは打ち負かされるべきものであった」とササキは回想する。「しかし我々の概念では、自然とは我々の経済と共働するものであった。」[10]

間もなく、ササキはプランナー、グラフィックデザイナー、建築家、そしてエンジニアを雇った。始めは土地のプランニングと敷地のデザインのためであったが、結局古くからの施主たちの希望により、建物もデザインすることになった。やがて１９７０年代以来エンジニアたちは、都市のウォーターフロントの隔壁や、環境への影響に関する長い陳述書といった、複雑な技術的問題を引き受けるようになった。その頃、この事務所は明らかにもう一つの一般的でない出発を遂げた。ササキ・アソシエーツの主任たちは、事務所の各活動分野の少なくとも一人は、株を持ち決定を下す地位にある主任のレベルにまで昇進することに合意した。

１９７０年代までに、ササキは出版を目的として書くことをやめてしまった。しかしながら、彼は数少ない、しかも殆ど１９５０年以降に発表された論説の中で、特にランドスケープ・アーキテクトの環境計画から都市デザインにまで及ぶ仕事の幅を明確化した。「計画される敷地や領域に影響を及ぼす自然の作用に基づく環境の調査が必要である」と彼は１９５３年に書いている。「こうした調査によって、いかにすれば文化的形態が最も好ましく自然の作用に一致するかが規定されるであろうし、様々な生態学的な緊張関係はそうした研究から明らかにされ、従って今日我々の現場で確認する以上にふさわしいデザイン形態がより一層生み出されることになるのである。」１９５５年には、彼は文化的側面を重要視して以下のように記している。「経済的機能としてのみならず、ある意味で、文明社会の文化的達成の基準となる十分な視覚的表現としても、ランドスケープ・アーキテクトは自身の技術を貢献できるのだし、他の職能の人々と一緒に良い環境を創造するであろう。」[11]

１９５０年代のササキと彼の事務所がボストン、フィラデルフィア、そしてシカゴのプロジェクトに取りかかっていた頃、ササキは根本的な都市問題について熟考していた。一つの機能そして文化的表現としての都市は危険に晒されている、と１９５５年に彼は書いている。１９５６年には、ササキは特に都市デザインの新しい分野を取り扱った。「ランドスケープ・アーキテクトは、その特有の知識の故に、都市デザインの分野に多大なる貢献をするであろう．．．ランドスケープ・アーキテクトはプランナーと共に土地利用に連関する諸要素を決定し、そして更にプロジェクト全体のデザイン構成や形態を決定するであろう。」[12]

１９５６年の四月に、ハーヴァードのグラデュエートスクール・オブ・デザインが開催した会議では、リチャード・ノイトラ、ガレット・エックボ、ジェーン・ジェイコブス、ルイス・マンフォード、チャールズ・エイブラムス、エドモンド・ベーコン、そしてチャールズ・エリオット等が、建築家とランドスケープ・アーキテクト、そしてプランナーが共に働くための共通基盤を求めて一堂に会した。当時、主催者である学部長サートは、ホリオーク・センター、既婚学生住宅、世界宗教研究所といった、都市デザインとキャンパス・プランニング及びそのデザインを含むハーヴァードの多数のプロジェクトを、ササキの事務所と共同で行っていた。この会議で、サートは、都市デザインの問題を解決するためには大がかりな諸専門家集団が必要であることを強調した。彼は、「何年にもわたる個人の孤立した仕事の後で、我々は必然的に統合の時代に来ている」と記している。都市計画の段階では最も少なく探求されてはいるものの「最も創造的」である都市デザインこそが、サートが専心する都市の再集中化の課程をもたらすべきであった。彼の視点によれば、都市は、ビジネスの場所としてのみではなく、文化と学問の中心としても、アメリカの偉大さに貢献するのである。[13]

ササキはこの機会を、現代における二三の厄介な進展について強調するために用いた。彼は、「意味のない折衷主義」と彼が名付けた、建築様式の理由のない符号（現代とも過去とも符合する）を憂えた。同様に厄介なのは、「意味のないモニュメンタリティー」やスケール感のなさであった。ササキは、技術に支えられた大がかりな規模の建物が、それまで目撃されたことのないような広がりを表現するであろうことを予想した。しかし、そこに住んだり、そうした建物を理解しなければならないのは人間なのである。第三の厄介な進展は、周囲との関係の欠如である。周囲の状況を認識しており、人は謙虚に、またはどちらかというと勇敢に、そして大胆に接近する。しかしながらササキにとって、目新しさのために壮観さを追求することは嫌悪すべきデザイン概念である。[14] プログレッシブ・アーキテクチャー誌に多く記載されたこうした論点は、ササキの理性的で分析的な思考と、人道的で繊細な感受性を示唆している。

実に、プランニングとデザインの実践における人道的側面は、ササキにとって最優先に重要であった。より大きな環境から彼が引き出そうとしていた調和と全体性もまた、事務所において彼が維持しようとした特質であった。このことはササキが隠さず認めるように、困難でデリケートな事柄であった。というのも、彼が自分の周囲から集めた才能のある所員たちは、往々にして強い個性と激しい気性を持っていたからである。またもやササキは自分自身の限界と責任に留意して、人格者として知られ公平な人物であるポール・ガーデスクを、彼の次に主導権を握るランドスケープ・アーキテクトとして選んだ。二十年以上にわたり最高指導者として、そして社長として、ガーデスクは、人間関係、契約、そして他の、デザインというビジネスの抱えるあまり知られていない側面に、その落ち着きと、いまだにササキ・アソシエーツのメンバーたちによって懐かしがられる幾分かの超俗性を携えて対処したのだった。

ササキは１９８０年に退いたが、事務所の顧問に留まっている。ガーデスクは１９８４年に退職し、公認会計士と経営学修士の資格を持つジェームス・A・スークフォースが社長に選ばれ、九年間勤めた。スークフォースの告白によれば、彼が事務所を自分一人で率いていくことは無理であった。どちらかというとスークフォースは、彼自身の財務上の主導権と四つの分野の主任たちによる専門上の主導権との間の、バランスを保ったのだった。その主任たちは、プランニングのリチャード・ゲールハウス、ランドスケープ・アーキテクチャーのケネス・バセット、建築のジョン・オーカット、そしてエンジニアリングのモーリス・フリードマンである。「我々五人で組織を本質的に運営した」とスークフォースは説明している。[15] 彼が１９９２年の終わりに社長を退いた後、新しいバランスが達成された。ケネス・バセットが社長になったが、彼は前任者のスークフォースと頻繁に協議を重ねたのだった。現在、バセットとスークフォースは隣り合ったオフィスを占有している。

今日のササキ・アソシエーツの社長であるバセットは、事務所の中で、一つのプロジェクトから他のプロジェクトへと円滑に移動してきた。彼は、自分が聴く耳を持っていること、与えられた状況の幅広い下部構造を理解できること、そしてササキの残した伝統を彼自身の言葉で伝えて行くことに、誇りを持っている。「我々の文化は、分野間のバランスをとることによって生まれるのだ」と彼は述べる。「文化を操る舵の手は、ゆるくなければならない。もしあなたが、自分の所属する分野の考え方に強く固執しているなら、息をつくための部屋を与え、それと同時に彼らをその分野に優しく連れ戻しながら、『だけど全体というものもここにはあるのだ。もし我々全員がこの同じことに関わっているなら、我々はあるチームの部分であり、チームのやり方で振る舞わなければならないということを悟る必要がある。そしてそのためには、あなたは自分の振る舞いと物腰、そして仕事のやり方を調節しなければならない』と論さなければならないとき、そうした文化の一番おもしろいところは失われる。しかし、あなたはこの与えられた休息のための部屋を、ただかしこまって通り抜けるのではない。あなたは多くの異なる分野の異なる考え方に注意を向けながら、そこを通るのである。私はそれが好きなのだ。」[16]

以下に続くページでは、事務所の仕事と展望を自分たちなりに解釈するササキ・アソシエートの現在の主役たちから、より多くの内容を聴くであろう。ここでは、ササキの残した伝統である「哲学と志と人間関係の融合」という視点が、まとめになるかもしれない。「（事務所の）初期の頃にヒデオと仕事をすることを好んだ建築家たちとの会話を、私は覚えている」と建築家兼プランナーであるデヴィッド・ハーツェルは思い起こす。「競争と相対立するものとしての協力、参加、そして援助を信条とする人と共に働くことこそだったら彼らは建築家たちの大いなる自尊心は、非常に喜んでそれを経験した。そしてこうしたヒデオの特性は、誰が事務所に留まり、だれが去るかを実によく反映した。自分のやりたいようにやることを望み、ドアに自分の名前を掲げたい人々はこの場所を通り過ぎていった。」[17]

事務所を去ったランドスケープ・アーキテクトのピーター・ウォーカーは誇りを持って振り返り、こう語っている。「ちょうど１９３０年代と４０年代に、トーマス・チャーチのサンフランシスコにあるアトリエがモダニズムをランドスケープ・アーキテクチャーの分野に先導したように、ヒデオのネオ・オルムステッド的視点は戦後の飛躍的発展というチャレンジを擁護しながら、１９５５年以来我々全てのために、ランドスケープの実践が抱える目的、方式、そして特質を定義づけて見せたのだった。バウハウス的理想である同等の能力を持ったデザイナーたちによる協力というものは建築の基盤のみではなかなか達成できないが、それは献身的なランドスケープ・アーキテクト、建築家、プランナー、そしてエンジニアたちによって四十年にわたり模索され続け、今日までササキ・アソシエーツにおいて持続している。あたかもそれは、全体的に精巧に構築された世界という理想が維持され続けているように見える。」[18]

そして事務所に留まったランドスケープ・アーキテクトのドン・オルソンは１９８１年にこう回想している。「多くの事務所が我々の軌跡を辿ったわけではないし、我々も彼らの後を追わなかった。我々以前に存在していた事務所は、多分、同様の成長の機会に対応するにあたって、より都合の良いポジションにいたのである。つまり全てがうまく行くためには、ササキの特別な素質が必要不可欠だったように思われる。」

キャンパス・プランニング

メラニー・スィーモ
訳／金　一

「大学というものの存在は、それが知識と人生への熱情との間の関係を保持していることによって、また、学ぶという構想力に富む思索において若者と老人とを結びつけることによって正当化される。大学は情報を提供するが、それを創造的に授けるのである．．．．事実はもはや単なる事実ではなく、それはあらゆる可能性を備えているのである。それはもはや記憶の重荷ではなく、我々の夢を生む詩人として、また、我々の目的を設計する建築家として活性化しているのである。」
アルフレッド・ノース・ホワイトヘッド

この一節は１９６８年６月２８日の日付のあるクリーブランド州立大学の基本計画図面の、題辞として使われたものである。ササキ・ドーソン・デュメイ・アソシエーツ（ＳＤＤＡ）は、ドン・M・ヒサカ・アンド・アソシエーツと共に都市に位置するこのキャンパスに取り組んだ。基本計画に加えて、事務所は様々な新しい教育用建物のためにランドスケープ・アーキテクチャーのサーヴィスも提供し、新しい大学センターのために広場をデザインしていた。これは、当時大きな発注であった。もし、ホワイトヘッドによって強調された大学の機能についての並外れたアイデアがなく、それがササキの事務所によって様々な価値の一表現として再発見されることがなかったら、この

計画は今日、ササキ・アソシエーツのキャンパス・プランニングとそのデザイン活動の印象的な歴史において、単なる脚注に留まっていただろう。

当時、若い建築家兼プランナーであったM・ペリー・チャップマンは、先ず最初にロチェスター大学の基本計画に従事すべく、１９６４年にササキの事務所に雇われていた。間もなく彼は、１９６０年代当時のササキ事務所にとって最も急速に成長する実践分野であった、複雑なキャンパス・プランニングとそのデザインとに没頭するようになった。三十年後、チャップマンが戦後のアメリカのキャンパス・プランニングについてエッセイを書こうと決めた時、彼はササキにインタビューし、１９６０年代の多作の時代から始まる草稿を書いた。そこで、ある編集者が更に前の時代から書くように勧めた。チャップマンは思い起こす。「１９５０年代について調査し始めたとき、私はとても面白くて大切なことが、その時代のキャンパス・デザインに起こっていたことに気づいた。」

チャップマンのエッセイ、「社会の変化とアメリカのキャンパス・プランニング」（１９９４）は、いつかは一冊の本に匹敵する研究となるであろう。[2] ここで、ササキの事務所が初期に果たした貢献について触れなければならない。１９５３－５４年にハーヴァードで教え初めてすぐに、ヒデオ・ササキはMITの新しい学部長、ピエトロ・ベルスキを招待した。ベルスキと彼の学生たちがハーヴァードのスタジオでどのようなことをしているのかを知るためであった。ベルスキは、ササキが自分と同じ精神を持つことを理解して、この招待を受け、主に大学の理事から来るプロジェクトへの協力をササキに依頼するようになった。当時のアメリカの大学は、軍兵権利法に支えられて学究に励む復員軍人たちの存在のおかげにもより、どこも記録的な成長を経験していた。ベルスキは、オレゴン州ポートランドで著しい実践を積み重ねた後、その頃再びケンブリッジに落ち着いたが、まだ地元での自分の事務所を持っていなかった。１９５０年代の終わりと１９６０年代の始めに、彼はロビンソン・グリーン・アンド・ベレッタなどの建築設計事務所と共に、ロード・アイランド・デザイン学校（RISD）の新しい学生寮やカール・コックの事務所、そしてベニントン・カレッジの新しい図書館に取り組んだ。それぞれのケースで、ベルスキは彼の友人ヒデオ・ササキをランドスケープ・アーキテクトとして雇った。

間もなく、これらや他の教育機関の学長たちが、キャンパスの拡張やプランニングといった、より大きな問題についてアドヴァイスを頼むようになった。調査事項をきちんと形にまとめたり、インフラストラクチャー、駐車、歩行者の動き、オープンスペース、そして建物の位置などの問題を扱うために必要な多分野にまたがるチームを組織するために、ベルスキはササキとそのまだ小さかった事務所に目を向けた。

スクール・オブ・デザインと教育学部が共同で指揮していたハーヴァードのいくつかのスタジオは、教育プログラムと三次元の物理的プランニングとの関係を模索し始めていた。こうした模索の結果、すぐにササキの事務所が行っている仕事の情報が伝わった。なぜなら、ササキと他の同僚の何人か（リチャード・ドーバー、ジャック・ロビンソン、ケネス・デュメイ、そしてドン・オルソン）もまた、スクール・オブ・デザインの学生に非常勤講師だったからである。ササキは、組織だった実践的建築技術を学生たちに伝えた。彼は自分の事務所を一種の学校と見なしていた。そこでは、キャンパス・プランニングのわき起こる問題を取り扱うために、探求心のみならず、急成長、歴史的連続、インフラストラクチャーと建物の用途、そして建築とランドスケープの視覚的質の統制といったリサーチへの、実務に通じた興味が必要で不可欠であった。こうした検討は、コンサルタントたちや大学当局によって様々な配置モデルを用いて行われた。建物のプログラムを決定していく課程が改善され、建設の様々な課程を監督するためのキャンパスの諸問委員会が組織された。焦点はもはや建物のみではなく、空間の組み合わせ、連続性、人の動き、そして戸外空間にも向けられた。開発のための新しい枠組みが生まれたのである。

こうした調査の結果は急激に蓄積され、ドーバーが「キャンパス・プランニング」を書くために用いた理論と客観的データになった。この本を出版直後に読んだチャップマンは好奇心をそそられた。本のインパクトは、ジェーン・ジェイコブの「偉大なるアメリカの都市の生と死」（１９６１）やゴードン・カレンの「タウンスケープ」（１９６１）のそれに匹敵した。これらの本は、人を日常の小さい、大切なディテールに立ち戻らせながらも、その人の視野を広げていくようなものであった。その上、大きな写真とスケッチを、そして確かな理想と現実とを提示していたため、これらの本はデザイン業界に急激に浸透していった。キャンパスのプランニングとデザインにおけるこの新しい仕事の重要さと新鮮さの故に、彼の幅広いが人道的で自然の法則にのっとったプランニングとデザインという非常に求められていたサーヴィスによって、アメリカ国内で急激に評判を高めていった。事務所は、ハーヴァードやMITや他の学校からの卒業生たちを魅惑し、成長した。ウォータータウン・オフィスでの二三年の後には、若いプランナーとデザイナーたちの幾人かは彼らの故郷に帰って仕事についた。何人かは教えるために事務所を離れたし、公共機関で職を得たものの、ササキの事務所が新しいプランニングの責任を全うするのを手助けするために、戻ってくる者もいた。[3]

ササキの事務所に留まった若いプランナーとデザイナーたちは、アメリカとカナダのいくつかの地方に散らばる、新しいか、もしくは既存のキャンパスのためのすばらしいプロジェクトに携わることが出来た。例えば、カリフォルニア州ロスアンジェルスにあるフットヒル・カレッジは、単なるアカデミックな建築物たちの集合体ではないプランニングの一つの典型となった。問題となる二つの丘陵の頂に位置するフットヒルの建物と戸外スペースを統合するために、１９５７年以来ササキと彼の同僚たちは二つの建築設計事務所、エルンスト・J・カンプ・アンド・アソシエーツとメイステン・ハード・と緊密に歩みを進めた。劇場、図書館、サンフランシスコ交響楽団が折折公演を行う体育館、そして大きくて儀式的な、または小さく打ち解けた広場や中庭。こうした全てが、学生たちや周囲のコミュニティーの人々で賑わう場所となったのである。間もなく、フットヒルは真のアクロポリスと考えられるようになった。アラン・テムコの見方によれば、それは若いコミュニティーの中で最も高い価値に捧げられた、一種の「至聖所」であった。それ故、フットヒルは新しいタイプの教育機関を発展に向けるための標準を設定した。つまり、コミュニティーとその地域のための「多角的文化活動の源」として機能する二年制短期大学である。[4]

後には、フットヒル・カレッジは、ササキの事務所を数十年間も従事させることになる巨大で複雑な、何段階にもわたるキャンパスのプランニングとデザインの一連の仕事に発展した。そして１９６０年代のササキ・アソシエーツには、とりわけリチャード・ゲールハウスやジャック・ロビンソンなどの建築とプランニングの両方でトレーニングされ、才能と個性がそうした仕事に適した若い専門家たちがいた。チャップマンやケネス・デュメイに加えて、こうした人物たちは、キャンパスのプランニングとデザインの実践において事務所を発展させるのに主導的役割を果たした。ブールダーにあるコロラド大学の戦後のキャンパス拡張のための総合計画が始まった。それは、ピエトロ・ベルスキ、ハリー・ウィーズ・アンド・アソシエーツ、デュメイ・アンド・レイ、そしてウィリアム・C・マチョウ・アソシエーツ、ホバート・D・ワジェナー・アンド・アソシエーツや他地域の頭角を現しているコロラドの事務所たちを含めた、多くの傑出した建築家たちと共同で行う一連の建築プロジェクトになった。振り返ってみると、フットヒルとコロラド大学が、最も注目され、数々の賞を獲得した初期のキャンパスの仕事であった。しかし、１９６０年代

と７０年代のササキ事務所には、他にも多くの重要なプロジェクトが持ち込まれた。それらは、アマーストにあるマサチューセッツ大学の拡張、キングストンにあるロードアイランド大学、シャーロッテスヴィルにあるヴァージニア大学の新しい建物、そしてバッファローにあるニューヨーク州立大学アマースト校の全体計画と建物のデザインであった。

アマーストのマサチューセッツ大学を含む、こうしたプロジェクトのいくつかにプランナーとして携わったゲールハウスは、異なるバックグラウンドを持つ意志の強い傑出した専門家たちと協力して問題を解決していく方法について、すばらしい思い出を沢山持っている。しかしながら、互いに堅い協力関係を築き、そうした労働環境で成長した二人、つまり彼にとっては年長の同僚たちにあたるササキとベルスキの功績ほどには、ゲールハウスは自分が初期に果たした華々しい役割について語ってこなかった。「ベルスキは、実に古き良き時代の紳士だった」とゲールハウスは溜息をもらす。「彼のスタイルと技術は驚くべきものだった。彼はヒデオとの関係を実に楽しんだと私は思う。」[5]

いくつかの論考で、チャップマンはキャンパス・プランニングにおける事務所の主な実績を、年代ごとに記している。１９５０年代と６０年代には、オープンスペースや人と物の循環について新しい構造を示唆した全体計画の多くが、ランドスケープ、サイトデザイン、そして時には建築の設計にもつながっていった。１９６０年代の終わりまでに、全体計画とは無縁の学術的用途の建物の依頼が来るようになった。そして、一層強力な土木技術に支えられた建築の分野は、すぐに当然のように伸びていった。１９７０年代には、南アジアでの戦争に対するキャンパスでの不穏な雰囲気の高まりや、経済不振、インフレ、エネルギー危機、そして基金としての有価証券の目減りによって、キャンパス・プランニングは一時期下火になった。７０年代の終わりまでに、いくつかの大学は彼らがキャンパスの外に所有する土地を、商業用地、企業用地、研究開発用地などとして複合開発するにあたっての助力を、ササキ・アソシエーツに依頼した。彼らのコミュニティーでの雇用や新しい歳入源を確保するためであった。

１９８０年代と９０年代には、キャンパス・プランニングが、多くの場合さらに切り詰まった予算と新しい配慮を伴って再び盛んになった。その配慮とは、新築よりは既存の建物の再利用であり、入学者数の減少の時期にあって学生の獲得に寄与する設備であり、未開発の土地の巨大な計画よりは選択的な拡張であり、既存のコンテクストに適合する伝統的な材料の使用であり、維持コストの安い植栽であり、より確かなセキュリティーである。さらには、既存のスペースにコンピューターや他の技術的装置を導入するための方法が必要であり、他方、伝統的には学術的生活の真髄であった、よりパーソナルな顔と顔を向き合わせての交流も推奨された。

ササキ・アソシエーツの多くの主任たちは、キャンパスや又はそれを越えたどんなスケールであろうと、シンプルで楽しい人間同士の交流のための出会いや集いの場所を作ることは、彼らの多分野にわたる実践の真髄に位置することであると考える。チャップマンは、一人のタウン・プランナーに最近聞かれた質問を好んで引用する。「どうして我々は、サイバースペースにかけるのと同じだけのエネルギーをパブリックスペースの必要性に注がないのでしょうか？」「これは逸話にすぎないのだが」とチャップマンは認めて言う。「しかし、何かがそこにあるのだと私は思う。」

都市デザイン

メラニー・スィーモ
訳／金　一

１９８６年の高層建築に関する国際会議でステュワート・ドーソンが論文を発表したとき、彼は聴衆に向かって、高層建築については少しの間忘れるよう頼んだ。「摩天楼に注意が向けられすぎている」と彼は始めた。「あまりに多くの関心が有効空間比、風変わりな窓割り、安全警備、トラバーチンなどにばかり向けられすぎている。自動車があまりに大切にされ、通りの人々への配慮が少なすぎる。」[1]

そのときのドーソンのトピックは、大きな通りの創造、特に彼が主任として担当した新しいダラス芸術地区のための都市デザインの全体計画についてであった。この計画では、ダラスのダウンタウンの北西部にある地域の、中心に広がる舗装されたどちらかというと寂しい一角を、歩行者に優しく且つ芸術に焦点を絞った、大きくて並木を従えた目抜き通りに変容させる必要があった。古くからの名前、「フローラ通り」は保持され、一方いくつかの新しい低層建築が通りの性格を定義づけて高尚化するのに役立った。その中にはI・M・ペイによるコンサートホールやエドワード・L・バーンズによる新しいダラス美術館、そして新しい商店、娯楽施設、レストランが含まれ、それらがオフィス・タワー、学校、そして歴史的なベロ家邸宅や他の建物たちの間を散在するように配置された。この大きな通りの建設について説明するにあたり、もしそれらがうまく調整されれば歩行者と自動車、高層ビルと「建築の小さな宝石たち」が共存していくための大きなスペースを生み出せるような、法的、資金的、園芸学的、そして建築的側面を、ドーソンは詳細に渡り披露した。しかしながら、ドーソンの最終的イメージは、自然界から導き出されたものだった。ウィリアム・H・ウィトを引用しながら彼は言った。「通りは都市にとっての生活の川だ。ベストなパブリックスペースというのは、どこで通りが終わってどこからスペースが始まるのか、区別のつかないものなのだ。」[2]

実際のところ、「川」はササキ・アソシエーツにほぼ４０年間にわたり繰り返されてきたイメージである。運動、連続性、生命力、そして自然自身の傾向とリズムによって鍛えられた速度を指し示しながら、同時に川は自然の一つの要素であり、川そのものでありながら、隠喩的でもある。このイメージは、１９５０年代と６０年代初期にドーソンやケネス・デュメイ、リチャード・ゲールハウス、ドン・オルソン、そして現在は事務所の年長の主任となった所員たちが、様々な都市デザインプロジェクトでその分野の頭角を現しつつあった人物たちと仕事を共にしたときに形成された。例えば、１９５９年に事務所は、アダムス・ハワード・アンド・グリーレイ、アンダーソン・ベックウィズ・アンド・ヘイブル、そして個人コンサルタントのケヴィン・リンチ、ジョン・R・マイヤー、ポール・D・スプレーアジェンらと、ボストンの新しい「施政センター」の中に建てられるいくつかの建物のための大きな枠組みをデザインした。都市を刷新する方法が既存の都市の構造から遊離したままであるという好ましくない傾向に留意して、このコンサルタントのグループは古いものと新しいものの統合や、人々が動きながら見たり経験したりする連続した空間を強調した。このコンサルタントたちはまた、低層の建物の間を、谷間を下る「川のように流れて」終いにはハーバーに人々を導く一連の公共オープンスペースを提案した。後には誰かがふとした思いつきで、この連続性を「海に向かって歩く」と呼んだ。このコンセプトは説得力があり、そのフレーズは生き続けた。[3]

特にプランニングの課程に環境保護と幅広い一般意見を導入するように、という無数の制限が課されるようになって以来、ササキの事務所は何年にもわたってさらに複雑なチャレンジをこなしてきた。間もなく、より多くの傾聴し

なければならない意見や考慮しなければならない要因が出てきた。最近の「クリーブランド・ゲートウェイ」計画に際しての微妙な交渉のように、事務所はアーバン・プランニングとそのデザインとして伝統的に知られるプロセスを始める以前に、頻繁に公共と私設のいくつかの団体の意見を調整しなければならなかった。クリーブランド・ゲートウェイ計画のデザイン主任であるアラン・ワードは語る。「二つの建築事務所が我々と共に採用された。球技公園担当のHOK・スポーツとスポーツアリーナ担当のイレーブ・ベケットだった。我々は敷地上で建物を整合させ、交通と駐車スペースを調整し、また公共の利益をも代表した。つまり役所と開発側、そして公共一般との間で、中立の第三者として活動することを目的とした組織であった。」[4]

キャンパス・プランニングのような都市デザインの問題は、ササキ・アソシエーツから彼らが最も満足を覚える「長期にわたり協力に努める精神」といったものを引き出した。そして驚くべきことに、彼らが最も「競争的」だったのは実にこうしたプロジェクトにおいてであった。問題は全て大きく複雑になりがちで、技術に加えて、どんな専門家も一人では解答を提示できないのだということを理解することが要求された。全然明白な前例がないような問題を扱うために、どちらかというと建築家、ランドスケープ・アーキテクト、エンジニア、そしてプランナーらはそれぞれ固有の理解を持ち寄った。

とはいえ、ササキの事務所がそうしたプロジェクトに興味を示し、且つそれに適しているのだという事実を説明する歴史的前例が存在する。その前例とは、単独のプロジェクトではなく、ある時期に限られたものでもない。それは、どんな専門家も、どんなに「すぐれた建築家」や「マントをつけたヒーロー」をもその大きな形態的解決のためには単独では頼れないような複雑な問題を解くための、徐々に展開するアプローチのやり方である。異なるトレーニングを受けた相互に尊敬し合う専門家のグループは、彼らの都市環境を改善するために、個々の自我を抑制しながら共に働くことを一様に強く希望した。もちろん、いかなる国のいかなる個人や事務所もそうしたアプローチを独占できるわけではない。しかしながらこうしたアプローチは、ある力を持ったデザイナーやグループもしくは流派の野心や理想が、異なる理想や価値によって鍛え上げられるような数少ない場でのみ発展した。それが起こった一つの場が、1950年代のハーヴァードだったのである。

1953年にジョセップ・ルイス・サートがグラデュエートスクール・オブ・デザインの学部長になったとき、それまで建築の上級の学生たちにウォルター・グロピウスが教えていた上級課程スタジオで重要な変化がなされた。学生の分野を問わなくなったのである。ランドスケープ・アーキテクチャーでのヒデオ・ササキの優れた学生たちとシティー・プランニングでのレジナルド・アイザックスの優秀な学生たちが建築の上級の学生たちに混じって、本質的に都市デザインの問題である、より複雑な建築の問題に取り組んだ。この上級課程スタジオが、1960年から61年にかけて建築の学生とランドスケープ・アーキテクチャーの上級の学生たちのための特別な分野として創設された新しい都市デザインプログラムのモデルとなった。このプログラムはアメリカ全土と外国から学生たちを集め、その卒業生たちは間もなくハーバード・スクエア近辺やボストン地域のデザイン事務所、とりわけササキ事務所に就職した。

ササキ事務所の多分野にわたる活動と、そのキャンパス・プランニング、都市の刷新、そして形態的デザインによって高まる評判に誘われたハーヴァードの都市デザインの学生たちが、事務所でアルバイトをし、そのうちの二三人は事務所に就職した。当時、リチャード・ドーバー、ジョン・エイデルバーグ、そしてリチャード・ゲールハウスを含む事務所にいる全てのプランナーたちは、主に建築デザインのバックグランドを持っていた。こうしたプランナーたちは、マサオ・キノシタのような初期の都市デザインプログラムの卒業生たちと仕事をした。その課程で、都市デザインという新しい分野の、プログラミングの要素と形態的要素が融合した。さらに、ハーヴァードを理論的拠点とし、ササキ事務所を実践の場として、都市デザインの分野は新しい問題が湧き上がるたびに再定義され続けた。

今日、ボストンやダラスからポツダムやタイペイにまで及ぶ、何十年以上ものササキ・アソシエーツの都市デザインを振り返ると、都市の統合されるべき成長し続ける複雑な問題を認識し、さらに事務所の一貫した幅広いヴィジョンとアプローチの取り方を理解することが出来る。都市は依然として、構造、パターン、コントラスト、そして力強い記憶に残るイメージを必要とする場所として捉えられている。足で、道の上で、そして空からも、ヒューマンスケールで体験できるスペースと視界の連続を作り上げようとする努力が、都市ではいまだに行われている。1963年に、ヒデオ・ササキがフィラデルフィアの都市プランナーであるエドムンド・ベーコン宛に、その都市のウォーターフロントを改善するための提案を事務所が準備した簡単なスケッチと共に送った時、彼はシルキル川の持つ線状に連続する性質を強調した。人々は、川縁の遊歩道に沿って座ったり散策したり、鉄道の上を越える歩道橋を渡ったり、静かな遊び場や草地で時を過ごすことが出来た。背後では、繁茂した並木が、川縁と都市構造の両方を定義づけていた。[5]

近年、いくつかの都市デザインの理論は伝統的近隣地区の開発に注目している。「ニュー・アーバニズム」である。これらは、60年か70年前に新鮮な傾向だったモダニスト的アプローチに対抗すべく、往々にして強力な環境的社会的目的に導かれた慎重な努力を重視する。ササキ・アソシエーツに参加する前に、1970年代の終わりにハーヴァードでランドスケープ・アーキテクチャーと都市デザインを学んだアラン・ウォードにとっては、最近の理論が提示する以上に、こうした近年の都市デザインのプロトタイプにはかなり多くの先例が存在するように思える。「それぞれの人々が、革命的変革を起こしたがり、自分たちが最初からやり直したと言う」と彼は見る。「しかし、実際には多くの連続があるのだ」。

イリノイ州のリヴァーサイドでフレデリック・ロウ・オルムステッドがカルヴァート・ヴォーと共にした仕事（1869）と、イギリスのハートフォードシャーにある所謂レッチワースでサー・レイモンド・アンウィンがバリー・パーカーと共にした仕事を思い起こしながら、ウォードはプランニングと都市デザインの考え方の進化を検出する。オルムステッド、アンウィン、そして20世紀初期のランドスケープ・デザイナー兼プランナーであるジョン・ノレンやエルバート・ピーツらの仕事から、20世紀の終わりのササキ・アソシエーツやその同時代の人々の仕事である新しいコミュニティーのデザインに至るまで、ある脈絡が流れているとウォードは信じている。この進化的発展からの劇的決裂は、モダンムーブメントの中で、唯一ル・コルビュジェ等による革命的プロトタイプにおいてのみ起こった。しかし、このムーブメントは、今日あと知恵で考えられているほど均質的なものでは決してなかった。その都市デザインの問題への解答の出し方は様々だった。今日でさえ、モダニスト的都市デザインの成功と失敗は、未だに評価がされていない。

同時にウォードは、アメリカ内外を問わず実在の都市で緊急に起こっている観念的でない具体的な問題にも、より多くの興味を持っている。彼はこう信じている。「実際の問題は、基本的にどうやって既存の都市を修理していくかである。アメリカのアーバニズムを実験として捉えた場合、フロンティアに住み初めて以来の数百年の歴史を我々は持っているように思われる。ヨーロッパで長期に渡り人々が行ってきたような、過去に時を重ね合わせていく様なこ

とはせずに、我々は何年にも渡って過去を改善しようとして単純に郊外へと動き、都市を広げてきた。今やある制限を設けて以前の間違った実験を修正し、それを正しく導いていこうと主張する時だと私は思う。そうすれば、既存の都市を矯正再建したり、公共的環境でコミュニティーの感覚を強化したりする努力が可能になる。もしもその環境をより密に都会化できるなら、パブリックスペースはもっと重要になるだろう。それが我々のこれからの課題の一つである。」

ウォードは、エコロジー、社会学、そして芸術に関する多くの事柄やその実現の機会について考え、一息ついてから言う。「私の感では、これからの基本問題は我々の文化がいかに自然と結びつくかである。それは我々が対峙する根本的チャレンジとして、未だに残されていると私は思う。」[6]

新しいコミュニティー

メラニー・スィーモ

訳／金　一

「大西洋岸をメインからフロリダまで旅してみても、このような場所は見つけられない。サンディービーチは切れ間なく数マイルも広がり、砂丘の背後では無限の塩生湿地帯が、曲がりくねった小川と浅い入り江で縁取られている．．．．ヴァージニアのイースタン・ショアーを経験することは、生活が土地に根ざし、家族が大地と海の恵みに支えられていた頃の人々に再び出会うために、時間をさかのぼるようなものである。」
カーティス・バッジャー、ザ・ネーチャー・コンサーヴァンシー誌

ヴァージニアのイースタン・ショアーでの人間の伝統的住まいと豊富な野生動植物の生息地との両方を維持する目的で自然保護局が始めた一連のプランニングの努力に、五年前からササキ・アソシエーツは貢献し始めた。四万五千エーカーほどの珊瑚礁の島々と、塩水湿地帯、そしてデルマーヴァ半島の大西洋岸に沿った高台のためのプランニングの努力は、現在、例外的に精密な調査の下にある。そして、その調査の全てが地元の市民グループやプランニングの依頼者側、商社、観光協会、住宅委員会、NAACPの地元の支部によってのみ行われているのではない。いかに人類は自然と共存するのかを問う本質的モデルとして、1979年に合衆国はヴァージニアのイースタン・ショアーを「国際生物圏保護地区」に指定した。自然保護局はこの例外的生態系に「最後の偉大な土地」という、戸惑い、喜び、そして多分なにがしかの予感や緊急性までをも暗示した呼称をつけた。

下記の「ヴァージニア海岸保護区」には、自然保護局の努力へのササキ・アソシエーツの貢献が、戦略、プロタイプ、デザインのガイドライン等の観点から概説されている。ただし、1969年に初めて事務所に入って以来いくつかの事務的または専門的役割を果たしてきたデーヴィッド・ハーツェルを含む、年長の主任たちの個人的信念は、そこには述べられていない。ハーツェルは当時ハーヴァードの経営学修士号を持った若い建築家であった。今日彼は、環境の維持可能性という主題について積極的に意見を述べるササキ・アソシエーツの主任たちの一人である。ヴァージニアのイースタン・ショアーの仕事を含む、自然保護局のプログラムにおいて推進されている幅広い独創的活動について、ハーツェルは1994年のAIAの環境維持可能性に関する会議で強調した。その活動の幅は、最も破壊されやすい場所や中心地域を守ることから、農業、漁業、芸術工芸、そして小規模産業によって地域の経済的発展を推進することにまで及ぶ。「いかなる単独のプロジェクトも全てを達成できるわけではないということに我々は気づく」と彼は同僚の建築家たちに想起を促す。しかし、それぞれのプロジェクトが環境維持可能性というゴールに向かって前進するチャンスを提供する。彼はこう結論する。「専門家たちが構築された環境のプランニングやデザインに焦点を絞るように、我々は、我々の時代の致命的問題の一つに率先して取り組まねばならない。」[1]

ササキ・アソシエーツの同僚の建築家兼プランナーであるリチャード・ゲールハウスは、根本的には環境の解決、美的解決を求めているが、彼の信念をハーツェルの様には表明しないだろう。「我々はいつも環境の解決、美的解決を求めているが、経済的意味での解決も求めている。土地の価値、その受け継がれてきた性格、そして何かを行うという経済状態に影響を及ぼす土地の特性についてはいつも考慮されてきた。」[2]　1960年に事務所に参加したゲールハウスは、新しいコミュニティーのプランニングとデザインに事務所が関わることについて、長期の展望を持っている。何年もの間ササキ・アソシエーツのプランニングの第一人者として、彼は会議で発表したり専門誌に書いたり微妙な新しいプロジェクトに施主を引き込んだりしながら、こうしたコミュニティーのプランニングにおける環境的側面を多く扱ってきた。彼の出発点はいつも、彼が来る三四年前に事務所に持ち込まれたシー・パインズ・プランテーションのプロジェクトである。サウスカリフォルニアの海岸から離れたヒルトン・ヘッド・アイランドにあるこの新しいリゾート・コミュニティーの第二期開発に、ゲールハウスはプランナーとして携わった。

「開発業者は、シー・パインズを第二次大戦後の国内で最初の現代的リゾート且つ退職者用コミュニティーとして捉えていた」とゲールハウスは言う。「その業者が設定した開発基準は実に業界全体の基準になった。」[3]　この成功の名誉は、1950年代の終わりに始まったこの新しいコミュニティーのプランナー、敷地デザイナー、そして建築家としてのヒデオ・ササキと彼の同僚のみに依るのではなく、行動制限や契約を含めた土地利用計画の法的側面に詳しい、当時はイェール大学法学校の若い卒業生であった施主、チャールズ・フレイザーの貢献にも依る。フレイザーは、植物群と動物群を含むこの島の自然の景観に変わらぬ興味と愛情を抱いてきた。（ジョン・マックビーが書いたように、アリゲーターとシカは、後に彼の私設警備隊によって守られた。）[4]　そこでの4500エーカーの土地の開発が始まってから40年近く経て、フレイザーのヴィジョンである「調和と融合」は広く認識された。「そこには汚れていないビーチと広々とした水の景観、頭上に連続した森の枝葉、そして水平線まで曲線状に続く湿地帯がある」とあるジャーナリストは1990年に報告している。「過去30年以上の集中的開発にもかかわらず、この静かな景観は、いまだにヒルトン・ヘッドの性質を最もよく代表している。」[5]

ゲールハウスは、近海の島々、川を望む絶壁、豊富な水路を伴った比較的平らな土地などの心地よい自然に恵まれたこの景観の中で、プランナーとして多くの仕事をした。ヴァージニアのウィリアムスバーグにほど近いある新しいコミュニティー「ジェームスのキングスミル」についての彼の論考に述べられているように、時折ゲールハウスは、開発の段階で他のファクターよりも優先されるエコロジカルな考慮について強調した。「干満のある湿地帯と、もろくて簡単に浸食されてしまう土からなる細谷は最も傷つきやすい自然環境の要素であることを、キングスミルの生態系分析は示している」と説明してから、彼は、1972年に完成した全体計画の主な構想を概説した。土地の造成、木々の伐採、そして汚水処理の技術的詳細は、経済コストを押さえながら環境への影響をも最小限に押さえ

るように実施された。開発プロセスをさらに複雑化していたのは、将来の建物の敷地に位置する植民地時代のプランテーションの残骸だった。開発業者の親会社であるアンヒューザー＝ブッシュ醸造社は、集中的な考古学的調査に資金を提供し、史跡を保存することに同意した。話し合いはいつも長く、時には退屈なこともあったとゲールハウスは認める。しかし最終的には、開発側、環境保護主義者、国立公園局、ウィリアムスバーグ郡、ヴァージニア州史的ランドマーク委員会、そして他の団体の主張は全て全体計画に取り込まれた。[6]

この無理のないバランスのとれた状態こそ、ゲールハウスが概説する、ササキ・アソシエーツによる新しいコミュニティーのためのプランニングとデザインを特徴づける。事務所の仕事に対してや、何が達成されねばならないかへの彼の考えを支配するような論点や普遍的な対応策（例えば、グリッド状の道や決まった開発の規模）は何もない。新しいコミュニティーの形態と構造に関しては、ゲールハウスは与えられた敷地と環境に基づくことを重要視する。「我々は、いつも土地に基づく決定をしてきた」と彼は説明する。「キングスミルには、尾根や渓谷からなる非常に様々な景観があり、そこにグリッドを引くことは出来ない。」マイアミの南14マイルにある、フロリダのデイド郡に位置する1100エーカーの新しいコミュニティー「ザ・ハンモックス」では、事務所は幹線道路による郡のグリッド区画に曲線を導入した。それにより、敷地の中にある湖と公園が組織づけられ、それぞれが15〜25エーカーの隣近を構成するスケールの小さな開発区画は、湖の方に向けられた。学校、教会、公有地、そして商業施設といったコミュニティーの設備は三つの村と一つの町の中心に集められた。ゲールハウスは思い返す。「70年代には『ザ・ハンモックス』は、ただ単にプランニングが独特だったから受け入れられた。」[7]

最近ゲールハウスは、現在ディズニー開発会社によってフロリダに建設中の新しいコミュニティー「セレブレーション」で開かれたプランニングとデザインの討論会に出席した。討論会の一つで、彼はチャールズ・フレーザー、ジャクリン・ロバートソン、ロバート・A・M・スターン、そしてディズニーの重役たちと、デザインとその市場開発の問題について話し合った。「ディズニーが、こうした場所に実際に住もうと考えている人々の層を調査すると、人々は決まってグリッドを望まないのであった」とゲールハウスは覚えている。「いつも、それが彼らの反応だった。」いずれにせよ、その敷地は建設困難な土地であった。総面積10,000エーカーのうちの半分しか建設に適さなかった。あとは保護された湿地帯であった。[8]

それとは対照的に、以下に述べるブランブルトンの敷地は、よりコンパクトで、より都会的な特徴を持っている。そこは375エーカーの土地に凝縮していた。ヴァージニアの田舎ロードン郡にあるそのプロジェクトの主任デザイナーであったアラン・ウォードは、基本的グリッドプランの持つ社会経済的可能性を考慮し、彼と同僚たちは、それを既存の道と比較的平らな地形に採用した。ジョージ・J・ピローズ、ロバート・C・ケトラー、サム・バス・ウォーナー・ジュニア、そしてルイス・D・ホプキンスと共に出席したランドスケープ・アーキテクチャー・フォーラムで、彼は「排他的な町並みや、全ての家がある特定の市場価値を付加される計画的なユニット開発よりも、グリッドパターンの中に幅広い種類のハウジングを導入する方が簡単だし、より味があると私は思う」と語った。ウォードは続けて言った。「それは単に色々な値段の幅をもったハウジングではなく、年長者のためのハウジングでもあった。ブランブルトンの計画では、ダウンタウンの中心部に歩いて行ける距離にあるメインストリートの近くに、年長者用住宅が配置された．．．．今や我々は、『間断ない医療保護を提供するコミュニティー』を殆ど一区画ごとのスケールで導入できるし、その方が年長者を排他的な住宅群の片隅に座らせているよりはずっと良い。」[9]

ウォードと彼の同僚たちはそのフォーラムで、最終的に好きな都市について話す機会を得た。「アナポリス（メリーランド）のどこが好きかと言えば、適度なスケールの通り、非常に活動的なこと、通りを美しくするような都市の表情、ちょうど良いスケールの一般建築物と地面である」とウォードは言い、自動車のための場所をデザインする必要性のために、今日のデザイナーの仕事が複雑になっている事を認めた。「あの歩行者スケールとタイトでコンパクトな空間がアナポリスを生き生きと活気に満ちた都市にしているのだが、それらは地域の幹線道路とは異なったスケールに基づいている。そして地域の幹線道路から目抜き通りや主要道路に向けてのスケールの移り変わりが必要なのである。それ故、我々は自動車を減速させてこの都市の構造の中に入らせ、おとなしく運転させるようにしなければならない。」[10]

ササキ・アソシエーツの中で主任たちが統一した立場を取らなければならないときもあるだろうが、個人的もしくはグループの会話でよく聞かれるのは、立場が明確にされたり修正されたりするときの、強い反対意見だったり、ほんの少し微妙に違っているだけの意見だったりするような多様な視野である。ハーツェルはこれを、事務所が維持しようと勤めている協力と包括の精神においては、きわめて普通なことであると考える。彼は言う。「人の意見を聞き、それに答え、多様な対立する意見を統合していく過程でこそ、より良い解決が得られるのだと私は思う。そして、この事務所を見回してみると、ケン・バセット、アラン・ウォード、ディック・ゲールハウス、そしてドン・オルソンは、物事にアプローチする際のこうした統合していく精神を自然に備えているのである。そして、それこそが、このビジネスに携わっている多くの他の事務所と根本的に異なるところである。」[11]

デザイン

メラニー・スィーモ
訳／金　一

ササキ・アソシエーツの主任の一人であり、ウォータータウンで建築分野の筆頭に立つアラン・レズニックは、最近事務所に入った才能のある活発な若い所員たちに非常に満足している。「彼らは新鮮なアイデアと、すばらしい熱意を持ってやってきた」と彼は言う。「彼らはこの事務所の経歴を完全には知らないだろうが、この事務所を特別な場所だと感じている。彼らが望むことは、良い人々とすばらしい仕事をすることだけである。」[1]

似たような意見は、事務所の他の分野のデザイナーたちからも聞こえてくる。強調されるのは、仕事（その複雑さ、多様さ、多くのチャレンジ）とそのチャレンジや機会を生きがいとする人々である。こうした人々は時を経るうちに、協力的なプロセスや多分野間のやりとりを通じて進展してきた、事務所の特筆すべき過去やその精神体系を学ぶのである。しかし、その歴史は遠い地平に留まったままであり、事務所の中でのみならず、より大きな環境の中でも繰り返し聞かされることによって、さらに遠くに押しやられる。戦争直後？「ここことは同じ場所である。」「ここことは同じ世界ではない。」「もしかしたらどこかに繋がりがあるかもしれないけれど．．．．」

実際のところ、1950年代初期から現在にかけての、ササキ・アソシエーツの仕事と人々を橋渡す脈絡がいくつか存在する。チームで働くことを良しとし、少なくとも一時的に個人のエゴを捨てて人の話を聞き、ある問題への最

も良い解決を求めて幅広い要素、優先項目、そして可能性の中を模索していくこと、つまり、協力的なプロセスで仕事をすることが、その一つの共通の糸である。自分の技術や洞察力を、プランニングとデザインの分野の中で異なるトレーニングを受けた他の人々のそれと統合しようという興味や熱意もまた、一つの共通の糸である。特に、キャンパス・プランニングとそのデザイン、新しいコミュニティー、企業のための大きなスケールのランドスケープや商業的ランドスケープといった、都市においても田舎においても事務所がほぼ45年間にわたり行ってきた様々なプロジェクトのタイプには、一貫性がある。ステュワート・ドーソン、ドン・オルソン、リチャード・ゲールハウス、そして他の同僚たちは、長期に渡る一連のプロジェクトを事務所に依頼し続けるクライアントたちとの関係を楽しんできた。この関係の継続は、機能的でプラグマティックな考察や、表現のクオリティ、そして文化的特質性の間の微妙なバランスと、事務所での織り糸を代表する。しかし、こうした糸より大切なのは、「デザイン」と呼ばれる物事を統合する偉大な技術によって生み出された、織布の糸である。

この問題に関してもまた、必ずしもユニゾンではないが、調和のとれた意見が聞こえてくる。ランドスケープ・アーキテクチャーの分野の主任ジョセフ・ヒバードは、二人とも師である師であるヒデオ・ササキ（彼が雇われてすぐに引退した）とドン・オルソンからデザインへのアプローチの方法を吸収した。つまり、「機能的問題を先ず処理し、表現と構成については後から考える。後者の存在を忘れてはいけないが、最初の日からそれらに捕らわれてはいけない」ということである。ヒバードは、彼とオルソンのデザインの問題への取り組み方が微妙に異なることにも気づいた。オルソンは一種の「科学的客観性」から始めるのだが、自分の直感を決してなおざりにはしない。彼はコンポジションや上手い方法について非常に鋭い直感を持っているとヒバードは言う。オルソンは出来るだけ幅広いコンテクストで問題を検討し、分析結果を参照し、特定のデザインの方向性を決める前に、多くの先例や可能性について考慮することを好む。ヒバードも、リサーチと分析にかける時間はやや少ないが、同様である。「私は演繹的な方法をしているが、非常に素早く仕事に着手する事も好きである」と、彼は説明する。最終的に、彼は同僚たちのように、どの変数や要素が最も重要かを決定し、それから、デザインの特別な問題を解くための構造的基礎を構想することに取りかかる。

このデザインへのアプローチの仕方だと、何人もの同僚や協力者から助言助力を受けられるし、それを積極的に歓迎できる。結果はより豊かで満足を得られる。なぜなら、異なる分野から寄せられる直感は問題点を明らかにするからである。しかしながら、解決に到着するプロセス、つまり物理的形へのデザインの統合は、まだ何となくそれぞれのデザイナーや最も責任がある人の心的なプロセスとしてミステリアスなままに残されている。ヒバードにとって、それは同時に起こるいくつかの活動の問題である。「ランドスケープ・アーキテクチャーはスタイル、形、美学、感覚的質を扱うと同時に、機能と有用性をも扱う」と彼は言う。「問題を上手く解決するためには、常に両方を同じレベルで扱わなければならない。」[2]

ササキ・アソシエーツのサンフランシスコ・オフィスを率いる建築家であり且つ主任の一人のスコット・スミスは、彼が事務所に惹かれたのはこの協力的な慣習のためだったと思い返す。「しかし、そこにしばらくいるまでは、それがいかに強力であるかを知らなかった」と彼は言う。1980年代の初め、事務所での彼の最初のプロジェクトの一つであるウェスタンワイオミング・カレッジの拡張計画で、スミスは関連する他の建築事務所に加えて、事務所内ではゲールハウス、ヒバード、ジョン・オーカット（当時の事務所の建築分野の筆頭）、ササキ（コンサルタントとして招かれていた）などの面々と仕事を共にした。特に、建築拡張計画の配置と形態に大きな影響を与えた二三の直感については、スミスはそれをヒバードに帰している。彼はこう述べる。「もし一人の建築家でも自分の決断に固執してグループを去れば、その建物は今日あるようにはなっていないと思う。この協調こそ、私が大切に思う我々の慣習の一つなのだ。」

デザインのプロセスそのものに関しては、スミスは幅広いコンテクストを最初に扱うことを好む。「建築は社会的芸術である」と彼は断言する。「それは、我々が住む文化と人々によって形成される。もちろん、専門家がこの建築という作品にインスピレーションを与えなければならない時もある。つまり、建物はデモクラシーではデザインできないのだ！建物をデザインするリーダーは必要である。しかし建物の成功は、いかに上手くそのリーダーが、敷地を訪れたり公開ミーティングや社内のプロセスなどから多くのことを吸収するかによる。我々は対象となるグループと共に多くの時間とエネルギーをかける。我々は質問をするが、クリエーティブなプロセスの真にチャレンジングなところは、よく聞くということである。」[3]

聞く耳を持つということは、45年近くササキ・アソシエーツが実践してきた、最も本質的なことの一つである。しかし、聞く事の性格も時代と共に変わってきた。ステュアート・ドーソンのそれに関する見通しは、1950年代までさかのぼる。当時彼は、ランドスケープ・アーキテクチャーを学んだ若い卒業生として、ランドスケープ・アーキテクト、建築家、そしてプランナーたちで構成された、まだ小さかった事務所に参加したのだった。今や年長の主任として、ドーソンは特に都会でのプロジェクトで一層傾聴すべき幅広い意見の大切さを強調してきた。そうした意見は社内や関係する事務所の同僚たちのそれに加えて、再開発業者、計画委員会、そのコミュニティーの組織や様々な利害関係にあるグループ、市場調査の専門家、そして時には芸術品の管理者や協力アーティストたちからも聞こえてくる。ドーソンは特にクライアントの意見に調子を合わせる。「生産的な傾聴のための余地は多くある」と彼は述べる。「クライアントの夢を少し自分のヴィジョンに近づけるためには、より成熟した専門家となる必要がある。それが私には面白くてたまらない。最初にクライアントと話したときには不可能だと思ったことを我々はやってみた。しかし、そのプロジェクトに関わる者たちは皆、だんだん上手いやり方があると確信するようになった。」[4]

1950年代と60年代に、もしクライアントが建築家の場合、ドーソンは自分がその建築家の意見より事務所の同僚たちの意見を多く聞いていることに時々気づいた。例えば、エーロ・サーリネンは彼の建物のランドスケープ・セッティングに、計画の早い時期から非常に興味を見せた。「それは面白い経験だった。彼はまだモデルの段階で気にしていた」とドーソンは思い出す。「しかし、それがどんな風に見えて、何色で、大まかなテクスチャーはこうで、といったディーテイルを、多すぎないように我々のヴィジョンとして彼に与えた後、担当者は一人残されて良い仕事をすることが求められた。それは、ケヴィン・ローチについても言える。彼はいつもプロジェクトの初期の段階の、ヴィジョンの構築に一番熱を入れていた。」当時、イリノイ州モリーンにあるディーアの本社に取り組んでいた頃、ササキが彼の作品を批評し、ある特定の植栽の方法（例えば、サンザシを一つのマスにまとめ、メープルとオークの木を緩やかに波打つランドスケープを渡る流れとして扱うよう勧めた）を受け入れた。このデザインプロセスから、サーリネンの建物は高貴だが控えめな環境を与えられた。ドーソンは、概念的デザインから始まり試練の数々を経てランドスケープ・インスタレーションの確かな成功に至るまでの全プロセスを経験した。これに満足したサーリネンとディーア・アンド・カンパニーはそれから何年もササキの事務所に仕事を依頼し続けた。

ドーソンにとって、このデザインのプロセスは移りゆく状況と共に変化してきた。彼は言う。「５０年代には問題はより単純だったと思う。我々が意見を聞くクライアントは非常に単純な協議事項を持っていた。だから、革新のための多くの余地があった。今日、人々はずっと洗練されている。彼らはもっと多くを要求する。そしてもし聴く姿勢があれば、より多くを語る。」　初期の頃を振り返れば、当時のサイズでの事務所の役割や、若かった社員たちといった逸話や偶発的な仕事のコンディションが思い返される。「初期には我々はもっと形式張らなかったと思う。よく夜通し働いたし、それから働き過ぎだったら遊びにも出かけた」とドーソンは言う。彼は込み入った記憶を追いはらうように、しばらく間をおいてから話す。「我々はすばらしい時を過ごした。あらゆる種類の原寸大モデルを作ったし、電灯設備を原寸大でデザインした。何でも探求心をもって実行していた。」[5]

社会に浸透していた拡張の気運は、戦争直後の若々しい昂揚心と楽観主義に支えられていた。この気運は一つには、合衆国のみならず外国も含めて、弾力性のある国内経済と、再建や新しい建設の差し迫った必要性から来るものであった。プランニングとデザインにとって本質的もしくは少なくとも適切だと思われた知識や理解の基礎もまた、拡大していた。社会学、都市論、人類学、美学、デザインにおける心理学といった諸学科や、高熱、換気、ソーラーシステムなどの環境の操作は、ますます専門のカリキュラムに取り入れられていった。

すでに述べたように、ササキの事務所は教育機関、特にジョセップ・ルイス・サートとピエトロ・ベルスキに導かれたハーヴァードとMITのデザイン学校と強い結びつきを持っていた。サートとベルスキが何年も事務所と緊密に仕事をしたことにより、こうした繋がりがササキの事務所に仕事をもたらしただけでなく、新しい考え方や理解の仕方が常に事務所の仕事に伝えられたのだった。初期のパートナーや所員たちは仕事をしながら非常勤で教えていた。こうしたデザイナーやその同僚たちにとって、学校でも事務所でも、学ぶことは絶えず続いていた。セミナー、出版予定の本、又はスタジオでの問題は、新しい理論や単純な予想をも生み出した。それらはあるプロジェクトで実際に試されたのだった。時空を越えて孤立している小さなプロジェクトもあれば、長期にかけてより多くの問題を考慮しなければならないような、大きなコンテクストと関わるキャンパスや都市におけるプロジェクトもあった。時には全く同じか、または同様のコンテクストのための一連のコミッションが事務所に持ち込まれることもあった。この場合、デザイン解決の手順が試され、デザイナーたちはより大きな問題に対して理解を蓄積していくことが出来た。

こうした大きくて複雑な問題の数々から、単なる部分の寄せ集めではない大きなヴィジョンが生まれた。言葉に明瞭に表現することは難しいが見ればわかるような全体性が展開した。この全体性が、単に大胆な幾何形態や強い個性によって支えられたものでなく、マテリアル、スタイル、又はスケールの一貫性によって確保されたものでもないことは、何人かのデザイナーたちにはすぐに明らかとなった。微妙ですぐにはわからないこの全体性という性質は、実体がなく、ほとんど説明不可能でまれなものにとどまっている。それは、人々、建設された形態やスペース、そして自然の要素がある均衡状態に達したように見える様な環境で、単に感じられるのであった。

ササキ・アソシエーツが雇用した最初の建築家たちの一人であるケネス・デュメイにとって、建てられた作品の醸し出す全体性は、一部にはササキ・アソシエーツで進展した建築の進め方から来たものであった。最初は小さな事務所がサート、ベルスキ、SOM、I. M. ペイ、アーネスト・カンプ、ウィリアム・ワースターなどの建築家たちから来た。皆、ササキと彼の事務所と共に仕事をすることを好んだ。（デュメイは思い返す。『全員が非常にハードに長時間働いた。あまりにハードに懸命に働いたので、その習慣が我々全員に深くしみこんでしまった。』）デュメイは色々な点で事務所に貢献し始めてすぐに、結果的に建物の依頼に結びつきやすい組織的全体計画を発展させることに集中した。本質的に総体的な観点からあるキャンパスを見ながら、彼とその同僚たちが最初に全体を形作り、それから建物のデザインという小さなスケールに取りかかっていった。もし、ササキ・アソシエーツの建築的実践がプランニングから成長したものだと言えるなら、彼らの他の分野の活動もそうだと言える。ゲールハウスが説明したように、アーバンデザインの仕事は、環境事業やグラフィックスの特性がそうであるように、プランニングの分野から育ったものである。こうした発展がきわめて自然に進化的に起こったという事は、ササキ・アソシエーツにおいて「プランニング」を常に物理的プランニングとして理解してきた事実において明らかである。その多くが建築の学位をも持つ事務所のプランナーたちの究極の産出物は、いつも建てられた作品もしくは一連の空間と構造である。「プランナーたちは、彼らが物理的ディメンションを真に体感する能力があるときのみ、この事務所で成功することができる」と、デヴィッド・ハーツェルは最近語った。例えば、方法的手腕は大切ではあるが、それだけでは十分ではない。ハーツェルは、またこうも述べる。「ここで生き残れる建築家たちは複雑なコンテクストを持った世界で生きられる者たちである。」[7]

スミスもまた、その「コンテクスト」が、あるプロジェクトの建築的なものや自然の環境以上のものを含むことに触れながら、これに同意するであろう。プログラム、地域、気候、そしてその土地で使われる特別な建築技術でさえも、全て彼の言う「コンテクスト」に貢献するのだということを、スミスは強調するだろう。彼は広い意味において、そうしたコンテクストに大いに適合した、ササキ・アソシエーツによってデザインされた一連の建物やランドスケープを示すことができる。しかし、そうした仕事の限界にも彼は気づいている。彼は言う。「ササキ・アソシエーツは署名性をもった建築を創らない。我々の建物を見ても、必ずしも人はその建物がどのように生み出されたのか、誰がそれを創ったのかを知らない。」　どちらかというと建物のデザインというものは、際だった自然のランドスケープや、また、建てられてから長い年月を経るうちに洗練されるような都会もしくは公共の場所といった様々な要素によって、受け手に伝わってくるものなのである。

この署名性のなさ、つまりランドスケープ・アーキテクトたちが経験し、何年にもわたりそれと戦ってきた「匿名性の形」もまた、ある含みを持っている。事務所の同僚たちに加え、関連する建築事務所とも協力するという変わらない伝統のために、この事務所のある特定の建物への貢献はいつも知られないままである。多くの州では、一般的に建物は、「記念すべき建築家」としての州内の建築家や設計事務所の作品として、公にも非公式にも記憶されてしまう。１９５０年代や６０年代のように、今日も事務所の多くの建築的仕事は他の建築家たちとの協力であり、彼らのためにササキ・アソシエーツがデザインのサーヴィスを提供しているのである。事務所がある仕事で公に認識されるかどうかは色々な条件次第であり、事務所の担当デザイナーのコントロールの域を越えている。しかしながらスミスは、事務所内外での協力の課程で形成される仕事上の人間関係には個人的に非常に満足している。クライアントや同僚は良い友人になるものである。そして時々ある建物が、デザイナーや事務所の署名ではないが、それ自身のコンテクストの中での、ある種の「署名」になることもある。「建物はキャンパスの上に立つ署名である」とスミスは自信を持って言う。

署名性について話すということは、個人のレベルでも集団のレベルにおいてもアイデンティティーの問題を持ち上げることになる。成熟し、自分たちの能力に自信を持っているササキ・アソシエーツのデザイナーたちの何人かは、彼らのプロフェッショナルとしてのキャリアの全てを、この事務所の協力的であらゆる分野を網羅した環境の中で過

ごしてきた。彼らは他の形式での仕事を知らない。余所で働いたことのあるものもいるが、一つには興味をそそる幅広いタイプの解決すべき問題や実現される成功の故に、彼らは協力して進める仕事のやり方を好むのである。何年時を経ても、所員たちは共働というアイデア（他の人と強調しながら物事を達成するために、日々努力するという力強い理想）に依然として惹かれている。皮肉なことに事務所の外では、デザインの専門家たちや一般人たちは、ササキ・アソシエーツをプランニング事務所、環境プランニングとそのデザインをする事務所、ランドスケープ・アーキテクチャー事務所、又はエンジニアリング事務所と見なしがちである。ゲールハウスは説明する。「我々は分野別に世間に知られている。共働の理想という一番大切なメッセージは彼らの脳裏を横切らない。」[8]

「我々がクライアントのためにしてきたことが、我々自身の姿である」と、ハーツェルは指摘する。詳細に説明するためには、言葉とイメージで、より包括的な歴史的なまとめをしなければならず、予定のページ数を越えてしまう。ここでは、いずれにせよ、ササキ・アソシエーツの専門家たちの最近の仕事の考え方に加えて過去の作品をざっと回顧することで、この事務所の全体的アイデンティティーといったものが理解できるであろう。

比較的最近事務所に入った所員たちの意見も興味深い。主任の一人であり、建築分野から成長独立したインテリア部門を率いるナンシー・ハロッドにとって、あるプロジェクトが最初のミーティングからプログラミングや概念的デザインを経て実施に至るまでの時間枠は、１９８７年に彼女が最初にササキ・アソシエーツに来て以来、急激に短くなってきている。締め切りは短く、資料は限られ、要求は大きくなっている。「年々、より多くのエネルギーが必要とされている」と彼女は認め、一番早いケースでさえ加速していると付け加えた。より早く効率よく働くチームは、それだけ早く彼らの仕事の結果を見るし、それから学ぶことができる。[9]　プログラミングの分野で、もう一つの発展が進行している。そこには今や他の分野と同様に、創造するという大きな機会がある。クライアントは、スミス、ヒバード、バセット、ゲールハウス、そして他の色々な分野の人々に対するのと同様に、ハロッドと彼女のチームに、必要性、欲求、そして抑圧がますます複雑に絡まった問題を定義する際に助けを求める。

デザインプロセスを飛躍的に進歩させているのはコンピューターなどの電子機器の導入である。ササキ・アソシエーツでは、コンピューターを使ったデザイン（CADシステム）や関連するテクノロジーへの熱意の度合いは人によって異なる。ほとんどのデザイナーはそれらをデザインのための道具、たぶん最終的にはなくてはならない道具として見ている。新しいテクノロジーもまた、デザインに関わる巨大化する解決されるべき問題の一要因である。なぜなら、コンピューターや他の電子メディアは非常に大きなスケールでキャンパス、会社のオフィス、金融業界などに導入されているからである。すでに触れたように、既存の場所に新しい装置を導入する必要性や、コンピューターのモニターの前に長時間座った後に学生たちが顔と顔をつきあわせて交際するための場所を新設又はデザインし直したりする必要性を、大学当局がますます強調していることに、ベリー・チャップマンは気づいていた。

ヴァーチャル・スペースに出現するはずの電子的出会いの場という観点から、物理的パブリックスペースの必要性が減少していくと理論化する者もいるが、アラン・ウォードはそれに対して慎重である。「電子メディアが、いかに我々が働き、世界を見るか、また我々が我々の仕事をどのようにしていくのか、に本質的に影響を及ぼすことは認める。電子メディアはそれらを変えていく。そして、電子メディアは、我々の住んでいる場所やコミュニティーの常識から我々を遠ざけた。しかし、物理的世界がヴァーチャルな世界に取って代わられることになるとは思わない。私は、どちらかというとその反対を見る。この我々の周囲の物理的世界が解体していくので、何か他のものに乗り移ろうと言うよりは、私は根本的にヒューマンなものを再生させたい。」[10]

これもまた、ササキ・アソシエーツがクライアントに対して行ってきたことである。根本的にヒューマンなことである、再生、再デザインそして改めて物理的場所を構築することは、過去には意義深い追求であったし、それは今後ともこの協力して仕事をする事務所の大きなゴールであり続けるだろう。やがては、こうして構築された場所もまた、団体としての事務所のアイデンティティーの一部を形成するであろう。

ダイアローグ

ハンター・モリソン
（プランニング・ディレクター、オハイオ州クリーブランド）

ジョセフ・ライリー
（市長、サウス・カロライナ州チャールストン）

採録／デヴィッド・ディロン
訳／金　一

ササキ・アソシエーツはクリーブランドとチャールストンで、プランナー、ランドスケープ・アーキテクト、アーバン・デザイナー、エンジニア、そして公共の代弁者として、また、幅広いプランニングのヴィジョンとそれを実施するための特別なガイドラインを供給しながら、３０年間に渡り仕事をしてきた。

３０年前には、多分野を網羅する事務所はまれであった。今日でさえ、ほとんどの大きな事務所はエンジニアやランドスケープ・アーキテクトを雇っていながら、彼らは皆自分たちをプランナーと呼び、ササキのように互いに協力して働く道筋に沿って、しっかりと進んでいる人は少ない。長いつきあいは永い結婚生活のように山も谷もある。成功したプロジェクトもあれば、失敗したものもある。良いデザインを奨励する市長もいれば、関心のない市長もいる。しかしながら、期待されることといえば、互いに良い意志を持つことや、お互いの強さと限界を尊重することで趣の添えられた「共有された歴史」というものが、見知らぬもの同志の功利的連合よりも結果的に良い仕事を生み出すということである。それが、チャールストンとクリーブランドでのササキのケースである。

ササキの、クリーブランドのダウンタウンとの関わりは、１９７０年代の終わりに、市の設立当初から続くフォーマルな市民スペースであるパブリックスクエアをデザインし直したことから始まり、１９８０年代と１９９０年代のゲートウェイセンターとノースコースト・ハーバーの計画に至るまで続いた。各計画の点と点をつなげると、現在のクリーブランド・ルネッサンスの地図になる。

１９７０年代は、クリーブランドにとって暗黒の時代であった。政治は混沌とし、金融は悪夢のようだった。何らかの活動の場で進歩的になろうとして、クリーブランドのガーデン・クラブとダウンタウン・クリーブランド会社によって率いられた私設の諸グループが提携して、パブリック・スクエアを刷新するためのプロジェクトを起こし、サ

サキを選んだ。ヤンキーの実利主義的傾向を持った保守的都市クリーブランドは、時流に乗ったデザインを軽蔑した。クリーブランドは単純さと慎みを要求したが、それこそササキが手渡したものだった。事務所は、広場の四分円のそれぞれに噴水、花の咲く木、ベンチを加え、あるところにはより多くの芝を、他の場所にはより多くの舗装を施すといった、いくつかの控えめな変更を付与した。最終的に、このプロジェクトはアーバンデザインのディーテイルというよりは、ほとんどテクノクラートたちから大きな公共スペースを無理矢理奪って人々に帰すようなものだった。市のエンジニアリング課と地域の交通機関の協力を得て、ササキは道幅を狭め、横断歩道を短くし、不必要なバス停を削減し、そして全体的には、歩行者にクリーブランドの歴史的中心部で権利のために戦うチャンスを与えた。「パブリック・スクエアの改装によって、ササキが市の方針を理解していることが示された」とクリーブランドのプランニング・ディレクターであるハンター・モリソンは言う。「彼らは要となるプロジェクトを、それが簡単ではなかった時に成し遂げ、しかも癇癪を起こさずにやってのけたのである。」

十年後、ササキが、40億ドルの予算を付与したダウンタウン南端の再開発計画であるゲートウェイセンターのマスタープランナーになったとき、この例は評価されないほどの非常に貴重なものとなった。クリーブランド・インディアンやクリーブランド・カヴァリエたちの新しい家々に占拠されていたゲートウェイ地区は、懸命な市による、悩み多いダウンタウンへの大きな賭を意味していた。マイケル・ホワイト市長は無愛想に、ゲートウェイが単なる一つのスタジアムやアリーナを作る以上の計画にならない限り、その計画が一ダイム以上の公共の金を受け取ることはないであろうと語った。ゲートウェイの計画は、ダウンタウン全体を活性化し、誰もが共有できる経済的利益を生み出さねばならなかったのである。

ササキの権限は、野球場とアリーナを親しみやすくして、それらがダウンタウンと境目なく調和するようにすることだった。建築的というより社会的なゲートウェイのその他の非難は、オンブズマン、苦情対策委員会、そして様々な当事者に対応する警官たちに向けられた。インディアンやカヴァリエたちがプライヴェートな協議事項を打ち出すのと同じだけ強く、事務所は公共のための協議事項を明白にしなければならなかった。「ササキは、他の事務所と異なり、チャレンジの大きさを感じていた」と、モリソンは付け加えた。「彼らは、単に建物のデザインに興味を持っている建築家として考えることを大きく捉え、問題を大きく捉えた。我々が、建築そのものを必要としていたのと同じぐらい、建築を置くための枠組みをも必要としていたことを、彼らは理解していた。」 この枠組みは、28エーカーの敷地の全体計画と、それによって市が担当チームと将来の開発業者たちに「これは良い」「これは良くない」と言えるようになった一連のデザイン・ガイドラインから構成されていた。

ササキの最初の動きは、野球場を北へ、つまりダウンタウンと歴史的通りのグリッドに向けて回転させることであった。インディアンと抜け目のない小売商人たちを牛耳るジェイコブス一家は、生産物を陳列することの価値を知っていた。つまりこの場合、インディアンたちと、彼らが開発を手伝ったダウンタウンのスカイラインのことである。ダウンタウンを野球の背景に用いることは、ひどい状態の川や羅起になっている市長たちで悪名高いクリーブランド市にとって、都会の洗練を想起させる。同時に、ササキは野球場担当の建築家たちであるHOKスポーツファシリティース・グループを説得して、メイン・コンコースを歩道の延長上に位置づけるために観客席のせり上がりを低く押さえるようにさせた。このことで、多くのスタジアムの概観を醜くしている渦巻き状の斜面や、人々が通ると鈍い音を立てる階段格子が取り除かれ、オンタリオ通りに沿った歯切れの良い都市の周縁が生まれた。事務所の歴史においても、全体計画において、周縁と連接は建物と同じだけの重要性を持っている。

その敷地では、ササキは儀式的というよりは社会的な一連の広場と景観を伴った大通りを創出した。それは、モールが消費者を気に入った店と店の間を往復させるやり方で、野球の観衆の大きな流れをゲートウェイとダウンタウンの間で行ったり来たりさせるためであった。野球場の角は外に開いており、通りがかりの人々が中の様子を見れるし、野球ファンたちもそこから街を見ることができた。

ササキの意図は実利的であると等しく詩的であった。「スクリーンを見たり、バットの打音を聞いたり。もしかしたら、その人の足下でホームランの球がバウンドするかもしれない」とデザイン主任であったアラン・ウォードは言う。「我々はゲームに行くつもりのない人々にも見たり聞いたり、公園を感じてほしかったのだ。」

ゲートウェイの大きなアーバンデザインのアイデアは、視界、材料、寸法、入り口、そして出口への細やかな数百ものアイデアから成り立っている。「緑の広がり、夢の球場」といった市側のロマンティックな、しかし概念的で感傷的なアイデアから、野球場の木の柵から駐車場までの大きな公共芸術のすべてを網羅したガイドラインを作った。その中には、試合の後に警察のバリケードをどこに置くのが適切か、といった微妙なものもあれば、ダウンタウンを大きく変えることになった提案もあった。ササキは、敷地内の駐車スペースを二つのガレージに分け、3200台分に制限した。それ以上の車には既存の駐車場を利用させることにした。インディアンとカヴァリエたちはより多くを要求したが、計画のゴールはダウンタウンを活気づけることであって道の舗装ではないので、市とササキは意見を変えなかった。既存の駐車場を利用させることによって野球ファンは通りを歩かされ、ウィンドウショッピングをし、そぞろ歩きをしてダウンタウンを再発見した。「我々は、野球場とアリーナを救ごしらえの注射だとは思っていない」とハンター・モリソンは説明する。「それらはダウンタウンを再建するための長期計画の一部なのだ。公園を都市構造に結びつけることによって、人々は自分たちの車に駆け込む代わりにそこを通り抜け、道すがら財布を空にするであろうと我々は信じている。」

二十以上のレストランやクラブが公園の周りや隣接する集合住宅に開店した。そこはクヤホガ川沿いの歴史的な倉庫地区で、今日、ゲートウェイに計画された連続する光のラインが、ゲートウェイとノースコースト・ハーバー（ロックンロールの殿堂と博物館の敷地）につながっている。いくつかのホテルが計画中であり、いくつかのオフィスビルが住宅に改装されている。それらのほとんどが50年以上も触れられることのなかったものである。ゲートウェイが計画されなかったら、それらはさらに50年間、一層朽ち果てていただろう。このプロジェクトによって一般人のダウンタウンに対する印象が変わった。急激に、そこは人々で溢れたのである。「ゲートウェイ再生のための最も大きな衝撃は駐車と交通計画であった」とアシスタント・プランニング・ディレクターであるリンダ・ヘンドリクソンは語る。「もしそれが失敗していたら、他の全てもまた失敗していただろう。クリーブランドが二つのスポーツチーム、そのオーナーたち、そして全てのこうした選手たちを獲得したのは、驚異的なことであった。」

ササキがチャールストンに関わったのは、ハーバータウンの敷地を含む、ヒルトンヘッド・アイランドにあるシーパインズ・プランテーションのための全体計画を、1957年に行ったのが始まりであった。チャールストンはハーバータウンのモデルであり、開発業者チャールズ・フレイザーは、ハーバータウンについて仕事をする人は誰でもそのオリジナルを知らなければならないと主張した。そこで、ケン・デュメイとドン・オルソンらはチャールストンを断続的に歩き回り、その歴史とランドスケープを調査し、建物を写真に収め、そして将来のプロジェクトのために全

般的印象を蓄積していった。主任として、ストゥ・ドーソンは後に皮肉を込めて言った。「事務所はニューイングランドに根を下ろす前に、サウス・カロライナでその地盤を固めた。」

その「将来のプロジェクト」は、1977年にやってきた。その年ササキは、7エーカーの敷地を持つチャールストンの新しいウォーターフロント・パークのデザインコンペに勝ったのだった。この時までに同市のウォーターフロントは、周囲の零落にわびしさを添える集合住宅の建物が点々とする、一連の朽ち果てた埠頭、見捨てられた倉庫、そして舗装のはがれた駐車場になり果てていた。

市長のジョセフ・ライリーは、ウォーターフロントとその近隣周辺を刷新する新しい公園を作ることによって、そうした全てを変えていくことを誓約した。それは、船長や退職した海軍の上級将校たちのための上品ぶった公園ではなく、チャールストンの人々が海との親密な関係を再構築するのを促す、釣りをする埠頭、庭園、そして噴水を伴った公共の場である。市長は、衰退しつつあるウォーターフロントを持つ二つの歴史的な港湾都市、ニューベリーポートとボストンにあるササキの出費で大きな建築的声明を作り出すことを嫌うササキ事務所を、評価していた。「彼らは大変評判の高い、大きな事務所だった」と彼は語る。「しかし、彼らは我々がここに持っているものに実に敏感に対応した。そこには、つまらぬ自尊心などなかった。」しかし、クリーブランドでのようにチャールストンの都市問題を的確に捉えたからこそ、ササキが最終的に雇われたのだった。「我々が公園だけを対象にしているのではなく、市の周縁全体を再開発しようとしていることを彼らは理解していた」とライリー市長は言う。

クーパー川に沿った全長1300フィートのウォーターフロント・パークは完成までに11年かかり、そのほとんどの時間は敷地の準備に費やされた。ササキ事務所の建築家たちやエンジニアたちが、仕事を主導していった。彼らは最初に、新しい公園の建設で追いやられる自動車たちを収容するための二つの駐車場をデザインした。それに三年がかかった。それから、彼らはチャールストニアンたちが「黒いマヨネーズ」と呼ぶ汚れた土を九フィートの砂をかぶせて固めねばならなかった。そのためにもう二年が費やされ、その間、砂の山は「ライリーの山」とあだ名されて彼の政治的敵対者たちのジョークになった。強く固められた後も、打ち杭や基礎なしの入念な下部構造の助けなしには、その土は噴水や広場や埠頭を支えられなかった。公園のコストの五十パーセントは見えない地面の下に掛けられた。新しい隔壁の建設によって干満のある湿地帯が影響を被った。ササキは、それを歴史的アッジャーズワーフと共に公園の南側に再生させなければならなかった。分野を越えて仕事をすることに慣れた、緊密な連携のとれた事務所のみが、こうした技術的問題を解決し、魅惑的で一貫性のあるデザインを生み出すことが出来た。

ライリー市長は驚くべき忍耐強い政治家で、熱心な協力者であった。彼は数々の会合に出席し、線を引き、色を選んだ。（ダウンタウンの駐車場のグリーンは彼の選択である。）そしていつも彼はデザイナーたちに、より大きな社会的責任を想起させた。「多くの都市では、仕事は若手に任され、市長を見ることは二度とない」と、ストゥ・ドーソンは思い返す。「決まってそうだ。しかし、ジョー・ライリーは例外だ。彼は全ての公開ミーティングに出席し、我々を紹介し、主催者としての役割を果たし、我々が適切な人々を前に話しているかを確めた。彼はこのプロジェクト全体をオーケストラの指揮者のように統率した。」

完成された公園は、クラシカルな格式とチャールストンに特有のその土地の気楽さを併せ持っていた。遊歩道、噴水、芝生の土地、樫の木の木立、そして、堅い舗装を施した北端から、より柔らかい景観を持つ南端に至るまでの変化、といったような大きな問題に対する決定は早かった。その一方、ディーテールに関しては延々と時間がかかった。市長と建築家たちは歩道に敷く砂利を選ぶのにサンプルを五十も取り寄せた。芝生を囲む座るための腰壁やキャベツヤシの配置については、徹底的に討論された。煉瓦の敷き詰められた小道は、ヘリンボン模様が正しくない方向を向いていたため、やり直されなければならなかった。もし、良いエンジニアになるためにこの公園の下部構造を学ぶだけで充分だとすれば、この低地帯にある公園で学んだランドスケープ・アーキテクトたちだけが、数百もの細かいディーテールを正しく収得しているといえる。以前はチャールストンのどこでも目にしたプライヴェートな庭の名残である八つの小さな庭を、その煉瓦の小道は結んでいる。それらの庭は、この巨大なパブリックスペースの前庭のような役割を果たしている。ライリー市長は、それらの庭は外見は同じに見えるが内では十分に変化を付けて、「庭の一つで恋人にプロポーズしたある紳士が、どの庭だったかを一生覚えているように」デザインして欲しい、と要求した。このプログラムは、この一節に現れている。

この公園を都市に結びつけるために、ササキは近隣の歴史的地区の通りや小路からの眺めを保持した。それによって、通りのグリッドが公園を突き抜けて水際に続いているように見えた。一つの軸は公共の釣り専用埠頭まで続いている。その埠頭は、最初に建築家たちの反対にあっても市長が建設を主張し続けたものだった。独特のパイナップル噴水は他の二つの軸の間に位置する。「我々は彼に、その埠頭がヨットを係留することに適していることを何度も伝えた」と、ドーソンは思い返す。「彼は、チャールストンはヨットを持たないような人々のための場所を必要としているのだと語った。彼は、我々が引く線に人間愛を導入する方法を知っていた。」

1990年にオープンしてから、ウォーターフロント・パークはチャールストンで最も人気のあるパブリックスペースとなった。この公園は、他のウォーターフロント計画の進展を刺激した。その中には、同じくササキの事務所によってデザインされ、チャールストンで苦闘していた海老を獲る漁師たちを収容したマラタイム・センターも含まれていた。むき出しの飾り鋲や、襞のついた金属製のかべ板といった低地帯独特の構造を持つこのセンターは、梱包室、小売り店、ギフト・ショップに加え、外にはコミュニティの集える芝生も広がっている。ウォーターフロント・パークの釣り専用埠頭が文化の表現だとすれば、マラタイム・センターは経済的な表現と言うべきである。「我々の文化のためにも、我々自身がアイデンティティーを実感するためにも大切である産業は、維持されなければならないのだということを私は明らかにしたかった」とライリー市長は説明した。最終的にウォーターフロント・パークに加えて、水族館、野球場、住宅をも含むことになる八マイルに及ぶ水際遊歩道のなかで、マラタイム・センターはもう一つの鍵になると市長は考えている。「全ての町に、そこを自分のものと感じられるような美しくてインスピレーションを湧かせる場所が必要である」と彼は言う。「ある都市がいかに優れているかは、公共の土地にどれだけ美しい場所が創造されているかによって決まるのである。」

【日本語訳／金　一、コロンビア大学大学院、美術史考古学科、博士課程、西洋建築史専攻.】
Japanese Translation: Il Kim, Ph. D. Candidate, Columbia University.

＊脚注：190～191ページをご覧ください。